how to
GROW
FOOD

how to
GROW
FOOD

A step-by-step guide
to growing all kinds
of fruit, vegetables,
salads and more

RICHARD GIANFRANCESCO

FIREFLY BOOKS

A FIREFLY BOOK

Published by Firefly Books Ltd. 2011

First printing

Publisher Cataloging-in-Publication Data (U.S.)

Gianfrancesco, Richard, 1972–
   How to grow food : a step-by-step guide to growing all kinds of fruits, vegetables, herbs, salads, and more / Richard Gianfrancesco.
[256] p. : ill., col. photos. ; cm.
Includes index.
ISBN-13: 978-1-55407-806-6
ISBN-10: 1-55407-806-7
1. Growth (Plants). 2. Plants — Development.
I. Title.
571.82 dc22   QK731.G536   2011

Library and Archives Canada Cataloguing in Publication

Gianfrancesco, Richard, 1972-
  How to grow food : a step-by-step guide to growing all kinds of fruits, vegetables, herbs, salads and more / Richard Gianfrancesco.
Includes index.
ISBN-13: 978-1-55407-806-6
ISBN-10: 1-55407-806-7
  1. Vegetable gardening. 2. Fruit-culture. 3. Herb gardening. I. Title.
SB324.3.G52 2011   635   C2010-906189-6

Published in the United States
by Firefly Books (U.S.) Inc.
P.O. Box 1338, Ellicott Station
Buffalo, New York 14205

Published in Canada
by Firefly Books Ltd.
66 Leek Crescent
Richmond Hill, Ontario L4B 1H1

Conceived, designed and produced by
Quarto Publishing plc
The Old Brewery
6 Blundell Street
London N7 9BH

QUAR.HGF

For Quarto:
Senior Editor: Ruth Patrick
Editor: Corinne Masciocchi
Designer: John Grain
Art Director: Caroline Guest
Illustrators: Kuo Kang Chen, Rob Shone, John Woodcock
Photographers: John Grain, Colin and Jenny Guest, Mark Winwood

Creative Director: Moira Clinch
Publisher: Paul Carslake

Color separation in China by
  Modern Age Pte Ltd
Printed in China by 1010 Printing
  International Ltd

10 9 8 7 6 5 4 3 2 1

CONTENTS

FOREWORD

When I was a child, the joy of gardening was all in the eating! Picking fresh peas, raspberries and plums from the garden and eating them was one of my favorite summer activities. As gardening has become a much bigger part of my life, the practice of growing and nurturing the plants has become much more important. Fortunately for me, I now have my own children who share my childhood passion, and as long as I grow what they like, I can spend as much time as I need tending my garden.

As a garden researcher for the past 10 years I've conducted many trials on how to use your time most effectively in the garden and how to get the best out of your plot. How to improve your soil, reduce watering, select appropriate crops and specific varieties and reduce pest and disease damage will all save time in the long run, whatever the size of your garden. Spending time on learning the basics as well as debunking some of the time-heavy myths that many gardening books still profess are worth learning now. But whatever you do, make sure gardening stays a pleasure and not a chore.

ABOUT THIS BOOK

This book is a practical step-by-step guide to planning, growing and maintaining a productive vegetable and fruit garden, with information on getting the most from whatever kind of plot you choose. Using the features described here will quickly provide you with all you need to know.

Part 1: Where to grow (pages 12–25)
Helping you to design your growing food garden and how to get the most from your plot.

DESIGN IDEAS
Packed with photographs of inspirational garden designs, helping you to visualize the layout.

STAR PLANT STAMP
Crops marked with a stamp are specially recommended.

STAR RATING
On a scale of one to five, each entry is graded for a range of criteria.

STEP-BY-STEP SEQUENCES
Detailing techniques such as sowing, growing and maintaining your crops.

Part 2: Growing directory (pages 26–193)
Information on how to grow, maintain, harvest and store vegetable and salad crops, fruit and nuts.

CALENDAR
What to do when for optimum results.

VARIETY SELECTOR
Lists of recommended varieties.

SUPPLEMENTARY INFORMATION
Features topics and techniques in more detail, helping you to raise and maintain your plants.

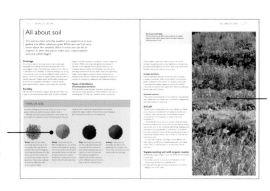

Part 3: How to grow (pages 194–227)
Core information on foundation gardening techniques.

INSPIRATIONAL PHOTOGRAPHY
Clear photography accompanies each topic, detailing techniques and providing inspiration.

STEP-BY-STEP TECHNIQUES
Clear photographs and descriptions of the key preserving techniques.

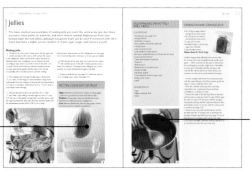

Part 4: Preserving your crop (pages 228–243)
How to make the most of seasonal gluts by preserving your excess crops.

RECIPES
Recipes included for each preserving technique.

INTRODUCTION

Is it because we're concerned about our diets, worried about the pesticides we're ingesting with grocery-store food or just a desire to get closer to nature? Whatever the reason, more of us than ever are gardening, and gardening to grow food has become an achievable reality for everyone. Whether you have a window box or an acre plot, it has become clear that growing food in your garden that you can take into your kitchen gives a real sense of achievement. Whether you're producing some herbs as a garnish, or growing all the ingredients you need for a dish, it can give the gardener and the cook an added dimension to both garden and food.

Fresh fruit and vegetables are good for you. Full of vitamins, antioxidants and other nutritional benefits, food from your garden couldn't be healthier.

Freshness affects taste too, and anyone who has eaten fresh strawberries, peas or asparagus from the garden will attest that the flavor is just so much better than those you buy in the grocery store.

Growing your own is good for the environment, too. No food miles, fewer pesticides and fertilizers, and less wastage. But if growing your own is so good, why isn't everyone doing it?

Growing your own food does take time. It also isn't necessarily the cost-saving hobby some would like you to believe either. However, the advice in this book will help you make the most of the time you have available, and where you do want to save money, the book points out some expensive grocery-store delicacies or those that produce large quantities of staple foods. So the arguments for growing some of your own food definitely outweigh the costs.

Perennial spring treat
Asparagus is actually one of the easiest crops to grow. Once planted, this perennial vegetable will reward you with tender green spears every spring for years to come.

Potato harvest
Digging up your own home-grown potatoes is one of the most
enjoyable events of the growing year.

How to grow For many, growing fruit and vegetables
can last just a single year, being put off by failure and a
lack of time to keep your plot in order.

This book will not only help you get started, but stay
gardening for years to come. The How to Grow section
(see pages 194–227) will provide reassurance to existing
gardeners, and straightforward advice to new ones.

To begin with, get to know your plot. Understanding
some of the basics, such as soil and climate, as well
as knowing about some of the problems that you are
likely to face, such as weeds and pests and diseases,
are all worth reading and thinking about. It's also worth
considering whether you'll be growing in the ground, the
greenhouse or in containers, whether you'll be growing
everything from seed and how and where you might do
this, or whether you want to devote more space to fruit
crops that require little maintenance, but more space.

Growing food doesn't need to be all about rows of
vegetables and spending hours watering and weeding.
Grow smart and select the right plants for your plot and
you can really enjoy your gardening without it becoming
a burden.

Seeds of potential
Just a few packets of seeds are all you need to start off your
growing food year.

The importance of design
Good garden design, for example, incorporating raised beds, not only
makes your garden look good, but makes growing food easier too.

Where to grow It's also worth thinking about what sort of gardener you are — are you into straight rows of neat crops, or do you prefer a more informal approach to your garden? Also, what sort of space do you have available? While those with large plots can afford to space their crops out well to get the maximum yield, others with smaller plots will want to cram their plants to cover every piece of soil with a plant. How to select the best site and design your plot are worthy of consideration before the spade is even lifted. The Where to Grow section (see pages 12–25) will help you answer all these questions.

What to grow Selecting plants that fit in with your lifestyle is of most importance. Not only choosing crops you enjoy eating and will use, but also plants that fit in with the time you have available. It's no point tending tomato plants all spring to find you're on holiday when they're ready to be harvested. Similarly, while growing rows of runner beans couldn't be easier, have you got a spare hour every week to pick them? And what will you do with several pounds of beans every week? Think about not just what you want to eat, but also how much time and effort the plants will need for growing, watering and picking.

Productive plants
If you're not careful, a single packet of seed will inundate you with a glut of vegetables. However, with most crops there are either ways to avoid a glut, or ways to store or preserve your produce for later use.

The Growing Directory (see pages 26–193) deals individually with every crop you may want to grow including fruit, salads, vegetables, nuts and even flowers. Each section begins with a star rating — a quick guide to how easy and productive each crop is. Importantly, we also consider how well the crop stores. While some will need to be eaten immediately, others can be stored for months, providing home-grown produce right through the winter. Climate zone information is supplied for perennial vegetables and fruit, so you can check that your winter isn't too severe to support these crops.

Each entry looks at the best way to grow the crop, and whether it's suitable for containers. There's also a calendar for each entry, providing a guide to when you'll need to do annual tasks such as sow, plant out, prune and harvest each crop.

Once you've decided what to grow, you'll then be presented with recommended varieties of each. Each entry features a variety selector, which provides some straightforward advice from either independent horticultural trials or from my own experience on the best varieties to grow. These have been selected on the basis of their yield, quality and storage of produce, and taste, as well as their ability to fend off pests and diseases where appropriate. Finally, each entry comes with ideas for use in the kitchen as well as specific methods for storing the crop for longer-term use.

Attractive display
Vegetables and edible flowers can make attractive ornamental — and functional — beds if you plan the positioning of your crops.

PART 1: *WHERE TO GROW*

Before you rip open your first packet of seeds, or purchase a bundle of raspberry canes, you need to consider your growing space. How big is your garden? Is it shaded or in full sun? What sort of garden style do you prefer? Spend some time designing your garden around your requirements. In the long run, having a growing food garden-space that works for you, your family and your kitchen will pay dividends.

Types of gardens

Wherever you decide to start growing your food garden, it's worth giving some consideration to the style of garden you want and how you might use it. Of course, this is determined in some way by the plot you have available, but whether you have a small balcony or patio, or a larger plot, it's worth thinking about not just what you want to grow, but how you want to use your garden.

Raised beds
Raised beds were first used where the soil or climatic conditions made gardening tricky. Now, they're used as design features in their own right. Raised beds are also easier to weed and tend to, being that bit nearer.

There are lots of garden styles to choose from when deciding how to lay out an ornamental garden, and it's similar for the vegetable plot too. Traditional vegetable gardens consist of neat, parallel beds with narrow paths in between to access the produce and maximize the growing space. Raised beds are a newer technique that, oddly enough, can evoke a traditional look. In smaller plots, the growing food garden often means incorporating it into the rest of the garden. A more ornamental kitchen garden, or potager, where flowers and vegetables sit happily side by side, can be both attractive and productive. On an even smaller plot, growing in containers and small raised beds may be the only option. While the space in these gardens may be limited, with decent planning they can still be extremely productive.

Perfect for smaller gardens
Patio gardening can be productive too. Crops like peppers, eggplants and tomatoes all do well on a sunny patio, as long as they're well watered and fed.

Productive plots
A large plot like this could require
16–20 hours per week to keep in good
order during the peak growing season.

The large plot

This is a term used to describe a large section of your garden given over entirely to growing food. The plot may be part of a community garden, where land is loaned to private individuals to grow fruit and vegetables. Just like your own garden, they'll need a big investment of time to get them right, so should be treated just like your own. The effort you put into the site when you first take it over will pay dividends in years to come, and creating a good basic structure to the plot is essential. There are some simple rules to follow here that should be considered before even a spade is sunk into the ground (see pages 18–25).

Large plots dedicated solely to fruit- and vegetable-growing do not always look fantastic. Winter especially will be fairly bleak, with bare stems and trunks, and little to look at and enjoy. There may be limited pickings too, except for winter brassicas such as Brussels sprouts, and root vegetables such as parsnips, and also perhaps lettuce and other greens, depending on your climate. If you want your garden to be attractive all year round, then this style isn't for you. If, however, your site is out of sight for most of the time, and you visit it only to garden and pick your produce, then this type of plot, where every square inch is devoted to productive gardening, will be both the easiest to manage and give the highest returns.

Most large garden vegetable and fruit plots are usually designed to have everything that's required in one spot: a shed, compost bin, and cold frames are all useful structures to have, as is a seat or bench to enjoy looking at the fruits of your labor. Plots are usually laid out as a series of narrow beds, sometimes raised off the ground, with paths in between. To make them easier to create, the beds are often not edged, but in the long run, it's better to edge them with planks of wood to help keep a distinction between your paths and beds. Paths are usually grass, chipped bark or straw, but for the more ornamental plot there is no reason why you can't use paving, brick or concrete paths. Whatever you use, in this type of garden it's about devoting as much soil as you can to growing produce.

Permanent fruit trees and berries, as well as perennial vegetables such as asparagus, will have their own areas of the plot. These will help provide the plot with some structure, especially in the winter months. The other beds should be devoted solely to annual vegetables and herbs, and a rotation system implemented (see pages 22–23).

The kitchen garden or potager

For many gardeners, growing food in their back yard is what gardening is all about. Being able to pop out into the yard and dig up some potatoes or pick a few snow peas for dinner makes this type of gardening very rewarding. However, many of us don't have huge plots of land where whole areas can be devoted solely to growing food — many of us want our garden to be not only productive but attractive too.

This is where the idea of the kitchen garden, or potager, comes in. Mixing flowers, vegetables, herbs and fruit is not a new idea, but it's a solution that can work extremely well for many modern gardeners. It is important to realize, however, that your plants may not grow to the size they would in a dedicated growing food plot, and crops will not be quite as bountiful. Managing a potager where plants are grown in a more haphazard fashion than in the straight rows or blocks of a larger plot may also mean more work for you. But in the end, it's about working with what you've got, and if you want your garden to produce cut flowers for your house as well as food for your kitchen, and for it to be full of scent, buzzing insects and color, then a kitchen garden is definitely for you.

Kitchen gardens vary in their formality and devotion to growing food. On the one hand, they can be truly ornamental gardens, with a selection of vegetables, herbs and fruit planted just occasionally around the flowers. On the other, they may be more dedicated to growing food, with the use of flowers limited to entrances and path edges. The best potagers, however, feature an equal mix of flowers and food — they are usually laid out in beds with a series of paths, just like an allotment garden, as whenever you're growing food you need to make sure you can always reach the middle of the bed from the path, without having to walk on the soil.

IDEAS: KITCHEN GARDEN

There are no clear rules to follow with a kitchen garden, and it's worth experimenting with flowers, vegetables and fruit to see what works for you. Here are some ideas for you to consider:

- You may choose a pear tree instead of an ornamental crabapple, and a blackberry or tart cherry to grow against a fence instead of a rose. These choices mean that while you may loose out on some color, you'll be rewarded with a harvest.

- Think about the vegetable varieties that you grow. While some can be plain and productive, others can be ornamental. A beautiful dinosaur kale plant looks incredible in any garden, as can the two-tone flowers of some varieties of climbing runner beans. Edging plants of frilly lettuce or herbs such as chives or parsley can be both ornamental and productive.

- Use height in the garden, not just for vegetables that climb such as beans and peas, but also for those that can be trained to climb such as pumpkins, squashes and marrows. Mix these with climbing annuals such as sweet peas that can be used as cut flowers.

- Add other flowers that can be used for cutting: marigold, chrysanthemum, sunflowers and cornflowers, for example, as well as flowers that you can eat (see pages 116–117).

Interplanting flowers and vegetables

Growing flowers alongside vegetables can provide extra benefits. Some flowers, such as nasturtiums, may be edible, while others, such as marigolds, may deter pests. Best of all, they brighten up your edible garden and turn a vegetable patch into a kitchen garden.

The patio garden

In smaller plots you may not have the luxury of being able to grow flowers and food side by side, but it doesn't mean that the productive patio garden has to look miserable for much of the year. Ornamental pots and bedding plants can still be used to great effect to make your patio or balcony a cheery and welcoming place to sit. The best productive patio gardens also include scented plants as well as a place nearby, situated in the sun, where you can sit and relax.

Some patio gardens will be big enough to squeeze in a single raised bed — a good idea to boost your productivity. This amount of space allows for growing larger vegetables such as brassicas and corn that don't typically do well in containers, but rows of cut-and-come-again lettuce, as well as fruit such as strawberries, and herbs, also look attractive.

Create a spectacle

Growing food doesn't have to mean an allotment-style with lots of bare soil. Edible plants can look good in the garden too as with this row of tomato plants growing in pewter-style containers. Kitchen and patio gardens should contain just as many flowers as they do crops.

IDEAS: PATIO GARDEN

Again, there are no hard and fast rules to growing food on the patio, but consider these options:

- If you're restricted to pots, the most productive patio gardens are those where just one type of vegetable per pot is grown. A number of pots all filled with different vegetables placed together means you wouldn't even notice this monoculture.

- Herbs always do well in pots, and evergreen ones such as bay and rosemary may help to provide a backbone.

- Some fruit in pots always do well — blueberries are a must, but even raspberries and currants can thrive in containers.

- Annual herbs such as coriander and parsley look attractive in containers and their diminutive size means they thrive.

- Position the best-looking containers at the front of the patio, and move the less attractive ones, such as potatoes, toward the back.

- Try growing vegetables and fruit in hanging baskets too, such as cucumbers, tomatoes and melons on a sunny patio.

Choosing the best site

Whatever your garden size, you will probably have some choice on where to site your productive garden. If you really have no choice, you'll need to select the plants that suit the situation you have. Otherwise, it's worth considering your options before you start to design it. Whatever you do, don't always opt for the piece of land at the end of the garden. Large trees, poor drainage, or frost pockets may mean that these areas will not be particularly productive. There are six physical considerations to bear in mind.

Sun and shade

It's a good idea to work out how sunny or shady your proposed plot is likely to be. While it may not receive much sun in the winter, it's important that the sun reaches it during the summer months. Although some fruit and vegetables grow well in shade, they will all be outperformed by those grown in sun. It's a good idea to have an open site away from large buildings, walls and trees. This may not be always possible, but it is worth attempting to maximize the amount of sun your plot receives. Consider, for example, reducing the height of any existing trees

Consider additional features
Selecting a position for all the additionals such as a water barrel, shed and greenhouse is important. The best place for a water butt is below a roof, but consider how far you need to carry the water, and if necessary invest in a water-butt pump.

or raising the canopy. Swapping fence panels for see-through trellises will not only allow you to grow climbing plants, but also allow more sunlight to enter into the garden.

Soil

Most sites will have the same soil right across the plot (see page 218). You'll need to consider what soil you have, and where necessary, how to improve its structure, texture and fertility. Where drainage is a problem, consider creating land drains to allow excess water to drain off your site.

Wind

It's worth avoiding areas of your garden that you know are exposed to strong wind. In coastal areas, this can be challenging, but there are some tricks you can do to increase the amount of shelter your plants receive.

The first is to consider the boundaries of your garden. Solid fences and walls may seem like a good idea, but this actually creates turbulence and the strength of the winds in the garden may actually increase. Much better are barriers that allow some of the air to come through but the barrier both filters and slows the air movement. Hedges are ideal for this, but will take some years to grow. Alternatively, windbreak materials can be erected as a temporary measure while the hedges develop.

Water

All plants need water, and it's important that you have a ready supply. If you tend to use the tap to water your plants, consider how far away the tap is from your plot, and if necessary add an extension to this.

Most of the watering, though, will come from the sky, but walls and especially trees can really reduce how much water reaches both the soil and the roots of your plants. In the summer, trees and ornamental shrubs will be taking up gallons of water from the ground and can make the surface dry and unproductive. For this reason, avoid siting your garden next to large trees.

A traditionally designed plot
A well-designed food garden means providing your plants with the best conditions available to you — lots of sunshine, good soil and little competition from other plants growing nearby. This open, flat plot provides just that.

Temperature

Temperature affects all gardens, but there is not really very much we can do to change it, except when it comes to frost. In some gardens, particularly those that lie on a slope, there will be areas that will remain frostier for longer. These are called frost pockets and occur when cold air runs down a slope and settles in a dip. Where you think you have a frost pocket, it's worth making sure you avoid that area for your growing food plot. If you find that your plot sits right on a frost pocket, consider ways of dealing with the problem area. Simply creating a gap at the bottom of a fence to allow the cold air to continue on its way may be possible, for example.

Slopes

Slopes can be tricky to use for the productive gardener. Very slight slopes shouldn't cause much concern, and if you're creating raised beds it may be possible to flatten out the slopes within the beds. Where slopes are steeper, creating terracing is the best option. Use terracing perpendicular to the slope to create a series of level beds with steps down.

Crops in blocks
Crops are often planted in blocks or squares. This allows you to get the soil and conditions right for each crop, as well as maximizing the use of space — as soon as one crop is harvested, another one should be planted in its place.

Designing your food garden

Once you've decided on the style of garden you are going to create and have set out the plot that is available to you, it's important to spend some time designing the plot. Once you've dug out the beds and planted some fruit, it's hard to go back and start again, so it's important to be organized. Your best bet is to sketch out some rough plans on paper. Only in this way can you really start to understand what you can fit in your plot and where it should all go.

CREATING THE PERFECT GROWING FOOD GARDEN PLAN

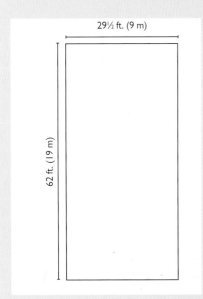

1 First take some measurements and work out the area you have available. Draw this to a known scale on a piece of paper.

2 Work out where north is in relation to your plot and draw this on the paper as an arrow.

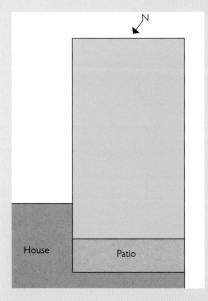

3 Draw in any structures that surround your plot or are within it, such as houses or garages. Think about the amount of shade they can cast.

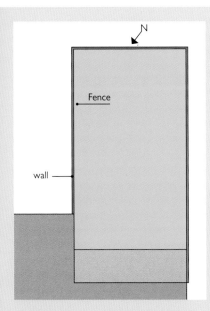

Fence

wall

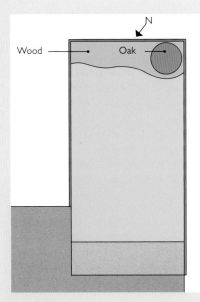

Wood — Oak

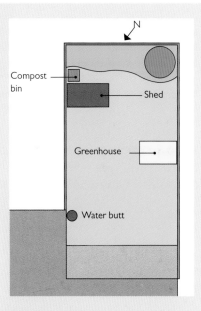

Compost bin

Shed

Greenhouse

Water butt

4 Draw in any fences and walls, particularly those that you can plant against.

5 Sketch circles for any other permanent plants or trees on your plot.

6 Add permanent structures: a shed, compost bins, cold frames and spigots that are either already present or that you plan to include.

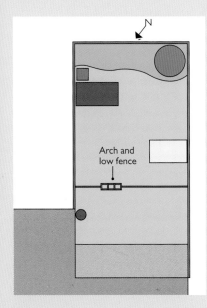

Arch and low fence

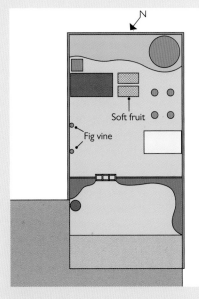

Soft fruit

Fig vine

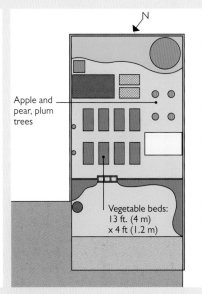

Apple and pear, plum trees

Vegetable beds: 13 ft. (4 m) x 4 ft (1.2 m)

7 Draw in any structures you plan to add: arches, arbors and pergolas allow you to separate the plot as well as open up space to grow more plants. Fences and walls can help to divide larger gardens and provide growing space for fan-trained trees such as figs, apricots and cherries.

8 Add beds or borders where you plan to plant long-lived plants and indicate what you plan to plant where. Any trees, berries (with fruit cages where required) and perennial vegetables should be added. Indicate where you plan to plant anything against walls or fences. Also add where you plan to place large containers and hanging baskets.

9 Sketch a series of beds, no wider than around 4 ft. (1.2 m). The length is up to you, but remember you'll have to walk right the way around every time you want to reach the other side of the bed. Ideally the beds should be in groups of either three or four to allow you to fit into either a three- or four-year rotation scheme.

Larger plots

These plots are often situated away from the house, either in another part of the garden or in a different location.

A shed may be useful to store your tools, pots, fertilizers and pest controls. Sheds should be positioned in the most shady and dry part of the plot so that they don't take up valuable growing space. It's a good idea to site some other essentials nearby, such as a compost bin for all your waste plant material. While these work best when sited in the sun, most people tend to keep them out of the way in a shady corner, but this does mean that decomposition will take a little longer. If you are thinking of having a greenhouse, this needs to be considered from the outset too as you'll need a sunny site on level ground.

Next are the beds. First think about any fruit trees you want to grow. Ideally, these should be positioned so they cast as little shade as possible onto your site.

Potagers and kitchen gardens

It's not necessary to lay out potagers and kitchen gardens in a very formulaic way. It is a good idea to have a series of paths that are intersected by narrow beds. These can be laid out in a pattern of symmetry to provide

CROP FAMILIES

Crops are put into families and these families move around the plot together.

Family		Why group together?	What soil conditions do they prefer?
PEA AND BEAN Includes all peas, fava beans, lima beans, soybeans, runner beans and dwarf beans.		These plants have root nodules that turn nitrogen in the air into nutrients the plants can use.	Because they make their own nitrogen, they require little fertilizer but need plenty of water, so prefer soil that has had plenty of organic matter, such as compost or manure, added.
POTATO Also includes tomatoes, eggplants and peppers.		Can suffer from blight, so best moved around together to stop re-infection. Other problems, such as scab and eelworm, can be avoided if moved around the garden together.	All like a decent amount of organic matter and nutrients.
ROOT CROP Includes carrots and parsnips, but also parsley.		Carrot fly can be avoided if the crops are netted together.	Don't like soil with fresh compost added. They don't require much in the way of additional fertilizer either.
BRASSICA Includes cabbages, cauliflowers, Brussels sprouts, Chinese vegetables such as Chinese cabbage and bok choi, radishes, kohlrabi, kale, as well as some salads such as mizuna and rocket.		These plants can suffer from clubroot and prefer an alkaline soil to keep it at bay. They suffer from the same flying pests so all should be covered with floating row covers.	Compost or manure should have been added for the previous crop. They require high levels of nutrients.
ONION Includes all onions, shallots, garlic, leeks and chives.		Plants can suffer from allium leaf miner and white rot. Floating row covers can be used on the crop to control insect pests.	An average amount of fertilizer and soil that has had compost or manure added to it for the previous crop.
EVERYTHING ELSE		All other crops should be moved around the garden, but it's not vital; they can be fitted in with any of the above families where there is space.	

some order to your kitchen garden. However, don't necessarily restrict yourself to rectangular beds. A series of 3 ft. 2-in. (1-m) square beds can work just as well, as can triangular or curved beds. Most importantly the kitchen garden has to fit in with the style of your house. Replicate and complement the materials used in your house and garden in the structure of your kitchen garden so it seamlessly flows on. Think about creating arches to enter and exit the garden, as well as some areas where fencing or walls allow you to grow climbing plants.

Because many of the plants take up residence for just the summer months, think about how you can fill in these gaps during the winter. Use permanent obelisks in the center of beds, which can be used by climbing plants in the summer, but provide a feature during the winter too. Consider the positioning of trees and berries. These can provide structure to your garden in the winter, but you don't want them to shade out your summer vegetables.

Patios and balconies

These are the gardens that provide the most design limitations. You are restricted in space, and have little choice when it comes to sun or shade. To maximize your growing space, consider any structures that allow you to grow in a three-dimensional space. Pergolas, arches and even simple posts allow you to grow plants vertically, making the most of the space you have available.

When choosing containers, go for a range of styles and sizes, but remember that the larger the pots, the less watering they'll require (if you have a balcony, make sure that it will hold the extra weight of the containers). Lastly, think about adding a series of hanging baskets or other systems to grow plants against walls and fences. These again open up growing space to you that otherwise wouldn't be available.

Crop rotation

Within your plan it's likely you'll have some space to grow vegetables each year. If you've followed the advice given on the previous pages, you'll have beds in groups of three or four. This allows you to rotate your crops around the garden each year.

The most important reason for this is to stop the build-up of pests and diseases. If you grew all your plants from the onion family in a single bed every year, for example, it's likely that onion white rot will strike and affect crops in future years. Moving crops regularly means this build-up of disease is less likely. Crop rotation ensures that additions of nutrients are kept to a minimum while ensuring plants grow to their maximum potential. With crop rotation, you should need to add bulky organic matter, such as compost or manure only every three years — while some crops like freshly manured ground, and others, such as carrots, dislike it.

Where full crop rotation isn't possible, try to move at least potatoes, onions and brassicas around the garden, even if it's just by a few feet.

THREE-YEAR THREE-BED ROTATION

YEAR I

Plot A Peas, beans and onions (add manure/compost)

Plot B Potatoes and root crops (add fertilizer)

Plot C Brassicas (add fertilizer)

YEAR 2

Plot A Brassicas (add fertilizer)

Plot B Peas, beans and onions (add manure/compost)

Plot C Potatoes and root crops (add fertilizer)

YEAR 3

Plot A Potatoes and root crops (add fertilizer)

Plot B Brassicas (add fertilizer)

Plot C Peas, beans and onions (add manure/compost)

FOUR-YEAR FOUR-BED ROTATION

YEAR I

Plot A Peas and beans (add compost)
Plot B Brassicas (add plenty of fertilizer)
Plot C Onions and root crops (no compost, little fertilizer)
Plot D Potatoes (add compost and fertilizer)

YEAR 2

Plot A Potatoes (add compost and fertilizer)
Plot B Peas and beans (add compost)
Plot C Brassicas (add plenty of fertilizer)
Plot D Onions and root crops (no compost, little fertilizer)

YEAR 3

Plot A Onions and root crops (no compost, little fertilizer)
Plot B Potatoes (add compost and fertilizer)
Plot C Peas and beans (add compost)
Plot D Brassicas (add plenty of fertilizer)

YEAR 4

Plot A Brassicas (add plenty of fertilizer)
Plot B Onions and root crops (no compost, little fertilizer)
Plot C Potatoes (add compost and fertilizer)
Plot D Peas and beans (add compost)

Crop rotation examples

Above are two crop-rotation schemes to try, depending on the size of your garden. Using a rotation scheme will ensure that your soil stays nutrient-rich and low in pests and diseases.

Growing undercover

Growing undercover gives you a head start with many of your summer crops, allowing you to sow earlier than you would otherwise be able.

GREENHOUSE TIPS

The most traditional-looking undercover space, a greenhouse is ideal for most vegetable and fruit growers. Greenhouses can be expensive, but it's worth investing in a decent one.

What materials? You'll be able to choose between an aluminum and wood greenhouse. While aluminum greenhouses are cheaper, they are much more difficult to dismantle and reassemble, so if you think you may move home in the next few years, wood is a better option.

What size? It's best to go for a greenhouse as big as you can afford and fit into your garden. 6 x 8 ft. (1.8 x 2.4 m) is a popular size and a good one to start with. Anything less than this and you'll soon run out of space.

What extras? Consider buying staging and shelving for at least one side. It's much easier to buy this with the greenhouse so it all fits into place. These give you space to raise plants from seed and grow vegetables in small containers. The other open side can be used for growing vining vegetables such as tomatoes and cucumbers.

Windows and vents Most greenhouse come with windows in the roof and the side. Consider buying some automatic openers, which open as the temperature rises.

Electrical supply It's well worth installing an electrical supply, with a waterproof socket or two. Always use a ground fault protected device when using electricity outdoors. An electric supply will allow you to use a thermostatically controlled electric greenhouse heater and a heated propagator to get your seedlings going.

Watering Consider fixing a water barrel next to the side of your greenhouse for a nearby supply, or run a fixed pipe and attach a tap next to your greenhouse, which will save both trailing a hose across your garden and carrying cans of water.

You can also fit an irrigation system inside your greenhouse, and using a water timer means that watering by hand twice a day in midsummer to keep your plants going becomes a thing of the past (see pages 214–215).

While we can improve our soil, select good-quality varieties and monitor pest control, one thing we can't govern is the weather. Investing in a frost-free environment for your plants means you'll be able to garden and harvest all through the year. For example, you can start tender vegetables early, which means harvesting comes earlier too. They also allow you to grow tender fruit as well as salads through the winter. Although a greenhouse is the most popular choice, there are other options.

Sunroom

If your house has a sunroom, it's an ideal space for growing food. It's likely everything will have to be grown in a container, but it's more than possible to grow all sorts of fruit and salad crops – anything from a nectarine to large pots of herbs. It may be difficult to keep a sunroom cool in the summer, so if yours receives lots of direct sun, consider installing blinds.

Polytunnel

A polytunnel is basically a plastic tunnel greenhouse. As they're made of aluminum hoops and sheet plastic, they are much cheaper to buy than a greenhouse and because they don't need a solid base, they're much cheaper to install too. They do not

Greenhouse
Western red cedar timber makes for a long-lasting and attractive greenhouse. Its natural oils means that it's not necessary to stain, and the coloring will slowly lighten with age.

Polytunnel protection
Polytunnels are cheap and quick to erect. They are ideal where the climate isn't quite warm enough for the crops you want to grow, or when you want to raise plants slightly out of season.

WHAT TO GROW IN A GREENHOUSE

- A great place to raise seedlings, both tender crops such as tomatoes and peppers, but also a good place to start hardy crops such as brassicas and onions.
- If you want an early crop of potatoes, carrots or summer squash, consider growing them in a pot and starting in the greenhouse very early in the season.
- Herbs can be overwintered in the greenhouse and remain productive for much of the year.
- Eggplants, sweet peppers and chilies can be grown in the greenhouse all summer. They can make the greenhouse both look good and be productive.
- Propagating plants such as strawberries can be left in a greenhouse where they will root quickly.

give the same insulation or light quality as a greenhouse but are perfectly good for growing all sorts of fruit and vegetables. Unheated, a polytunnel will allow you to extend your season by a month or two, but if you add a heater, you can use it just as a greenhouse. However, they're no thing of beauty so are best used in a devoted vegetable garden.

Cold frame

For those with little space, a cold frame is a worthy investment. Even for those with a greenhouse, a cold frame provides a space to transfer your plants to harden them off.

Many plants will suffer if you move them straight from the protection of a greenhouse to outside, so a cold frame, where the lid can be opened in the day and closed at night, allows a plant to acclimatize to the harsher conditions outside.

Mini greenhouse

If a cold frame doesn't give quite enough space, a mini greenhouse can be perfect. These come in a range of materials and prices. The cheapest are plastic covers over a thin metal frame, the more expensive are fixed to the side of the house and made of wood or aluminum and glazed with glass. While expensive versions should be avoided unless you really cannot fit a full-sized greenhouse in your garden, a cheap version is perfect for raising seedlings in a small garden. Choose one with plenty of shelving, and a width to fit a standard seed tray. This way you can raise lots of plants in one go.

If the shelves can be removed, it can be used later in the summer for larger crops such as a couple of tomatoes or cucumbers.

Pest and disease problems

The one problem of growing in a hot environment is that the seedlings can be a magnet for lots of pests and diseases. And the fact that they never become really cold means these pests and diseases rarely die out naturally. At least once a year it's a good idea to take all your plants out of the greenhouse and give it a wash and scrub. There are proprietary greenhouse cleaning products available. It's also worth cleaning all pots and trays as

this can reduce your exposure to damping off — a disease that will quickly kill off seedlings. Greenhouse-grown crops can also suffer from more pests and diseases in the summer as the pests can thrive in a warm humid environment, away from any natural enemies. Consider using biological controls, which are perfect for using in a greenhouse (see page 217).

Mini greenhouse
A mini greenhouse is perfect for raising seeds in spring. Some will also allow you to remove the shelves and grow tomatoes and other tender crops in the summer.

PART 2: GROWING DIRECTORY

Out of the hundreds of vegetable and salad crops, fruit and nuts in this book, realistically you will be able to grow just a few, at least in your first year. First, pick out the crops you especially like, particularly when picked fresh. Make sure you choose ones that suit your cooking style and your family's tastes too. Second, consider your garden space and the time you have to devote to the crop — grow only those that are likely to succeed in the space you have and the time you can spend caring for your plants.

VEGETABLE AND SALAD CROPS
28

VEGETABLE AND SALAD CROPS

If you want rewards quickly, vegetable and salad crops are a good place to start. With just a couple of packets of seed, you can be harvesting your first crop of salad leaves within four weeks, and your first radishes in five. And with the multitude of different vegetable and salad crops that can be grown successfully in the garden, with careful planning you can pick fresh food all year round.

ROOT CROPS

Root crops such as potatoes, carrots and onions are an important addition to any vegetable plot. Despite produce being widely available and mostly cheap to buy, there is nothing more rewarding than growing your own. Tasty and fresh, garden-grown carrots and new potatoes can't be beaten. Many root crops can also be stored, giving you access to your harvest for much of the winter too.

Potato

One of the easiest and most productive crops to grow, no kitchen garden should be without a row or two of potatoes.

- ✪✪✪✪✪ VALUE FOR MONEY
- ✪✪✪✪✪ MAINTENANCE
- ✪✪✪✪✪ FREEZE/STORE
- CROPPING SEASON: EARLY SUMMER–MID-FALL

Potatoes have been grown by humans for over 7,000 years, and it's not difficult to understand why this American native has become a favorite across the world. In fact, it's the world's most popular vegetable, with an annual production of over 330 million tons (300 million tonnes). Plant a seed potato (one of the tubers from the previous crop) in the spring, and by midsummer, many more will have been produced. Harvest in the fall, and the potatoes can be used in the kitchen right through the winter. Potatoes are tender plants but can be grown in most parts of the world, as long as there are plentiful amounts of water to help the tubers swell during the summer.

Where to grow Potatoes are a common sight in kitchen gardens and often follow on from brassicas on a rotation (see page 22–23), but they'll do well anywhere there are plenty of nutrients. In fact, potatoes are often used on new plots to help break them in, since they do well on all soil types. They are large plants, however, and do require a fair amount of space. If space is short, go for early varieties that don't put on as much growth before they need harvesting. If space is really short, containers are the best option. Potatoes grow very successfully in containers, and many companies exploit this fact by selling special bags or pots to grow potatoes in, but any large container, which holds at least 2.5 gallons (10 L) of soil, will do.

Types and varieties Around 7,000 years of breeding has left us with all manner of potatoes, available in a variety of colors — from cream to blue — as well as a selection of shapes and sizes. However, the most useful variation for the gardener is the speed of growth. While some potatoes are ready for harvesting after as little as 80 days of growing,

Harvesting potatoes
Depending on the variety, you can harvest potatoes from mid- to late summer, then store what you don't need for use through the winter.

others take much longer. This allows the gardener, with one planting, to keep harvesting potatoes from midsummer right through the winter. There are three main groups:

Earlies From a mid-spring planting, these potatoes will be the first to make it onto the kitchen table by midsummer. These young potatoes often command a high premium in the supermarket. Plant earlies 16 inches (40 cm) apart in rows 20 inches (50 cm) apart. Dig up plants as you need them.

Second earlies These are more likely to be waxy, salad-type potatoes, which will be ready for harvesting around three and a half months after planting — usually in mid- to late ➡

VARIETY SELECTOR

Earlies

- 'Caribe', 'Red Norland', 'Yukon Gold'.

Second earlies

- 'All Blue', 'Kennebec'.

Maincrops

- 'Butte', 'Rose Finn Apple'.

COLORFUL POTATOES

Potatoes are available in lots of colors, so why not try some more unusual varieties?

- **'Blue Danube'**: fine bright blue tubers, but sadly the flesh is white. Some blight resistance.

- **'Mayan Twilight'**: red and white patched tubers, with a deep yellow, sweet flesh.

- **'Congo'**: dark blue, both inside and out — great for kids' parties.

Colorful potatoes
Potatoes come in many colors — try blue or red for unusually colored mashed potato!

IN THE KITCHEN

Best for mash
- 'Accent', 'Kestrel'.

Best for roasts
- 'King Edward', 'Maris Piper'.

Best for chips
- 'Golden Wonder', 'Valor'.

Best for baking
- 'Picasso', 'Marfona'.

Best for salads
- 'Charlotte', 'Anya'.

summer. Dig these up as and when you need them. Leave any plants you don't need in the ground. They'll be fine for a couple of months and you can harvest when you need them.

Maincrop The largest harvest usually comes from maincrop varieties. The potatoes need a long growing season, and if you have plenty of storage space, they will stay fresh right through the winter. Space the rows 30 inches (75 cm) apart, to give the plants plenty of space to grow. Harvest in one go in the fall.

In the garden Potatoes will give you a decent yield wherever you grow them, but to maximize your harvest, grow them on rich, deep soil, and if you can, supplement the soil with plenty of homemade compost or other soil improver (see page 220–223). It's also worth adding a balanced granular fertilizer to the soil when you plant.

When you buy your potatoes in winter, they come as tubers, with small "eyes," which, if left on a cool windowsill, will start to sprout. Potatoes are sensitive to frost, and any growth that emerges can be hit by frosts. Plants will recover from some damage, but if frosts are forecast, cover the stems with floating row covers, straw or even a layer of compost.

As the plants start to grow, it's worth drawing up soil onto the young shoots, leaving just the young leaves exposed. This can protect the stems from frost and increase the yield.

Pests and diseases Potatoes are susceptible to a variety of pests and diseases, but only a few (some of which are easy to prevent) cause major problems to gardeners. To avoid virus diseases ruining your crop, it's best to buy fresh tubers each year — these

GROWING POTATOES IN A CONTAINER

1 Choose an early or second early variety. Fill a large container (2.5 gallons/10 L or more) or potato bag one-third with potting mix. Place one tuber with the shoots uppermost and cover with 2 inches (5 cm) of potting mix, before watering in well.

2 As the potatoes start to grow, add more potting mix, covering the stems. Add a slow-release fertilizer, mixing the recommended rate in with the potting mix.

3 Keep adding potting mix until just below the rim of the pot.

will have been produced from virus-free stock.

Common scab Scabby areas develop on the tubers, but can mostly be avoided by ensuring the soil isn't too alkaline. Avoid adding lime to the soil and work in plenty of organic matter.

Late blight The most devastating potato disease for gardeners is blight, where brown freckles on the leaves lead to a brownish rot developing in the tubers. The same disease that caused the Irish potato famine over 150 years ago is still causing problems today. There are a number of chemicals that can be sprayed on the crops to prevent the disease taking hold, but for organic gardeners there is little to help. If blight does strike, cut off all the foliage; this will limit the spread of the disease to the tubers. Wait a couple of weeks, then harvest all the potatoes.

Intensive breeding has developed some varieties that are resistant to the disease, but often this resistance lasts only a year or two before the disease mutates and works out how to infect the plant. Recent breeding in Hungary has produced some varieties (usually prefixed with the name 'Sarpo'), which do, for now anyway, keep the disease at bay.

PESTS AND DISEASES

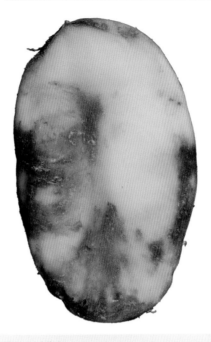

Potato blight
Late blight can ruin your crop, so you'll need to keep a close eye out for it.

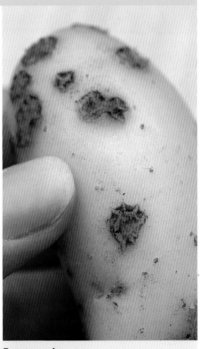

Potato scabs
If potato scabs are a problem in your garden, you'll need to improve your soil conditions.

4 Keep watering the potatoes. As the plants start to flower, the potatoes will begin to form.

5 The pot is best kept on a sunny patio. Keep watering your container as this will help the tubers to swell.

6 Try feeling into the pot with your hand, and once you feel decent-sized potatoes, tip the pot out.

Harvesting and storage Harvest earlies and second earlies as they are ready. Dig up a single plant to check the size of the potatoes. One plant should produce more than enough potatoes for a meal. While these types of potatoes don't store too well and should be dug up over the summer as you need them, maincrops will store for much longer. Once lifted in fall, store in paper or burlap sacks in a cool, dark place. If your potatoes were struck with blight, keep checking the tubers because infection can quickly spread.

In the kitchen Potatoes can be used in all sorts of cuisines — from Asian to European. Potatoes can be harvested all year round and are a versatile crop. Earlies, which you harvest in early summer, work well in warm or cold salads, or just as plain boiled potatoes as they have plenty of flavor. Second earlies are also usually waxy-type potatoes that don't mash well but are great boiled and used in salads. These types of potatoes are also delicious roasted with Mediterranean vegetables or used in soups. The large harvest from your maincrops comes in all shapes, sizes and colors. These can be used for mashing, baking, roasting or chipping. You could also try making your own chips, adding thinly sliced potatoes to other root vegetables, such as carrots and parsnips.

CALENDAR

EARLY WINTER

Order your seed potatoes and unpack them as soon as they arrive. Leave the tubers in trays in a cool, dry and light spot (but out of direct sunlight). The potatoes will start to "chit" or sprout (see below).

MID-SPRING

Put a sprinkling of fertilizer onto the ground and plant the tubers 6 inches (15 cm) deep and 16 inches (40 cm) apart. Separate the rows of potatoes by around 20 inches (50 cm) (this will depend on the variety).

LATE SPRING

Draw soil from between the rows over the shoots. Keep doing this until you create a ridge of around 12 inches (30 cm) in height.

EARLY SUMMER

Water any earlies because the tubers will be swelling now.

MIDSUMMER

Start to harvest your earlies. Use a garden fork to carefully dig out the potatoes. Use immediately.

LATE SUMMER

Your second earlies will start to be ready now. Give the plants a good soaking each week for a few weeks before harvesting. Make sure your maincrops are well watered too, and watch out for blight.

FALL

Maincrops can be lifted through the fall. These can be stored in paper or burlap sacks.

HARVESTING POTATO CROPS

1 Through the early part of the season, draw up the soil around the young stems of potatoes. This will help even more tubers to form. Once the foliage starts to die down, this is a sure sign that your crop is ready. Your potatoes will come to no harm if you leave them in the ground, so you could just dig them when you need them.

2 The best tool for lifting potatoes is a garden fork. Gently push the fork into the ground about 18 inches (45 cm) away from the main stems, and ease the potatoes out of the ground. It's impossible to avoid stabbing one or two potatoes, but this method should keep it to a minimum.

3 Collect your potatoes still attached to the plant, but also have a good dig around the area to make sure none are left in the ground. The foliage can go on the compost heap, and the potatoes taken indoors for immediate cooking.

Sweet potato

This crop can be tricky to grow, but it's well worth it if you're successful.

○○○○○ VALUE FOR MONEY
○○○○○ MAINTENANCE
○○○○○ FREEZE/STORE
CROPPING SEASON: MID-FALL–LATE FALL

Sweet potatoes naturally grow in sunny climes. They need a long frost-free period and plenty of sun and warmth to grow successfully.

Where to grow For those in colder areas who have tried growing sweet potatoes and failed, you are not alone. Grown in the soil in your vegetable patch, your tubers will likely be small. To increase the yield, try growing them under black polythene, which helps the soil warm up. A better approach is to grow sweet potatoes in large 2.5-gallon (10-L) containers, either on the patio or in a very warm greenhouse.

In the garden Sweet potatoes come as slips when bought from mail-order vegetable suppliers. Slips are small, unrooted cuttings taken from tubers that have sprouted. When they first arrive, put them in a jar of water to perk them up. If you're growing them in the garden, pot them up in small containers in the greenhouse or sunny window and wait until the last frosts before planting outdoors. If you're growing the plants in a pot in a greenhouse or window, plant straight into this.

Pests and diseases Sweet potatoes are trouble free.

Harvesting and storage Tubers should be harvested before any chance of frost. Lift as you would potatoes (see page 34), or if in a tub, just tip them out — but don't expect more than a couple in each pot. Clean off and store as you would potatoes (in paper or burlap sacks in a cool, dark place).

In the kitchen Sweet potatoes can be roasted and served in risottos or on pizzas. You can also make fantastic soups or boil and mash them to serve with Sunday roast.

(see page 34)

CALENDAR

MID-WINTER
Order your slips from mail-order suppliers.

MID-SPRING
On arrival, pot up slips into small pots for planting outdoors later.

LATE SPRING
For planting outdoors, dig over the ground well, add some organic matter and plant. Use floating row covers to protect plants from late frost.

EARLY SUMMER
If growing in pots, keep the plants well watered, and water with a tomato fertilizer.

MIDSUMMER
In the ground, make sure plants don't go short of water, and weed the crop regularly.

LATE SUMMER
Continue watering and feeding your sweet potatoes in containers.

EARLY–LATE FALL
You can start to harvest in early fall, but the sweet potatoes should get bigger if left even longer. Dig up plants or turn out your tubs. Clean off and store in paper or burlap sacks. Harvest by the first frost.

PLANTING OUT SWEET POTATOES

1 On arrival, place your slips in a jar of water for a day or two. Once perked up, plant deeply in small containers.

2 In the garden, plant out through black plastic sheeting once all risk of frost has passed.

VARIETY SELECTOR

• **'Beauregard Improved'**: a good American variety from Louisiana. These grow to grocery store-sized tubers and have red skins and sweet orange flesh.

• **'Georgia Jet'**: recommended for cooler climates, but it can still be tricky to get a good crop. The bright red skin hides the pale orange flesh.

Carrot

Quick and easy to grow, it's possible to keep
your kitchen stocked with fresh garden carrots
for most of the year.

OOOOO	VALUE FOR MONEY
OOOOO	MAINTENANCE
OOOOO	FREEZE/STORE
CROPPING SEASON: LATE SPRING–LATE FALL	

After potatoes, carrots are probably the most
important root crop to gardeners, and for
some they're even more rewarding to grow.
Spotting the developing orange crowns pushing
through the soil and pulling these out is a real
joy. Carrots are invaluable in the kitchen —
everyone knows how good they taste raw,
steamed and roasted, but they can also be
used in cakes and puddings. They're rich
in carotenoids, which help to protect the
body from cancer and heart disease, as
well as helping to maintain healthy skin. For
some, however, growing carrots can prove
very difficult.

Harvesting carrots
Carrots can be harvested
from early summer
right into winter, but for
the sweetest crop, pick
them when they're long
and slender.

Where to grow Carrots grow best on
sandy soil — this way, the carrots can grow
undeterred. In stony or heavy soil, carrots
can become twisted or forked. If your soil
doesn't suit, opt for a container filled with
multipurpose potting mix.

Types and varieties Like many
vegetables today, there is a range of colors
to suit all. The traditional orange carrot was
developed in the Netherlands in the 17th
century — in support of the royal House
of Orange. Today, other colors are making
a comeback, with cream and even purple
carrots available.

Then there are the shapes — most are
cylindrical, but one or two varieties are
spherical. Of the cylindrical varieties, you
can go for shorter, stubby roots or longer,
thinner roots. If you're growing in stony or
heavy soil, the shorter varieties will prove
more successful.

Like potatoes, there are earlies and
maincrop types. Earlies tend to grow quicker
and can be harvested in as little as 10 weeks
after sowing. Maincrops are slow but steady
growers. Harvest these in the fall.

GROWING CARROTS IN A CONTAINER

1 From early spring onward, fill large
2.5-gallon (10-L) containers with potting
mix and sprinkle a seed every inch (2.5 cm)
or so. Cover with a dusting of potting mix.

2 Water well and continue to water as the
plants start to grow. Feeding shouldn't
be necessary.

In the garden Don't add any organic matter to your soil, but dig it over well, then make a shallow drill in which to sow the seed. Water the drill if the soil is dry. Sow in bands (see pages 200–203) and aim for three seeds every inch (2.5 cm). If you sow too thickly you can always pull up some baby carrots later to make more space.

You can sow early varieties from mid- to late spring, but the seed is more likely to grow once the soil has warmed up. Late spring is the time to sow your maincrop carrots. Push a garden fork deep into the soil around the carrots, gently easing them out of the ground.

Pests and diseases Carrots are relatively pest-free, except for one major insect: carrot root fly. This pest flies at low heights, smelling out your crop. It lays its eggs on the carrots and the larvae drill into the roots, spoiling the crop. There are no chemicals worth bothering with, but you can outwit this pest. Either put up a low fence of polythene or floating row covers around your crop to a height of 2 feet (60 cm) or cover your crop with floating row covers. Alternatively, go for a relatively resistant variety, such as 'Flyaway' or 'Resistafly', or try companion planting (see page 226). Growing in alternate rows with onions has proved to be successful, supposedly because the scent of the onions masks that of the carrots.

Harvesting and storage While early carrots will give you a crop of sweet baby vegetables through the summer, a maincrop variety will keep you going through the winter. As long as the soil doesn't freeze, carrots can be left in the ground and pulled when you need them. If long periods of cold weather are expected, add a layer of straw or potting mix to protect the crop until needed.

Don't lift or store carrots, as the old methods of storing in clamps or boxes of sand are too much effort for the modern gardener. However, they freeze beautifully: they need to be chopped, blanched, chilled, then frozen.

In the kitchen Young baby carrots can be used in fresh-tasting, warm summer salads. As the season progresses, use maincrop carrots in stews, or slow roast them for sweetness.

CALENDAR

EARLY SPRING
You can start to make sowings now, but germination may be sporadic. Create a 5/8-inch (1.5-cm) drill and sprinkle seeds along it. Aim for three seeds every inch (2.5 cm). Cover the drill with soil.

MID-SPRING
In cooler areas, repeat as above.

LATE SPRING
To be safe, and in cooler conditions, make late spring your main sowing date.

EARLY SUMMER
Start pulling young carrots from the soil, leaving others to grow bigger.

MIDSUMMER
It's not too late to sow another row of carrots — at least 6 inches (15 cm) away from your last row.

LATE SUMMER
Keep pulling baby carrots, leaving a plant every 2–4 inches (5–10 cm), which will continue to grow right into fall.

EARLY FALL
Start to harvest your main crop of carrots. They can be left in the ground if you don't need them yet.

3 Leave the containers in a sunny spot on the patio, and as the shoots start to grow, carrots will start forming below ground.

4 Start pulling baby carrots when they're around finger-sized, leaving others in the pot to grow bigger.

VARIETY SELECTOR
Earlies
• 'Mokum', 'Nelson'.

Spherical
• 'Parmex'.

Maincrop
• 'Bolero'.

Colorful
• 'Purple Pak', 'Rainbow', 'Deep Purple'.

For stony soil
• 'Chantenay Red Cored', 'Parmex'.

Parsnip

Once a mainstay of the winter kitchen garden, parsnips can be harvested from summer right through to late winter.

✪✪✪✪✪	VALUE FOR MONEY
✪✪✪✪✪	MAINTENANCE
✪✪✪✪✪	FREEZE/STORE

CROPPING SEASON: EARLY FALL–LATE WINTER

Perfect parsnips
A bumper harvest of parsnips will add sweetness to soups and stews right through the winter.

Parsnips are related to carrots, and so many of the techniques used and pests encountered are the same. It's a good idea, therefore, to grow them side by side. Parsnips are renowned for being tricky to germinate; this is mostly due to parsnip seed losing viability quickly with age. If you start with fresh, good-quality seed each time and sow when the soil has started to warm, you should end up with a bumper crop.

Where to grow Like carrots, parsnips do best in rich, deep soil. Stony or heavy soil will result in the roots forking, making them difficult to clean and prepare in the kitchen. In the garden, grow parsnips alongside other root crops. If your soil doesn't suit parsnips, they can also be grown in containers — follow the advice for carrots (see pages 36–37).

In the garden If you are growing in rows, plant ½ inch (1 cm) deep and leave 8–12 inches (20–30 cm) between rows. Parsnips can get quite large, so aim for a plant every 6 inches (15 cm) along the row. As they can be awkward to germinate successfully, it's best to put in two or three seeds each time, and thin out later. Alternatively, sow a seed every 2 inches (5 cm) and thin out baby parsnips in the summer, leaving the others to carry on growing.

Pests and diseases Like carrots, the biggest threat to parsnips is carrot root fly. Prevention is the only way to avoid this dreaded pest, so go for floating row covers, barriers or companion planting (see above, and page 226).

GROWING PARSNIPS

1 Make sure your bed is well weeded — remove any perennial or annual weeds. Dig over well and rake to a fine tilth. Draw out a row with the back of a rake and sow a few seeds every 6 inches (15 cm).

2 Seeds should start to germinate in a week or two.

3 If you have more than one plant every 6 inches (15 cm), you can thin them out now. If there's more than one plant growing next to each other, be careful when removing the extra seedlings. If you have any gaps, these extra seedlings can be used to fill in.

PROTECTING YOUR PARSNIP CROP

1 Insert canes around your crop in spring, once it is established. Ideally, sow parsnips next to carrots, since they suffer from the same pests and can be protected in the same way.

2 Wrap floating row covers or polythene sheet around the canes up to 2 feet (60 cm) high and secure in place with pegs or wire. Alternatively, you could use floating row covers (see page 53).

Harvesting and storage You can start harvesting baby parsnips in summer, but the tastiest ones are picked later. Parsnips are renowned for sweetening up after the first frosts, so make sure you leave some for early winter and beyond. They can be left in the ground until required — in very cold areas, cover the row with straw.

In the kitchen Use parsnips to sweeten up stews and soups, or cut lengthwise and roast. Parsnips can also be boiled and mashed.

4 After the first frosts, the parsnips should start to sweeten up. These can then be lifted with the aid of a garden fork as and when you need them.

5 The object of the exercise: a bumper harvest of parsnips.

CALENDAR

MID-SPRING
Start seed off in mid to late spring and sow seeds ½ inch (1 cm) deep direct into a well-prepared seedbed.

LATE SPRING
Keep an eye on the seedlings and resow extra seed if any fail to come up.

EARLY SUMMER
Parsnips are slow to get going and can struggle if there are lots of weeds, so ensure you keep weeding your plot.

MIDSUMMER
Water if very dry and start to harvest baby parsnips once the tops are around 2 inches (5 cm) in diameter.

LATE SUMMER
Continue weeding.

EARLY FALL
Parsnips should be starting to swell, but leave in the ground for a larger crop.

MID-FALL
Start to harvest your main crop of parsnips. Dig up what you need for each meal, but leave what you don't need in the ground to be harvested at a later date.

VARIETY SELECTOR
Go for F1 varieties as the seed quality is likely to be better.
- 'Hollow Crown': sweet, mild, nutty flavor. Grows up to 12 inches (30 cm).
- 'Harris Early Model': deliciously sweet.

Beet

This earthy-flavored vegetable comes in a variety of colors, and is quick and easy to grow.

STAR PLANT LONG LASTING GREAT TASTE

- ⬤⬤⬤⬤⬤ VALUE FOR MONEY
- ⬤⬤⬤⬤⬤ MAINTENANCE
- ⬤⬤⬤⬤⬤ FREEZE/STORE
- CROPPING SEASON: EARLY SUMMER–MID-FALL

Red roots
Bright red beets add color to your garden and your plate.

This versatile vegetable is a mainstay in any kitchen garden. It is quick-growing, is simple to raise and suffers from few pests and diseases, and best of all, it looks and tastes great.

Baby beets can be grown in as little as nine weeks and so it's a great crop for continuous sowing — from early spring to midsummer. As well as the traditional purple roots, there are yellow, white and striped versions.

Where to grow Beets can be grown in containers, but they are also easy to grow in the ground. It's a good idea to add some general fertilizer to the soil before sowing.

In the garden Beet seeds are a type of fruit, each of which contains up to four individual seeds. Therefore, with each seed you sow, you'll probably get a few plants coming up. Let these grow together and they'll naturally push each other apart to form separate beets. Plant seeds 1 inch (2.5 cm) apart and ⅝ inch (1.5 cm) deep, with 8–12 inches (20–30 cm) between rows.

Pests and diseases Beets are pretty trouble free, but the roots can split following periods of drought, so keep the plants watered.

Harvesting and storage Start the beet harvest early by picking some of the leaves, which can be eaten in salads. Baby beets can be pulled up when the roots reach around 2 inches (5 cm) in diameter. If you started sowing in early spring and continued until midsummer, you'll have beets from late spring to late fall. Once they're lifted, brush off the soil and twist off the foliage — avoid cutting the root because it will start to bleed.

In the kitchen Slice baby beets raw and add to salads. Beets can be roasted, made into soup, or boiled, then skinned and served with sauces or salads. For pickling, use small beets.

CALENDAR

EARLY SPRING
Start off in early spring on well-cultivated soil. Sow a single row of seeds and repeat this every two to three weeks.

MID-SPRING
Keep sowing beet seeds in individual rows every few weeks. If the soil is looking dry, water the drill before adding the seeds. Keep watering until seeds start to emerge.

LATE SPRING
If you really like beets and have the space, you can carry on sowing seeds in late spring. You can also harvest some of the young leaves from previous sowings to eat fresh in salads.

EARLY SUMMER
Start to harvest your first baby beets. Just pull up by the leaves and twist off. You can keep sowing for a longer supply of beets into fall.

MIDSUMMER
Make this your last sowing. A crop of baby beets will be ready in mid fall and larger roots by late fall.

GROWING BEETS IN A CONTAINER

1 Fill a large container with multipurpose potting mix.

2 Scatter seeds over the surface, at least 1 inch (2.5 cm) apart.

3 Cover with around ⅝ inch (1.5 cm) of potting mix and then water. Leave in a sunny spot, pulling the beets when they are the size of golf balls.

VARIETY SELECTOR
Choose colorful varieties to brighten up your kitchen garden.

- **'Detroit Dark Red'**: a good-tasting old stand-by.
- **'Albina'**: a good white variety.
- **'Burpee's Golden'**: golden flesh.
- **'Chioggia'**: striped (red and white) variety.

Turnip

Turnips are excellent space fillers and grow in as little as six weeks.

- ●●●●● VALUE FOR MONEY
- ●●●●○ MAINTENANCE
- ●●●○○ FREEZE/STORE
- CROPPING SEASON: EARLY SUMMER–MID-FALL

Rapid roots
Summer turnips are quicker and easier to grow than most people think.

Another member of the brassica family, turnips can be separated into two groups. Slow-growing or winter types, grown in the same way as rutabagas (see page 44), will be ready for harvest from fall. Then there is the more interesting group: the quick-growing or summer varieties. Sow from early spring onward in succession (see pages 200–203) and small, golf-ball-sized turnips will be available for pulling from your kitchen garden all summer.

Where to grow Summer turnips make a great catch crop. They don't take up much space and can be fitted into gaps in the vegetable garden through summer.

In the garden For winter turnips, sow seeds around 8 inches (20 cm) apart in midsummer. You'll be rewarded with large roots that can be left in the ground and harvested through the fall and winter in mild winter regions (zone 8 and above). From a late

spring planting, summer turnips can be ready in as little as six weeks. This quick turnaround means that summer turnips will also do well in containers with minimum maintenance.

Pests and diseases As with all brassica crops, pests are a problem. Use floating row covers and incorporate (and protect) with your other brassicas. For the slow-growing turnips, grow with your other brassicas, such as rutabagas and Brussels sprouts.

Harvesting and storage Summer turnips don't keep, so pull them up as you need them. Don't let them get bigger than the size of a golf ball or they will become tough. Leave winter turnips in the ground until mid-winter in mild winter regions (zone 8 and above).

In the kitchen Turnips can be boiled and mashed with carrots and butter. They can also be roasted or even eaten raw grated in salads.

CALENDAR

EARLY SPRING
You can start to sow summer turnips direct in milder areas. Create a fine seed bed and add some balanced fertilizer. Make drills 5/8 inch (1.5 cm) deep and sow seeds thinly.

MID-SPRING
Every couple of weeks sow another row of turnips 6 inches (15 cm) away from the last row. As plants grow, they'll push each other apart, but thin them out if they're too dense.

LATE SPRING
Water during dry spells, and keep sowing further rows. Rows of turnips should be ready for pulling in succession.

EARLY SUMMER
Keep pulling up your turnips. If they get any bigger than golf ball size, throw them on the compost heap.

MIDSUMMER
Sow a row or two of winter turnips, plant seeds 8 inches (20 cm) apart, around ¾ inch (2 cm) deep.

LATE SUMMER
Keep watering and weeding winter turnips.

EARLY FALL
Start harvesting winter turnips, and leave in the ground and pull up when needed.

GROWING BEST-QUALITY TURNIPS

1 Prepare a seed drill 5/8 inch (1.5 cm) deep, and sow turnip seeds 2 inches (5 cm) apart. Cover with soil and water in well.

2 Keep watering and pull out turnips when they are the size of golf balls.

VARIETY SELECTOR
Best summer turnips

- 'Purple Top White Globe', 'Oasis'.

Best winter turnips

- 'Golden Ball'.

Radish

Radishes add spice to salads or can be grown for Asian-inspired cooking. Best of all, they're one of the easiest brassicas to grow.

✪✪✪✪✪	VALUE FOR MONEY
✪✪✪✪✪	MAINTENANCE
✪✪✪✪✪	FREEZE/STORE
CROPPING SEASON: LATE SPRING–LATE FALL	

Wintery morsels
Black-skinned radishes can be a useful crop when there is little else around in cold winter areas (zone 7 and below).

Summer radishes should be sown little and often from early spring onward. Quick to grow, they take as little as four weeks from sowing to harvest. Best of all, they come in a range of interesting colors: the traditional red, as well as white and purple.

Winter radishes are best known for their use in Asian cusine. One of the best known are the white daikon, but there are red as well as black types too.

Where to grow Grow winter radishes alongside other long-growing cabbage-family crops. Treat summer salad radishes as a catch crop and fit into brassica beds as well as other areas of the garden as space becomes available, but watch out for pests. Sow them little and often to keep a regular supply of salad radishes for your kitchen.

In the garden If you are new to growing food and just can't wait to get started, summer salad radishes are a good place to start. Apart from sprouting seeds and some quick-growing baby-leaf lettuces, radishes will be your first proper crop. To sow them in a pot, aim for a seed every inch (2.5 cm), and as they grow, the roots will push each other apart. Alternatively, sow in short rows spaced around 6 inches (15 cm) apart, with a seed every inch (2.5 cm).

Winter radishes are best in the vegetable bed. You'll need to sow in midsummer and they'll be ready for pulling by mid-fall.

Pests and diseases As they are members of the brassica family, radishes are susceptible to the same pests and diseases (see page 55).

Harvesting and storage Successional sowing of summer radishes will give you a continual supply of small roots all summer. Pull them as you need them. If any radishes go to flower, allow them to set seed. Their green pods are edible, with a hot and fiery taste. Winter radishes can be left in the ground, but can be damaged by frost. Protect with straw until required.

In the kitchen Keep pulling salad radishes when they reach around ¾ inch (2 cm) in diameter. These mild and crunchy roots make a tasty addition to salads. Winter radishes can be very hot and are better cooked. Marinate in soy sauce and add to stir-fries.

GROWING SUMMER RADISHES

1 Make sure your bed is well weeded — remove any perennial or annual weeds. Dig over well and rake to a fine tilth. Draw out a row with the back of a rake.

2 Sow a few seeds every 6 inches (15 cm). Seeds should start to germinate in a week or two.

3 Sow short rows every couple of weeks 1 inch (2.5 cm) apart and about ½ inch (1 cm) deep from early spring onward.

Peppery roots
Radishes come in a variety of colors and are the quickest vegetable to grow from seed to plate.

CALENDAR

MIDSUMMER

Sow winter radishes now. Make sure your soil is well watered and sow in drills 12 inches (30 cm) apart.

LATE SUMMER

Keep watering your seedlings. Thin them to 6 inches (15 cm) apart.

EARLY FALL

Make sure your plants don't go short of water and weed regularly.

MID-FALL

Start to harvest your winter radishes when they've reached a decent size and taken on the color suggested on the seed packet.

LATE FALL

If you haven't harvested all your crop, cover with a layer of straw, or similar, to protect from frosts.

VARIETY SELECTOR

Summer radishes

- 'Cherry Belle', 'French Breakfast': red.
- 'White Icicle': white.

Winter radishes

- 'Summer Cross' F_1: white daikon.
- 'Black Spanish Round': black-skinned.
- 'Red Heat': white-skinned, magenta flesh.

4 Cover with floating row covers if pests are a problem.

5 Start to harvest when the radishes start to form.

Rutabaga

A much-forgotten member of the brassica family, these yellow-fleshed roots are worthy of a small spot in your garden.

⬤⬤⬤⬤◯ VALUE FOR MONEY
⬤⬤⬤⬤⬤ MAINTENANCE
⬤⬤⬤⬤◯ FREEZE/STORE
CROPPING SEASON: MID-FALL–EARLY WINTER

Versatile vegetable
Rutabagas are a tricky but rewarding crop to grow.

You rarely see rutabagas growing in gardens today, but this once-popular crop is worthy of increased interest. It's a slow-growing crop, taking all season to reach maturity, and one that also suffers from the same pests and diseases as other brassicas. So while it's not the easiest to grow, if you provide the right conditions and protect this crop well you'll be rewarded with large, bulbous roots, which can be roasted, boiled or mashed.

Where to grow You'll need a sunny and fertile spot for your rutabagas. Grow them with your other brassicas such as turnips, radishes and cabbages and move them around your plot each year on a rotation (see pages 22–23).

Pests and diseases Like all brassicas, rutabagas suffer from a range of pests, most of which can be kept at bay with the use of floating row covers. Rutabagas can also split in the ground — often caused by an irregular supply of water — so it's best to water the crops evenly, especially in dry spells. Watch out for slugs and snails (see page 227).

Harvesting and storage After a spring sowing, rutabagas will start to mature in fall; however it is worth leaving them until they develop fully. You can leave them in the ground for some time — but don't let them freeze. Once harvested, twist off the leaves at the top and either use in the kitchen immediately, or store for a limited period in a cool place.

In the kitchen Rutabagas are much milder than other brassicas, such as turnips, but still retain that slight cabbagey flavor. Cutting off the skin will reveal a large yellow root — cut into cubes then boil, mash or roast. Like turnips, try mashing them with carrots, adding plenty of butter for a delicious vegetable accompaniment.

CALENDAR

MID-SPRING
Sow seeds directly in the ground, into a well-prepared seedbed. Place seeds about ½ inch (1 cm) deep and 12 inch (30 cm) apart. Cover crops with protective floating row covers to prevent pests from attacking them.

LATE SPRING
If you didn't get around sowing seeds in mid-spring, you can still do it now.

EARLY SUMMER
Keep watering your crop — rutabagas hate to dry out.

MIDSUMMER
Water and weed, check plants for pests.

LATE SUMMER
Keep watering your crop, especially during any dry spells.

EARLY FALL
Pull out of the ground with the top growth intact. Roots will be ready for lifting from late summer to late fall.

PRODUCING BEST-QUALITY RUTABAGAS

1 Watch out for slugs and use controls such as organic pellets where necessary.

2 Keep flying pests off your crop by using floating row covers over the top.

3 Water your crop in all but the wettest of climates through the summer.

VARIETY SELECTOR
• 'Laurentian': traditional purple-topped rutabaga with sweet, yellow flesh.

Onion

Onions are one of the most popular vegetables used in the kitchen.

Onions come from a group of vegetables and flowering plants called alliums. Used since Egyptian times in cooking, they were then developed by the Romans. Not only were brown-skinned onions used by this time, but red- and white-skinned varieties too. Today there are many varieties available in a selection of shapes, colors and flavors.

There are also a couple of growing methods (by seed or set — see below) as well as some variation in timings (you can plant either in fall or spring). Select your variety, harvest and store your onions carefully, to ensure they last you well into the winter.

Where to grow Onions belong to the same group of plants as shallots (see page 48), garlic (see page 49), spring onions (see pages 106–107) and leeks (see pages 104–105), and where possible it's a good idea to grow all of these near to each other. As they suffer from similar pests and diseases, you should rotate them around the garden together too. Use well-cultivated ground for growing onions, preferably with some well-rotted compost added the previous year. Add 1¼ ounce (35 g) per square yard of general-purpose fertilizer before you plant. Onions can also be grown successfully in containers; however, they are not the most attractive container vegetable!

Types and varieties Onions are biennial, meaning they take two years to flower and set seed. In the first year they produce a storage organ — the bulb — which is what gets harvested.

Onions can be grown in the garden in two ways. The first is from seed, where seed is sown in pots and transplanted to the garden, or sown direct in the ground. The second is through sets. Sets are small bulbs that have been grown from seed very ➡

Dry off your onions
Once harvested, onions need to be dried off to ensure they store well through winter. Either leave on the soil surface to dry, or if it's wet, move them to a greenhouse or cool sunroom.

GROWING ONIONS FROM SEED

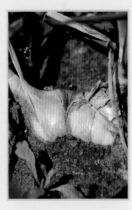

1 Sow about six seeds in individual small pots in mid spring.

2 Plant out the whole clump of seedlings four to six weeks later from each pot, about 8 inches (20 cm) apart.

3 As the bulbs swell, they'll push each other apart, creating a clump of small onions.

densely by the supplier. Their small size means that in their second year (the year you'll be growing them) they'll continue to grow the bulb rather than setting seed. There are pros and cons to both methods. Growing onions from seed is generally cheaper—there's a larger selection of varieties available. Sets, on the other hand, are simple to plant and easy for the novice vegetable grower. Growing onions from seed is slightly more tricky, since onion seed is small and fussy. Using sets is generally more expensive than seed and the choice of varieties isn't as great.

VARIETY SELECTOR

- 'Copra', 'Ailsa Craig', 'Candy', 'Walla Walla Sweet': medium or long-day varieties for northern regions (above about 35° latitude).
- 'Pumba', 'Yellow Granex': short-day varieties for southern regions (below about 35° latitude).

Pests and diseases Onions don't really suffer from pests — their sulfurous compounds seem to put most flying pests off trying to nibble them. However, they do suffer from a couple of diseases:

White rot The most prevalent fungal disease is white rot, which can remain in the soil for many years. You'll see white fluff growing on the bulbs, and the leaves will turn yellow and die. Unfortunately, there is no treatment for white rot, and once it's in the soil you won't be able to grow onions or any other allium in the same patch for at least 10 years. Rotate your crop to another part of the vegetable patch, and if necessary, grow onions in containers.

Downy mildew This is another fungus that affects the leaves, causing oval lesions, which eventually cause the leaves to die. Downy mildew is at its worse in cool, wet summers — remove and destroy any damaged plant material as and when you see it.

Harvesting and storage When the bulbs have grown and the leaves start to yellow, your onions are almost ready for harvesting. Don't bend the tops over, but do lift the bulbs slightly with a fork. This breaks the roots, encouraging them to ripen, and their skins to harden off. You can leave them on the surface of the bed for a couple of weeks, but in a wet summer it's best to move them into a greenhouse to dry off. Be careful when handling onions, as any damage will mean they will rot in storage. Use any damaged onions first. The others can be suspended in braids or bunches and kept in a cool shed or garage. If braiding or bunching your onions, make sure you don't cut off the long stems.

In the kitchen Onions are used in all sorts of cusines, from Italian to Indian. When chopped finely, they add texture and flavor to a variety of sauces. Brown onions store longest and are best used for cooking, whereas red and white onions are less pungent and sweeter, so are great in salads.

GROWING ONIONS FROM SETS

1 Using sets in either spring or fall, rather than seed, is a quicker and easier way to grow onions. Whichever season you plant, make sure your soil is fertile and weed free before you begin.

2 Push the sets into the ground, pointed end up, around 4 inches (10 cm) apart, with 8 inches (20 cm) between rows. Leave just the point sticking out, but watch out for birds that have a habit of pulling the sets out of the ground. You could use a guide as shown to ensure that your rows are straight.

3 By mid- to late summer, the onions should be ready to harvest. Using a garden fork, gently lift them out of the ground.

KNOW YOUR ONIONS

There are lots of types of onion to grow in your garden. Select the varieties that suit your cooking requirements.

BROWN ONIONS

The traditional brown onion is a staple in all kitchens. Tough, shiny skins mean they store well through winter and are best used for cooking.

JAPANESE ONIONS

These are varieties that have been specially bred for fall planting. They are ready for harvest before your main crop of onions, but don't store well beyond the fall.

PICKLING ONIONS

These are regular onions sown very densely, resulting in small bulbs. Some onion varieties have been specially bred for pickling, but really any variety will do.

RED ONIONS

Often sweeter and milder than brown onions. The red color used to be skin deep, but newer varieties have been developed to extend the color right through the onion. They add color and a lovely taste to salads.

WHITE ONIONS

Often called sweet or Spanish onions, these are milder and often larger than traditional brown onions. They contain fewer sulfur compounds that make your eyes water and are ideal for eating raw in salads. They do not grow well in cooler climates.

CALENDAR

LATE WINTER
Visit your local garden store and buy your onion sets.

EARLY SPRING
Start to plant onion sets. Push sets into the soil so the tips are just sticking out. Plant sets 4 inches (10 cm) apart for decent-sized onions, with at least 8 inches (20 cm) between rows.

MID-SPRING
Keep your rows of onions well weeded — no additional watering should be needed.

LATE SPRING
Keep weeding — the plants will look after themselves.

EARLY SUMMER
Plants should start to form large bulbs, but these aren't ready yet.

MIDSUMMER
Maintain your regime of weeding. Some varieties will be ready for harvesting. Lift carefully with a fork, and leave on the ground so the skins dry off.

LATE SUMMER
Most onions will be ready for harvesting in late summer.

EARLY FALL
Order in your fall sets or Japanese onions.

MID-FALL
In mild-winter areas (zone 8 and above), plant fall sets now, following the advice above, but use a different part of the garden as part of your rotation.

4 Knock the excess soil off the roots, which will encourage the bulbs to dry out.

5 Leave the onions either on the ground (if it's sunny) or move them to a greenhouse until the skins and stem have completely dried. This will encourage the skins to dry off before storing.

Shallot

If you're looking for a more refined cooking onion, you can't go wrong with shallots.

✪✪✪✪✪	VALUE FOR MONEY
✪✪✪✪✪	MAINTENANCE
✪✪✪✪✪	FREEZE/STORE

CROPPING SEASON: LATE SUMMER–MID-FALL

Shallot set
A single shallot set will produce a whole slump of new, sweet and mildly flavored shallots in a matter of months.

Shallots are similar to onions in the way they are grown and in the problems you'll face. The rewards, however, are somewhat different. Plant a single bulb in the ground in spring and, unlike onions where you'll just get a single larger bulb in return a few months later, the shallot set will have multiplied into over 10 small oval bulbs.

Where to grow Shallots can be grown with onions and other members of the allium family. Use ground that is reasonably fertile, but preferably not an area that has recently had organic matter added to it because they won't grow as well.

In the garden More often sold as sets (small bulbs), you will now find shallot seed for sale too. Sets can be grown in exactly the same way as onions (see page 45); however, it's better if you space them slightly wider apart — 6 inches (15 cm) apart, and 12 inches (30 cm) between rows — to allow the multiple bulbs plenty of space.

As with onions, shallots cannot compete against weeds, so it's important to keep your onion bed well weeded, otherwise your crop won't develop.

Pests and diseases As for onions (see page 46).

Harvesting and storage Shallots will start to ripen up from midsummer. They can be lifted and left to dry off on the soil surface. If the weather is wet, dry them off indoors. There is no need to split the shallots up, as they'll start to break up on their own. Store in net or mesh bags or string together as with onions (see page 46). Stored in a cool, dry place, shallots can keep for up to nine months.

In the kitchen Shallots are well loved by chefs. Their flavor is more subtle than their larger counterparts. Use as you would regular onions, or use whole in stews and casseroles.

CALENDAR

MID-SPRING

Plant your shallot sets individually in rows, 6 inches (15 cm) apart, next to your onions. Push individual sets into the ground so their tips are just showing. Use floating row covers to cover the sets until they start to sprout to prevent birds from pulling them out of the ground.

LATE SPRING

Keep your crop well weeded.

EARLY SUMMER

Keep weeding, but additional watering shouldn't be necessary except in the driest of summers.

MIDSUMMER–LATE SUMMER

Gently push a fork underneath the clumps of shallots and lift out of the ground, leaving them on the soil surface for a couple of weeks for the skins to harden, then take in for storage.

VARIETY SELECTOR

- Sets: 'Yellow Moon', 'Topper'.
- Seed: 'Prisma', 'Ambition'.

GROWING SHALLOTS FROM SEED

1 Ensure your area is well weeded and the soil dug over to create a fine tilth.

2 Using the edge of a rake, draw out a seed drill around ⅝ inch (1.5 cm) deep.

3 Place 6 to 8 shallots seeds every 12 inches (30 cm), then draw the soil back over with the rake.

Garlic

Indispensable in the kitchen, garlic is simple and rewarding to grow.

⬤⬤⬤⬤⬤ VALUE FOR MONEY
⬤⬤⬤⬤◯ MAINTENANCE
⬤⬤⬤⬤⬤ FREEZE/STORE
CROPPING SEASON: LATE SPRING–EARLY FALL

Push a single garlic clove into the soil, and as long as you don't allow weeds to swamp the area, you'll be able to lift a full bulb of garlic from the ground several months later. Garlic is well known for its health benefits and has been used in cooking since ancient times.

Where to grow Grow garlic alongside onions and shallots and rotate them collectively around the garden. Garlic doesn't do well in heavy or very wet soils.

In the garden Garlic is a hardy plant and needs a period of cold to succeed (30–60 days below 50°F/10°C). Plant garlic in the fall or early winter.

Pests and diseases Garlic is relatively trouble-free.

Harvesting and storage Unlike onions, garlic bulbs form well below the soil

Ripe garlic bulbs
From a single bulb of garlic you can expect to harvest a dozen or so bulbs. These can be used fresh or dried and used through the winter.

surface. In midsummer, carefully lift a single bulb of garlic to see if it's ready. If not, leave the others for another couple of weeks. Ease out of the ground, being careful not to bruise the bulbs, and leave on the surface to dry. Make sure all your garlic is lifted by midsummer to avoid the cloves resprouting. You can use fresh garlic immediately, otherwise dry and store it with your onions and shallots in braids (see page 46) or mesh sacks.

In the kitchen Garlic bulbs can be roasted whole, or stuffed into a chicken to add flavor. Use cloves peeled, chopped and fried in Mediterranean, Indian and Asian dishes.

CALENDAR

EARLY–LATE FALL
Plant now. Break individual cloves from the bulb and plant flat-end down. Push down 1¼ inches (3 cm) into the soil.

MID-WINTER–LATE WINTER
Don't plant your cloves during this time — it is too cold and inhospitable.

MID-SPRING
Make sure the plants aren't being smothered by weeds.

LATE SPRING
Continue weeding and water if the weather is dry.

EARLY SUMMER
Bulbs should start to swell and can be harvested from now onward. Check by digging up one plant — if the bulbs are very small, leave for one or two more weeks.

MIDSUMMER
Keep harvesting your bulbs and hang them up to dry.

GROWING GARLIC

1 Break up bulbs and plant garlic, pointed end upward, as individual cloves direct in the ground.

2 When ready, use a fork to carefully dig up the bulb growing below the ground.

3 Brush off the soil and leave to dry in a greenhouse.

VARIETY SELECTOR
- **'Music'**: hardy with large, succulent cloves. A hardneck variety, which is more cold-hardy.
- **'New York White'**: softneck variety, purple blush.
- **Elephant garlic**: technically a type of leek, this mild-flavored garlic look-alike produces bulbs up to 4 inches (10 cm) in diameter.

Jerusalem artichoke

An easy vegetable to grow that will reward you year after year with sweet-flavored, nutritious tubers, perfect for soups and stews.

○○○○○ VALUE FOR MONEY
○○○○○ MAINTENANCE
○○○○○ FREEZE/STORE
CROPPING SEASON: LATE FALL–WINTER

A native American plant, Jerusalem artichokes (also called "sunchokes") grow tall and produce pretty sunflowers, as well as tasty tubers below ground that can be dug up from fall through to winter. Before you start planting, there is one word of warning: It is extremely difficult to dig up every tuber from the soil and you will find that once planted, Jerusalem artichokes will reappear year after year, so grow this plant only if you know you like the taste as it's not to everyone's liking. Grow it somewhere out of the way, in an enclosed area so that it can't spread across your borders.

Where to grow
Jerusalem artichokes are tough plants and will do well in all but the most extreme climates.

Jerusalem artichokes are happy growing almost anywhere in the garden, whether in sunny or shady areas. However, they are best positioned out of the way and in a sheltered spot as they can grow to over 10 feet (3 m) tall. Because of their spreading habit, select a bed with enclosed sides. About 21 square feet (2 sq m) are more than enough to devote to this plant.

Growing in containers is an option as this will prevent plants from spreading. However, they are vigorous growers and will need constant watering in the summer, so consider this option only if you don't mind watering every day or have an automatic irrigation system. Use soil or a soil-based potting mix for your containers, since this is generally much heavier than multipurpose potting mix, which often contains peat or composted bark which, when they dry out, are very light. The heavy soil will help to prevent the plants from toppling over when they grow tall.

Pests and diseases
Jerusalem artichokes are usually trouble free.

Harvesting and storage
Once the foliage is hit by the first frosts, the plants can be cut down to around 2 inches (5 cm). Being hardy, the tubers can be left in the ground until they are needed. Work your way along the bed and dig up as many as you need for each meal. This way they'll last throughout the winter. If very hard frosts or snow are likely, cover the ground with a thick layer of straw for protection. The tubers can also be stored in plastic bags in the fridge for a few weeks.

In the kitchen
Similar to potatoes, Jerusalem artichokes can be roasted, baked, fried and boiled, and are harvested from the fall onward (harvest as you go).

Winter produce
The knobbly tubers of Jerusalem artichoke can be lifted as you need them right through the winter.

CALENDAR

LATE WINTER–EARLY SPRING
Order your tubers in the winter and plant out 4–6 inches (10–15 cm) deep and 12 inches (30 cm) apart. For container growing, plant a single tuber.

SPRING–FALL
For the best crop, water in dry weather.

LATE FALL
Cut stems down to 2 inches (5 cm) and dig up tubers when required.

WINTER
Either leave a few tubers in the ground (even in cold-winter areas — zone 7 and below), or replant a few that you dug up for a crop the following year.

VARIETY SELECTOR
• Many suppliers may just sell Jerusalem artichokes unnamed or called 'Common'. All artichokes are good croppers, but some are more knobbly than others. If you do have a choice, go for 'Feseau' since this named variety is considered to be less knobbly and therefore easier to prepare than other unnamed varieties.

Celeriac

With its distinctive celery-like flavor, celeriac can be used in salads, soups and more.

●●●●○ VALUE FOR MONEY
●●●●● MAINTENANCE
●●●●○ FREEZE/STORE
CROPPING SEASON: EARLY FALL–LATE WINTER

Delicious, nutritious and from the same family as carrots and celery, celeriac is one of the most underrated vegetables. It is easy to grow, but does need a long growing season and moist soil to allow the roots to swell to the size of a beefsteak tomato by fall. It can be left in situ and harvested throughout the winter (just like Jerusalem artichokes, opposite).

Where to grow A close relative of celery, celeriac is much easier to grow but requires plenty of water. It thrives in a cool, damp climate with a long, frost-free growing season.

In the garden Favors an open site in the main part of your vegetable patch, reaching 20 inches (50 cm) high. It needs plenty of moisture and nutrients, so plant out in rich soil and plenty of organic matter.

Pests and diseases Celeriac is trouble-free.

Harvesting and storage Celeriac can be harvested from early fall onward. The leaf stalks will start to rot over the winter so these should be removed — leave the roots in the ground until required. The flavor will improve after a mild frost or two, but a layer of straw may be required to protect it from severe frosts. The colder your climate, the more straw you will need.

In the kitchen Leaves can be picked off celeriac through the summer and used in soups and salads to add a celery flavor. Once harvested, the knobbly roots will need to be scrubbed and peeled. Chop into cubes to use in soups and stews, or slice very finely in salads. Boiled and mashed, it can be eaten alone or mixed with mashed potato.

Tastier than celery
Try the root sliced very finely in salads, or boil and then mash.

VARIETY SELECTOR

There isn't much breeding work on celeriac, and it's likely the varieties on offer will be limited. Look out for these two:

• 'Monach': smooth skins, with a good flavor and texture. Creamy colored roots.

• 'Brilliant': white flesh that doesn't discolor. Also fairly smooth skins.

CALENDAR

LATE WINTER–EARLY SPRING
Buy seed of one of the recommended cultivars. Sow seed into trays or pots. Don't cover the compost with soil as the seed needs light to germinate. Raise in a cool greenhouse or sunroom (around 54°F/12°C or less). Once germinated, prick out the seedlings and grow on individually.

MID-SPRING
Harden plants off in a cold frame or somewhere sheltered outside, then in late spring plant out in their final position, with about 12 inches (30 cm) between plants. Protect plants from slugs and snails. Add a layer of organic matter, such as garden compost, to retain moisture, and some granular fertilizer rich in nitrogen. Water well in dry spells.

MID-FALL
Remove dying leaf stalks and start to lift when required in the kitchen.

LEAFY CROPS

Packed full of vitamins and antioxidants, leafy crops such as cabbage, mizuna and spinach make a healthy choice for your kitchen. Their ornamental value, with crops such as lettuce, endive and kale, means they look great in your garden too.

Cabbage

Cabbage is a versatile crop with enough types and varieties to ensure an all-year-round supply.

●●●●○	VALUE FOR MONEY
●●●●●	MAINTENANCE
●●●○○	FREEZE/STORE
CROPPING SEASON: ALL YEAR ROUND	

While cabbage may not be your first choice of vegetable to grow, if you are going to grow any brassicas, you should include a row or two of cabbages. As well as cabbages, the brassica family includes other leafy crops, such as sprouts, kale and Chinese cabbage, as well as the root crops turnip and rutabaga and the flower crops broccoli and cauliflower. Most are fairly slow-growing crops and should be rotated around the garden together. If you are growing any of the above, you may as well devote a whole bed to them and grow a wide selection. Brassicas have a few pests and diseases to contend with, so it's worth grouping them together, since your attempts to keep the pests at bay will be most effective when crops are side by side.

Where to grow Cabbages are fairly large, slow-growing crops and don't do particularly well in containers. However, with the ability to grow baby-sized versions and squeeze more plants into a tight space, they are definitely worth trying in a small garden. Clubroot, a common disease (see page 55), can be offset with alkaline soil. If your soil isn't around pH 7, it can be increased to that level with the addition of lime (see page 219).

Types and varieties There is a wide variety of cabbage types, often termed by the season they are harvested. Summer and fall varieties include some interesting red types; winter varieties include the 'Mammoth Red Rock' (large coleslaw cabbage), the crinkly green 'Savoy' and pointy-headed 'Early Jersey Wakefield'; and spring cabbages are basically ones that give you spring greens and small hearts in the spring and early summer.

In the garden Cabbages like rich, organic soil with plenty of organic matter. ➡

Colorful cabbages
Leafy cabbages are a magnet for pests, but if you manage to keep them off, you'll have a bumper harvest.

INSTALLING FLOATING ROW COVERS

1 Insert pairs of 12-inch (30-cm) canes at 3-foot (90-cm) intervals over your vegetable bed.

2 Cut lengths of plastic water pipe to the desired length using a hacksaw and slip over two canes. Floating row covers can also be draped right over the plants.

3 Drape floating row covers over the top, and either bury the edges or secure with pegs, bricks or lengths of wood to stop pests from getting underneath.

PLANTING CABBAGE FROM SEED

1 Sprinkle a few seeds in a pot of potting mix, allowing around a finger width between each seed. Cover with a layer of compost and water.

2 Keep the seedlings well watered and under cover until they are strong enough to be planted out.

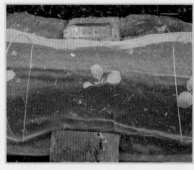

3 Plant out cabbages once they've grown on. The distance between plants will affect the ultimate size of the cabbages.

4 Cover your crop with floating row covers to deter flying pests.

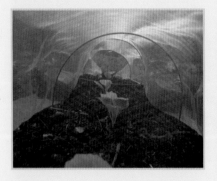

5 Ensure there is enough space under the floating row covers to allow the young plants to develop.

6 Once the heads are formed, cut carefully at the base of the plant.

They're a greedy crop so it's worth applying a generous amount of balanced fertilizer before planting out. The plants also need to be well watered, particularly during dry spells. Plants are most often raised in small pots before being planted out. Whichever types you are growing, grow them in small pots, then plant out when they've grown on. Sow a single seed in each small pot. Cabbages don't need much heat, so keep them in a cold frame or on a sunny windowsill. Once the plants have about four leaves, they are ready for planting out. For large cabbages aim for a plant every 20 inches (50 cm) or so. If you want to squeeze as much into your space as possible, place them much closer together, up to every 6 inches (15 cm). This should produce miniature versions — ideal for a small household. Cover crops with floating row covers.

Harvesting and storage Spring heads will be ready for harvesting in early spring. Cut the heads when required. As they grow they'll start to heart up, so keep cutting for the kitchen until they're all used up. Hopefully by this time your summer cabbages will be ready. Keep cutting as you need them, leaving the others in the garden. For winter cabbages, they too should keep in the garden until needed. If you do grow winter cabbages, they'll need storing indoors in racks at the start of winter.

In the kitchen With cabbages being available from the garden almost all year round, you'll need to be inventive to find enough dishes to include them in. Spring greens are fresh and tender and can be steamed like spinach. Other cabbages such as 'Early Jersey Wakefield' and some red cabbages can be used shredded in salads. Other types such as 'Savoy' are fantastic shredded and fried lightly.

Cutting your cabbages
Heads of cabbages can be picked once they're formed.

BRASSICA FAMILY PESTS AND DISEASES

Cabbages, as well as all other brassicas, suffer from a large number of pests and diseases.

This group of diseases can be avoided if you use floating row covers, well secured to keep the pests at bay.

CABBAGE ROOT FLY

The grubs feed on the roots of young plants, stunting and even killing them.

CABBAGE WHITE BUTTERFLIES

If the butterflies lay their eggs on the leaves, the resulting caterpillars will quickly devour your crop. Use BT spray on your crop.

FLEA BEETLES

These small beetles feed on the leaves of plants, peppering them with holes. While they can kill very young plants, older plants will survive but will be seriously spoiled.

MEALY CABBAGE APHID

Gray-green insects that cluster on the undersides of leaves, causing yellowing and distortion.

RABBITS

These larger pests love brassicas, especially in winter. Fencing will keep rabbits at bay.

CLUBROOT

Clubroot affects all members of the cabbage family. It's a disease that causes roots to swell and distort and plants usually wilt and die.

Once your soil is infected it's difficult to eradicate. Keep rotating your crop and avoid planting brassicas on soil where you know plants have been affected in the past. Clubroot is less severe in alkaline soils, so if you have this type of soil but still want to grow cabbages, then consider creating a high pH bed, devoted just to brassicas year-on-year.

POWDERY AND DOWNY MILDEW

Both these diseases can affect brassicas. Keep your plot well watered and remove any dead or yellowing leaves. If mildew continues to be a problem, try increasing the spacing between plants.

VARIETY SELECTOR

Summer and fall varieties
- 'Castello', 'Hispi': green.
- 'Metro', 'Primero': red.

Winter and spring varieties
- 'Dutch White', 'Holland Winter White', 'January King', 'Hardy Late Stock No. 3', 'Savoy', 'Celtic', 'Colorsa', 'Spring Cabbage', 'Durham Early', 'April'.

CALENDAR

EARLY SPRING

In mild winter climates (zone 8 and above), if you sowed your cabbages last summer, you should be able to start harvesting them now. Keep harvesting until early summer. Start to sow your summer/fall varieties in small pots.

MID-SPRING

You can still sow summer and fall varieties now.

LATE SPRING

Start to sow your winter cabbages in small pots. Plant out your summer/fall varieties in the garden.

EARLY SUMMER

Plant out the winter varieties you sowed six or so weeks ago. Start harvesting summer varieties.

MIDSUMMER

Watch out for pests, water well and keep harvesting your summer cabbages. Sow spring cabbages in pots.

LATE SUMMER

Keep plants well watered.

EARLY FALL

Plant out spring cabbages. Harvest fall cabbages.

MID-FALL

Keep harvesting.

LATE FALL

Check over your spring cabbages, and keep them protected from birds pecking and destroying your crop.

EARLY WINTER

Finish harvesting fall cabbages and start harvesting winter cabbages.

Brussels sprouts

Make sure you have room in the vegetable garden as this relative giant takes up lots of space!

○○○○○ VALUE FOR MONEY
○○○○○ MAINTENANCE
○○○○○ FREEZE/STORE
CROPPING SEASON: MID-FALL–LATE WINTER

This hardy winter vegetable is a member of the cabbage family. It has been bred to produce tight, leafy buds up its tall stem. Picked over winter, sprouts have a spicy, pungent flavor. The plants need a sizeable area of space to allow them to reach their full potential, growing to around 20 inches (50 cm) wide and up to 30 inches (75 cm) tall.

Where to grow Grow Brussels sprouts alongside other brassicas, such as cabbages and swede. They need a long growing season, plenty of space and fertile soil in a reasonably sunny spot. Avoid adding organic matter just before planting.

In the garden Because plants grow tall and become very bulky, they're liable to fall over, so it's a good idea not to dig over the soil before you plant your sprouts, maintaining a firm soil bed. It may also be necessary to push in canes and tie the plants to the cane to provide additional support. Sprouts are best planted out on a bed that has had beans in the previous year or a limed brassica bed (see pages 22–23 for more on crop rotation). Add 3½ oz (100 g) per square yard of general-purpose fertilizer when you plant.

Pests and diseases As with cabbage (see page 55).

Harvesting and storage Early varieties such as 'Falstaff' and 'Oliver' can be ready for picking as early as late summer. Others, such as 'Diablo', will be ready by fall. Check the plants and wait until the buds are tightly formed. Leave sprouts on the plants and pick from the bottom up. Sprouts are reputed to taste sweeter after the first frosts but if you

Ripe for the picking
Tight buds of Brussels sprouts will be ready to be picked from autumn right through the winter in zone 7 and above.

have very cold winters, pull out the whole plant and hang in a frost-free but cool shed.

In the kitchen A traditional choice for Christmas dinner, sprouts can be steamed and sautéed with chestnuts. You can also make hearty soups with sprouts, adding other winter vegetables from the garden.

VARIETY SELECTOR

• 'Diablo': a good choice for sprouts at Christmas.

• 'Falstaff': produces red leaves, and sprouts. Sadly, the color disappears on cooking.

• 'Oliver': has a short season so is good for northern climates.

CALENDAR

EARLY SPRING
Sow a single seed in individual small pots. These can be left outside in a sheltered spot. You'll probably want half a dozen plants at most.

MID-SPRING
When plants are 6 inches (15 cm) high, plant out, leaving around 3 feet (90 cm) between each plant. Draw soil around the stems and firm down. Water the plants well, protect from slugs and snails and cover with floating row covers.

MIDSUMMER
Stake plants when they get too tall. It's a good idea to add another dose of general fertilizer.

FALL ONWARD
Start picking from the bottom upward.

Kale

An old favorite in the kitchen garden. With its architectural appearance, kale is now making a comeback in the home garden.

✪✪✪✪✪ VALUE FOR MONEY
✪✪✪✪✪ MAINTENANCE
✪✪✪✪✪ FREEZE/STORE
CROPPING SEASON: EARLY FALL–LATE WINTER

Kale, or borecole as it used to be referred to, is another leafy brassica. Traditionally grown from spring for a fall and late winter crop, you can also grow it as a salad crop from late summer onward, similar to mizuna (see pages 58–59). Some of the prettier varieties, such as 'Dinosaur', are also popularly grown in ornamental gardens and make an enjoyable snack while you're working in the winter garden.

Where to grow Kale fits in with other brassicas and should be grown alongside them so pest protection can be applied easily to all. If you are after a crop of cut-and-come-again salad, consider growing kale in a pot or any area of the garden where you have space.

Types and varieties The traditional varieties of kale include curly kale varieties that produce crinkly leaves. Most are green but there are also some attractive red varieties. Making a comeback are the strap-shaped leaves of the black kales or 'Dinosaur', widely grown in Italy. They can reach over 6 ft 5 in (2 m) tall.

In the garden Kale requires the same soil and site as Brussels sprouts and other brassicas. It is normally grown as a winter vegetable (see calendar) but can be grown as a salad too. For a cut-and-come-again crop of salad leaves, seeds can be sown direct in the ground in rows spaced about 8 inches (20 cm) apart, or alternatively every inch (2.5 cm) in a 12-inch (30-cm) diameter container. Sowings can be made almost all year round. You should be able to start cutting the young leaves at the base of the plant after around six to 10 weeks. They should resprout a couple of times, but won't be as good as the first harvest.

Pests and diseases As for cabbage (see page 55). Protect with your other brassicas. Floating row covers will help to keep any pests off.

Harvesting and storage Tender leaves grown as a cut-and-come-again crop should be cut as required. Pick individual leaves as you need them and plants will continue to grow.

In the kitchen Packed with iron and vitamin C, young leaves can be used in salads. The slightly tougher leaves can be stir-fried or steamed like Chinese vegetables. Kale can simply be steamed with a little butter added for a delicious vegetable accompaniment.

VARIETY SELECTOR

• **'Blue Curled Scotch'**: traditional green variety of curly kale.

• **'Redbor'**: unusual and attractive red-colored curly kale.

• **'Dinosaur'**: traditional black kale variety.

Statuesque vegetable
'Dinosaur' (black kale) can bring color and structure to your garden in winter, as well as useful leaves for your kitchen.

CALENDAR

MID-SPRING

Plant a couple of seeds in small pots, weeding out the smaller one if both come up. Leave to grow in a cool greenhouse or sheltered spot in the garden.

EARLY SUMMER

Carry on growing in the pot. Leave in a sheltered spot, but watch out for pests nibbling your plants. Cover with floating row covers for added protection if necessary.

MIDSUMMER

Plant out into the garden, 18 inches (45 cm) apart. Keep well watered and protect from slugs and snails.

FALL ONWARD

Start to pick leaves as you need them. Leave crops through the winter as they'll continue to grow, if somewhat slowly.

Mizuna

This group of Japanese plants from the cabbage family provides a welcome addition to the salad bowl throughout the winter.

✪✪✪✪✪	VALUE FOR MONEY
✪✪✪✪✪	MAINTENANCE
✪✪✪○○	FREEZE/STORE

CROPPING SEASON: MIDSUMMER–MID-WINTER

Fast-growing and delicious, mizuna produces highly attractive spiky and serrated leaves in huge quantities. If you want to keep your salad bowl well stocked late in the season, this should be one of your regular crops. Mizuna has a peppery, cabbage flavor. It is fairly hardy and will survive outside throughout the winter. If you keep your crop covered, the leaves will remain undamaged and perfect for the kitchen.

Where to grow These greens can cope with a fairly wide range of soils, but they prefer rich, fertile soil — much like other brassicas — and can cope with light shade. They will do well in a pot, hanging basket or window box.

Types and varieties Often sold just as mizuna, there has been some recent breeding, with a few new varieties available. All are fairly hardy and productive.

Other winter salads Mizuna is a great winter salad and is perfect to keep you in fresh leaves through the winter — if you're growing under a cloche or floating row cover (zone 6 and below), or in a greenhouse.

However there are other winter salads that can also be grown in the winter. Aim to sow all of these in early fall and they should start to crop through the winter.
Mustard 'Red Frills' This crops between early winter right into early spring. This variety is particularly fine-leafed — other varieties can be much coarser. Growing in the winter means that the usual brassica pests aren't around to cause it any trouble, but it does do better with some protection, such as floating row covers. It will start to run to seed in the spring.

Corn salad 'Cavallo' This is a great salad for padding out the winter salad bowl. Also known as lamb's lettuce, its flavor is very mild, but the leaves are soft and tender. It forms rosettes of round leaves that can be picked right through mid-winter and into spring. Again, since the weather is cold, it should be untroubled by diseases and pests such as slugs and snails.
Claytonia Also known as miner's lettuce, this salad produces lots of small leaves on long stalks. Again, it's a good filler to your salad bowl, but useful if you find the leaves of mizuna and mustard quite spicy. It should crop from mid-winter right into spring.

In the garden Mizuna can be grown throughout the summer, but with so many other vegetables and salads available at that time of year, it's best to wait until the fall. When most other vegetables start tailing off,

GROWING MIZUNA

1 When leaves reach a decent size, cut them down around ¾ inch (2 cm) from the base and enjoy the leaves.

2 Make sure the soil is kept moist, and water with a general-purpose fertilizer.

3 Recut the leaves when they've regrown. Mizuna leaves can be cut down up to three times.

Winter leaves
The spicy leaves of mizuna make an interesting addition to the winter salad bowl.

CALENDAR

EARLY FALL

Sow in rows, sprinkling seed every inch (2.5 cm) with 16 inches (40 cm) between rows. Cover with soil, water and sprinkle with organic slug pellets.

MID-FALL

As plants appear, cover with a protective cover, such as a cloche, floating row cover or polythene tunnel.

LATE FALL ONWARD

Cut leaves as required.

it's time to sow your mizuna. Given some protection (zone 7 and below), it will happily sit in your kitchen garden throughout the winter just waiting to be picked.

Pests and diseases As with other brassicas (see page 55), but less likely to be affected through the winter. A crop cover — cloche, tunnel or floating row cover — over the top of the plants will help prevent the leaves becoming too tough and nibbled.

Harvesting and storage Cut leaves off at the base as you need them. Leaves should be ready for harvesting in as little as six weeks. Cut stems may resprout in mild areas. Leave the plants in the ground throughout the winter, since they can survive temperatures down to 14°F (-10°C).

In the kitchen These spicy leaves can be used to pepper up a winter salad. Alternatively, they can be wilted and added to tomato

sauces and spooned onto pasta. They can also be used in stir-fries, steamed and in soups in Asian cooking.

Miner's lettuce
Like mizuna, Claytonia is a winter lettuce, but it has a milder flavor.

VARIETY SELECTOR

Often sold as mizuna, or even as part of a spicy salad mix. However, you may have some luck finding specific varieties such as the following:

• 'Early Mizuna': has serrated leaves.

• 'Tokyo Belle': mizuna variety that has broader leaves.

Chinese cabbage and bok choi

Chinese cabbage and bok choi will make a rewarding harvest.

⬤⬤⬤⬤⬤ VALUE FOR MONEY
⬤⬤⬤⬤⬤ MAINTENANCE
⬤⬤⬤⬤⬤ FREEZE/STORE
CROPPING SEASON: LATE SUMMER–EARLY WINTER

A common problem with Asian vegetables is bolting (running). Bolting is exacerbated in hot and dry conditions and long days. Some modern varieties claim to resist the urge to bolt. As with other members of the brassica family, Chinese cabbage and bok choi suffer from slug attacks as well as flying pests. But these tasty, tender leaves and stems will allow you to create some authentic Asian dishes. If you struggle with bolting, plants can be grown as cut-and-come-again crops — follow the advice for mizuna (see page 58).

Where to grow A late summer planting can follow on from early potatoes or fava beans (see page 72). Alternatively, these crops do well in containers if protected from pests. They are quick-growing vegetables, but need a good supply of water to keep them growing fast. Use an area of good-quality ground.

Types and varieties Chinese cabbages are much faster growing than the Western types of cabbage, and are usually white and light green in color with a pungent brassica flavor. The hearted Chinese cabbages — often known as Chinese leaves or Napa cabbage — form crisp hearts of tightly folded leaves. Bok choi produces broad leaves, either green or red depending on the variety, as well as broad white edible stalks that widen at the base.

In the garden To prevent plants bolting, the best chance of success is to sow in the summer. Add a handful of general fertilizer to the soil prior to planting out. It's a good idea to mulch the plants with compost after planting,

VARIETY SELECTOR

Chinese cabbage
- **'Greenwich'**: narrow heads, bolt resistant.
- **'Bilko'**: large heads, bolt and disease resistant.

Bok choi
- **'Joi Choi'**: large white stems and dark green leaves. Good bolting resistance.
- **'Red Choi'**: leaves have a touch of red.

GROWING BOK CHOI IN CONTAINERS IN SUMMER

1 Plant up to six seeds, equally spaced, in a large container. Cover with a dusting of potting soil and sprinkle with a few organic slug pellets.

2 Protect the container from flying pests by covering it with floating row covers.

3 Keep watering and feeding with a general-purpose liquid fertilizer.

4 Crops should be ready to harvest in eight weeks.

Stir-fry perfection
The bolt-resistant Chinese cabbage 'Mei Qing Choi' has vigorous growth and crisp, tender leaves.

CALENDAR

MIDSUMMER
Add a general-purpose fertilizer or one high in nitrogen. Sow in the ground. Aim for a Chinese cabbage every 12 inches (30 cm) or bok choi every 8 inches (20 cm). If you sow more than this, you can thin seedlings later. Alternatively, sow individual seeds in small pots.

LATE SUMMER
Transplant pot-sown plants once they have grown to a reasonable size. Carefully remove plants from the pots and space as above, leaving 12 inches (30 cm) between rows. Mulch plants with compost and water every week.

EARLY–MID-FALL
If plants are looking weak, water with a liquid fertilizer. Start to harvest. Cut Chinese cabbage around 1 inch (2.5 cm) above the base to encourage reshooting.

LATE FALL
Cut the remaining crop. Start picking the re-shooted stumps of Chinese cabbage.

EARLY–LATE SPRING
If you live in a mild area (zone 8 and above), plants will survive the winter and start producing flowers. Cut these like broccoli.

MORE ASIAN GREENS
As well as Chinese cabbage and bok choi, there are a range of other Asian vegetables that form loose heads and are suitable for stir-fries or steaming. Grow in exactly the same way as above.

• **'Tatsoi'**: produces dark-green, rounded leaves that form rosettes (often called rosette bok choi). Look for **'Ryokusai'** and **'Yukina Savoy'**.

helping to keep them weed-free and retain moisture. The shallow roots benefit from watering little and often.

Pests and diseases Growing in containers helps to reduce slug damage, but you may still need to apply controls as any damage can spoil the crop. Using floating row covers generally prevents all the common brassica pests (see page 55).

Harvesting and storage Crops can be ready in as little as 10 to 12 weeks. However, if you time your plants to harvest in late fall and cover them with floating row covers to protect from light frosts, they should remain intact for several more weeks. If

heavier frosts are forecast, then the heads can be removed and stored for several weeks in the fridge. Cut the vegetables at the base, which should resprout and produce a fresh flush of leaves.

In the kitchen Young leaves can be used in salads and are commonly used in Asian cooking, steaming or stir-frying.

Spinach

A much-loved, leafy vegetable. Sow close and pick young for salads or sow farther apart for fresh leaf spinach for cooking.

○○○○○	VALUE FOR MONEY
○○○○○	MAINTENANCE
○○○○○	FREEZE/STORE

CROPPING SEASON: EARLY SUMMER–MID-FALL

Famous for its health benefits, spinach is an often forgotten crop. However, it's useful in the garden as it will fit into the smallest of spaces, and for a salad crop, will be ready for harvesting just a few weeks after sowing. Long days, especially when hot, can cause spinach to run to seed. An easier, but similar crop is New Zealand spinach and chard (see opposite). However, for the smallest and freshest salad leaves, spinach is difficult to beat.

Where to grow Best grown as a quick-growing salad, spinach will do well in containers or in the ground. It isn't too fussy, as long as the soil is reasonably fertile and well drained. Quick-growing spinach can be squeezed in between other crops that are slower growing, such as corn or brassicas.

Types and varieties Spinach varies little in taste between varieties. However, some are hardier than others.

In the garden Spinach can be sown in early spring and again in late summer. Spinach doesn't do well when the weather is really warm. Spinach does well in containers because leaves can be picked when they reach just 2 inches (5 cm) across. Fill a large container with potting mix, sprinkle seeds every 2 inches (5 cm) or so, and cover with a dusting of compost and water.

Pests and diseases Generally trouble-free, spinach is sometimes troubled by aphids (see page 227) and downy mildew but some varieties claim resistance to this disease. Slugs also need to be controlled.

Harvesting and storage Repeated sowings of spinach will provide a crop intermittently throughout the year. Pick when young for salads, or allow to grow on for use in cooked dishes. Spinach is liable to bolt, and when this happens, just pull up the unwanted plants.

In the kitchen Use small leaves in salads. Larger leaves should be washed and cooked in a pan (water not necessary) and wilted.

Crisp and fresh
Spinach is an elegant-looking and healthy vegetable that can be used in the same way as Swiss chard.

CALENDAR

EARLY SPRING
Make your first sowing of seed, ½ inch (1 cm) deep, in rows 12 inches (30 cm) apart. Cover with cloches or floating row covers if the weather is still cold.

MID–LATE SPRING
Keep sowing rows of spinach every few weeks for a continuous supply of salad leaves. If you leave a plant every 6 inches (15 cm), this can be left to grow on.

EARLY–MID- SUMMER
Keep watering your spinach during dry spells and harvest as required.

LATE SUMMER
Sow winter-hardy spinach for an early crop next spring in zone 6 and above, ½ inch (1 cm) deep, in rows 12 inches (30 cm) apart. Aim for a plant every 8 inches (20 cm).

VARIETY SELECTOR

- **'Bordeaux'**: good choice for baby-leaf spinach.
- **'Tyee'**: productive with crinkled leaves, slow to bolt.
- **'Space'**: very slow to bolt.

New Zealand spinach and Swiss chard

Providing alternatives to spinach, New Zealand spinach and chard taste great and make attractive ornamental plants.

✪✪✪✪✪ VALUE FOR MONEY
✪✪✪✪○ MAINTENANCE
✪✪○○○ FREEZE/STORE
CROPPING SEASON: EARLY SPRING–LATE FALL

New Zealand spinach is easier to grow than true spinach (see opposite) because it does not bolt. The leaves look and taste very similar, but they are usually much larger.

Swiss chard grows bigger still, when stalks and leaves are best separated prior to cooking. Some varieties are brightly colored and will liven up both the garden and the plate.

GROWING SWISS CHARD IN CONTAINERS

1 Fill a large pot with multipurpose potting mix. Sow six to eight seeds and cover with a sprinkling of compost.

2 Keep your pot well watered and cut stems as required in the kitchen.

Where to grow These leaves prefer rich, moisture-retentive soil. Add extra organic matter if you have any. Plants should cope with some shade.

Types and varieties As members of the beet family, Swiss chard is a biennial, meaning that it shouldn't flower in its first year.

New Zealand spinach is thin-stemmed, with slightly thicker leaves than spinach, but taste-wise, there is little difference between them.

Swiss chard is a much larger plant, reaching up to 18 inches (45 cm) high. Leaves can be picked young, but leave it to grow and the plant will produce thick stems in a range of bright colors.

In the garden New Zealand spinach and Swiss chard are very easy to grow. Sow once and they will keep growing all year. Sow twice and they'll crop well into the next year too. Fast-growing and thirsty, they do prefer a rich, moisture-retentive soil, but will do well in a container. The bright colors of chard stems are often used in containers and in ornamental borders for their color alone.

Pests and diseases Relatively trouble-free, but can be affected by downy mildew, as with spinach (see opposite).

Harvesting and storage The outer leaves can be picked regularly for a continuous supply. Alternatively, cut whole plants down to ¾ inch (2 cm) above soil level and they should resprout. Leave the plants growing throughout the year and harvest as required.

In the kitchen Use New Zealand spinach in the same way as regular spinach. Young chard leaves can be used in the same way too, but on mature plants the stems become much thicker. Separate the stems and leaves, steaming or using both in stir-fries.

CALENDAR

MID-SPRING
Make a single sowing of New Zealand spinach and Swiss chard. Raise in small pots and plant out later or sow direct, ⅝ inch (1.5 cm) deep in rows 12 inches (30 cm) apart.

LATE SPRING
Thin out seedlings to around 12 inches (30 cm) between plants. Spacing can be greater for Swiss chard to allow the stems to be displayed.

EARLY SUMMER
Start to pick outer leaves, or cut whole plants as required.

MIDSUMMER
Sprinkle over a general-purpose fertilizer and keep well watered. Sow some more seed now, as above, for a crop well into next year.

LATE SUMMER
Keep picking leaves for use in the kitchen from now right into winter.

VARIETY SELECTOR

New Zealand spinach
• No named varieties.

Swiss chard
• 'Bright Lights': red, yellow, gold and white stems.
• 'Fordhook Giant': large, meaty stems; thick, tasty leaves.

Lettuce

Dating back to Egyptian times, lettuce has always been a popular food.

○○○○○ VALUE FOR MONEY
○○○○○ MAINTENANCE
○○○○○ FREEZE/STORE
CROPPING SEASON: EARLY SUMMER–LATE FALL

The first lettuces were grown for their oil-rich seed, but it was probably the Romans who popularized eating the leaves, which were bred to be palatable and sweeter than plants found in the wild. Now, after many centuries of intensive breeding, there is a wide range of lettuce varieties. A staple crop of our salad bowls, there are crispy and soft, or buttery-leafed types, as well as more colorful varieties.

Recent developments in growing methods have introduced the idea of baby-leaf salads and cut-and-come-again leaves. Here, lettuce makes a great quick-growing salad crop that can make it from the seed packet to your plate in a matter of a few weeks.

Where to grow Lettuce can be squeezed into the smallest of spots. It is happy in a slightly shady bed and prefers good, rich soil with plenty of organic matter. Because it's a quick-growing crop, you can plant it in between other slower-growing vegetables, such as corn or brassicas, earlier in the year. You can also plant it into gaps when other vegetables, such as peas and fava beans, are pulled out. However, you should also bear in mind that it is best to rotate lettuces around the garden to avoid pests and diseases.

Lettuce can be grown in containers. Plant during the growing season for a decent crop from your garden, or sow in pots on a sunny windowsill both early and late in the year for a late-fall, winter and early-spring supply.

Types and varieties Lettuces can be broadly separated into two groups — lettuces that form hearts (hearting varieties), and ones that do not, often called loose-leaf types. *Hearting types* Hearting types can be further broken down. Firstly, there are the butterheads. Usually with fairly thick leaves,

butterheads are soft and flavorsome. The second type, the crispheads, are generally not so popular as they don't work as well in the salad bowl. These crispy, hearting lettuce varieties can be further separated into cos or romaine types, which are extremely popular in the kitchen. Sweet, crispy and flavorsome, they come in a wide range of sizes from the little gems to the larger, sweeter romaines. Then there are the icebergs, best known for their use in fast-food outlets and sandwich bars. Their leaves remain crisp, but lack flavor. Finally, there are the Batavian types, which are more of a cross between a cos and a butterhead, often with good flavor.

Loose-leaf types The loose-leaf types don't form any sort of heart. They are particularly good, therefore, for use as a cut-and-come-again lettuce. The red and green lollo types are well known and often frilly, but unfortunately, they don't taste as good as they look. Better tasting are the oak-leafed types, with thicker, juicy, sweet leaves.

Pests and diseases Lettuce suffers from a few pests and diseases. If slugs are a problem, one way to avoid them is to grow in a container. Alternatively, cut-and-come-again crops grow so quickly that often the pests and diseases don't have time to take hold.

GROWING CUT-AND-COME-AGAIN LETTUCES

1 You don't need a deep pot — a shallow, wide one would do fine. Fill it with multipurpose potting mix.

2 Sprinkle seeds across the surface, aiming for a seed every ⅝ inch (1.5 cm). Cover with a dusting of potting mix.

Crisp leaves
Grown in the garden, lettuce can provide the kitchen with a regular supply of leaves right through spring and into fall.

While lettuce can be sown direct, slugs will often eat the seedlings before they make it above ground. It is better to plant out larger plants and protect them from slugs and snails. Aphids such as greenfly are a problem too, and once on the leaves they are difficult to clean off. If the problem gets worse, reach for an organic trigger spray. Root aphids can also damage plants, making them wilt. Downy mildew is a disease that affects lettuce, causing yellowing leaves and mold growth — worse in cool, damp conditions. Avoid getting the plants wet and don't plant them too closely together. If plants are badly affected, pull up and discard.

Harvesting and storage Lettuce should be harvested as you need it and depending on the type, when it's ready. Store in the fridge and use within a week.

In the kitchen Lettuce is the most widely grown salad crop. Its sweet, fairly bland flavor makes it an excellent basis for all

Red lettuce
Red leaves make a colorful addition to the salad bowl.

sorts of salads. Mix with more spicy leaves of arugula or mizuna, or combine with the bitter leaves of endive and chicory to spice up salads. Crispy varieties are used in Caesar romaine salad, or go for a soft butterhead type to fill out sandwiches.

CALENDAR

LATE WINTER
Start sowing seeds in small containers. Keep the pots out of direct sun and well watered.

MID-SPRING–SUMMER
Keep sowing batches of seed, planting out into the garden when large enough to handle — this way you'll have a constant supply of leaves through the season.

MIDSUMMER
Stop sowing now as lettuce seeds don't germinate well when it's hot.

LATE SUMMER
Another sowing from now will provide leaves into fall. Keep harvesting your earlier sowings. Pick leaves off the loose heads or cut whole crispheads at the base.

FALL
If you have a greenhouse or cold frame, sow a variety such as 'Winter Density'.

WINTER–SPRING
Harvest your greenhouse- or cold frame-grown lettuce.

3 Water the plants, and after four weeks they should be ready for cutting. Snip off 1 inch (2.5 cm) from the base.

4 Keep watering and they should resprout. You should be able to get three cuts from one container.

Chicory and Endive

You either love or hate the slightly bitter leaves of chicory and endive — if you enjoy them, they're definitely worth growing.

●●●●●	VALUE FOR MONEY
●●●●○	MAINTENANCE
●●●○○	FREEZE/STORE

CROPPING SEASON: MIDSUMMER–EARLY WINTER

As easy to grow as lettuces, chicory and endive are their slightly bitter cousins. Popular in France and Italy, they're a staple ingredient in grocery-store salad bags. Many people blanch the leaves by covering the plants with a large pot to exclude the light a week or two before picking. This tempers their slightly bitter flavor.

Where to grow Can be grown in a container as a cut-and-come-again crop, as with lettuce. Alternatively, grow in rows in your vegetable garden. The crinkly leaves of endive and the bright colors of radicchio endive will brighten up any space.

Types and varieties You can get green or red chicory, but it's the red variety that is most popular (often known as radicchio, it forms dense heads of bitter red leaves). Certain types of chicory can be forced into chicons — tightly packed blanched shoots often seen in supermarkets.

The most popular endives are the curly types, with heads of finely divided, crinkly leaves. They are often dark green, but blanching them can turn them yellow.

In the garden Chicory and endive can be sown throughout the spring and summer to keep the crop coming right into winter.

Pests and diseases Chicory and endive tend to suffer from the same problems as lettuce (see page 64) but are generally free from pest problems.

(see page 64)

Harvesting and storage Pick as required. Plants are fairly hardy so can last throughout the winter depending on climate and protection.

In the kitchen Use raw in salads. Forced chicory or radicchio can be grilled and used in warm salads and appetizers.

VARIETY SELECTOR

Radicchio

- 'Indigo': balls of bitter, red leaves.

Endive

- 'Très Fine Maraîchère': excellent, bitter leaves.

For forcing

- 'Witloof Zoom'.

CALENDAR

EARLY–MID-SPRING
Sow in small pots as with lettuce. Plant out in rows 12 inches (30 cm) apart when at a reasonable size.

LATE SPRING
You can still sow now as above.

EARLY SUMMER
This is the last chance to make your spring and early summer sowing.

MIDSUMMER
When endive plants are large enough to be picked, blanch by placing a plate over the leaves for a week or two before picking. Resow another batch of seed for a winter crop.

LATE SUMMER
Plant out small plants sown last month 12 inches (30 cm) apart for a crop throughout the winter. Cover with floating row covers in cold areas in the fall.

EARLY FALL
Keep harvesting plants as they become ready.

FORCING CHICORY

1 Once you've grown the plant outside, you'll need to lift the roots in late fall after cutting off all the foliage. Alternatively, try growing them in a pot.

2 Plant several roots in pots filled with multipurpose potting mix. If you've grown them in a pot, just leave them in situ.

3 Cover the plants to exclude the light. Place somewhere warm with a minimum temperature of 50°F (10°C). In a few weeks, a chicon should have grown from each root. Cut off just above the base.

Arugula

Hot and peppery, arugula is a firm favorite in the kitchen — and it's easy to grow!

⚫⚫⚫⚫⚫	VALUE FOR MONEY
⚫⚫⚫⚫⚪	MAINTENANCE
⚫⚫⚫⚪⚪	FREEZE/STORE

CROPPING SEASON: LATE SPRING–MID-FALL

Once seen only in Italian cuisine, arugula has become a firm favorite on dinner plates all over the world. It adds spiciness to salads and is even used in pasta sauces and on top of pizzas. Arugula can be grown easily throughout the year.

Where to grow As it is fast-growing, arugula can be grown in with other brassica crops to keep the rotation together. Arugula can be ready for harvesting in as little as six weeks, so if you're using floating row covers on your other brassicas it's worth sowing some arugula in the gaps early and late in the year. In fact, arugula doesn't do well in the middle of summer because it tends to bolt (run to seed).

Easy to grow in containers too, a sprinkling of arugula seeds will provide you with a quick supply of leaves. Cut them down and they should resprout, at least once, to give you a double crop.

Cut and come again
Cut arugula at the base to encourage it to produce more edible leaves.

Types and varieties Wild arugula has deeply serrated leaves and is slightly tough and chewy, and very peppery. Salad arugula varieties have much larger, less-serrated leaves that are softer and not as peppery.

Pests and diseases Usually the only pest with this quick-growing crop is flea beetle, which peppers the leaves with small holes. Early and later crops may avoid flea beetle, or use floating row covers to protect the crop.

Harvesting and storage Snip off as many leaves as you need. If you have sown successional batches of seed, arugula should be available for most of the spring, and from late sowings, fall, and depending on climate and protection, winter.

In the kitchen Sprinkle into salads, pasta sauces, and on top of pizzas.

VARIETY SELECTOR
- Wild arugula: 'Sylvetta'.
- Salad arugula: usually no named varieties.

CALENDAR

MID-SPRING

Don't start arugula off too early — mid-spring should be fine. Either sow direct in rows, aiming for a seed every ½ inch (1 cm), or sprinkle into a large but shallow container filled with multipurpose potting mix.

LATE SPRING

Start to harvest the first leaves — pick them off or cut down plants 1 inch (2.5 cm) from the base.

MIDSUMMER

Start sowing a pot or a row of arugula every month. This way your salad will be perfect for picking when you need it.

EARLY FALL

Make this your last sowing of arugula as it doesn't do so well during the winter. Switch to mizuna (see pages 58–59) for peppery leaves throughout the winter.

SEED AND FRUIT CROPS

If you think peas and beans can easily be bought in the grocery store, you've obviously never tasted their freshly picked garden flavor. Easy to grow too, both the pole and bush varieties are worth finding a space for.

Also included here are the curcubits, from summer squashes to cucumbers, all of which are straightforward to grow and very bountiful.

Pole beans

If you want a productive, easy-to-grow crop, then pole beans come top of the list.

⊕⊕⊕⊕⊕ VALUE FOR MONEY
⊕⊕⊕⊕⊕ MAINTENANCE
⊕⊕⊕⊕⊕ FREEZE/STORE
CROPPING SEASON: EARLY SUMMER–MID-FALL

The legume family of crops are grown worldwide and include all beans and peas. Pole beans are those that twist themselves around supports as they climb upward. They're tender crops, but are quick to reach maturity so from a spring sowing, beans can be ready for picking as early as midsummer. The best thing about beans is that the more you pick, the more they produce. They just keep on growing until the first frosts.

Peas and beans are also known for their ability to fix nitrogen from the atmosphere and use it as a nutrient for their growth. In fact, this process is possible because of certain species of bacteria that reside in their roots, but still, this means the plants need little in the way of additional fertilizer.

Where to grow All pole beans need supports and plenty of space to allow them to grow upward. Peas and beans should be fitted into your rotation (see pages 22–23) and grown as a group.

They often follow on from brassicas, which are greedy crops, and will have used up much of the fertility of the soil. Because of the amount of foliage they produce, pole beans need a plentiful supply of water, so grow in rich, moisture-retentive soil and add lots of compost. They can cope with some shade but prefer a sunny spot.

Types and varieties Runner beans, which are extremely productive, produce ugly but tasty beans. Also, runner beans are pollinated by insects and sometimes suffer from pollination problems early in the season.

For a much earlier crop, go for conventional pole beans, which come in a wide number of colors and shapes — flat and cylindrical pods, as well as green, yellow and purple pods. All should be picked over ➡

Bountiful beans
Pole beans will provide you with a long supply of tasty beans right up to the first frosts.

regularly, taking off pods when they're still fairly small and tender.

Pests and diseases
Aphids and bean beetles are occasionally a problem — use an organic spray.

Harvesting and storage
In the height of the season, pick the beans every few days. If you leave it longer, they will become tough and stringy. Be careful not to damage the remaining beans when pulling the pods off the plant.

Excess beans can be blanched in boiling water and frozen. Beans saved for drying should be left to dry, shelled and stored in an airtight container.

In the kitchen
Fresh beans can be used throughout the summer — they are best steamed. Dried beans can be incorporated into soups and stews throughout the winter.

VARIETY SELECTOR

Runner bean

- **'Red Flame'**: red flowers.
- **'White Lady'**: white flowers.

Pole bean

- **'Blue Lake'**: cylindrical green pods.
- **'Hilda Romano'**: flat, purple pods.

MAKING A SUPPORT FOR POLE BEANS

1 Choose a sunny site, but an area that won't cast shade on your other plants. In early spring, make a bean trench and dig in as much potting mix as you can spare.

2 Select canes 6 ft. 5 in. (2 m) high, and push 6 to 10 of them positioned at least 6 inches (15 cm) apart into the ground to form a wigwam shape.

3 Tie the canes securely at the top with string.

4 When planting your beans (one plant per cane), guide them around the canes to encourage them to climb.

CALENDAR

MID–LATE SPRING
Don't sow beans too early because they are a tender and fast-growing crop. Plant beans singly in small pots filled with multipurpose potting mix.

EARLY SUMMER
When all threat of frost has passed, plant out beans along your supports. If you have more plants than supports, plant a couple of plants at the base of each support or sow seeds directly in the ground.

MIDSUMMER
Pole beans should be ready for picking, but runner beans may take a little longer. Pick your beans every few days. Water in dry spells.

LATE FALL
Pick beans left on the plant for drying. Leave them somewhere cool and dry, such as a garage or greenhouse, and wait until the pods have dried. Remove the beans from the pods and store in a paper bag until next spring.

TIP
Before you go on vacation, make sure you pick off every bean you can find — this will ensure the plants carry on producing beans when you return.

Bush beans

If you are short on space but love beans, select a bush variety, ideal for containers and hanging baskets.

✪✪✪✪✪	VALUE FOR MONEY
✪✪✪✪○	MAINTENANCE
✪✪✪✪○	FREEZE/STORE

CROPPING SEASON: EARLY SUMMER–MID-FALL

Crunchy pods
Stringless, tender bush beans are easy to raise from seed, require very little maintenance and provide a huge harvest.

Like their larger, climbing cousins, bush beans come in a wide range of colors and shapes. There are also some varieties that are perfect for drying. You have a choice of two types of bush beans: runner beans or bush beans. There are not that many varieties of runner beans available, but there are lots of bush beans, and generally these are more popular.

All bush beans are easy to grow and are generally free from pests and diseases. While runner beans need insects to pollinate their flowers, bush beans do not, meaning there is usually no problem with the beans setting, even if you are growing them in a greenhouse, or growing them slightly out of season.

Where to grow Similar to pole beans, bush beans are tender, so need to be grown in a frost-free place. They also like rich soil and will do fine in a slightly shady spot, but full sun would produce the highest yields.

If you have plenty of space, grow them in the garden, with other peas and beans, and rotate each year to prevent pest problems building up. They prefer light but moisture-retentive soil.

If you are short on space, a pot or hanging basket is ideal. They're attractive plants too,

especially when in flower or when the colorful beans have set. If you have a greenhouse, you can grow bush beans in the soil border or in containers either for an earlier or later crop than you would get outdoors.

Types and varieties There are only a few bush runner bean varieties and all look attractive, reaching about 1½ feet (45 cm) high. They're a good choice if you have only a small space and prefer fewer beans than are produced by their climbing cousins.

The choice of bush beans is much greater. Filet types produce very fine, pencil-thin pods. Standard bush beans produce cylindrical green, yellow or dark purple pods.

Pests and diseases Aphids and bean beetles. As with pole beans, use an organic spray if the problem worsens. Alternatively, encourage natural predators such as ladybugs and lacewings.

Harvesting and storage Start picking pods when they're about 4–6 inches (10–15 cm) long. Picking can damage the plant so don't pull the plant too hard. Blanch excess beans and freeze.

In the kitchen As with pole beans, bush beans are best steamed and served with butter. The most tender beans taste just as good as asparagus!

VARIETY SELECTOR

Bush runner bean
• 'Dwarf Bees': red flowers.

Bush beans
• 'Bush Blue Lake 274': ideal for containers.
• 'Roma II Bush': straight and stringless.
• 'Royal Burgundy Purple Pod Bush': deep-purple pods.

CALENDAR

MID-SPRING

Bush beans are sensitive to frost, so sow in small pots about four weeks before the last frosts. In milder areas, sow direct into the soil. Separate rows by around 12 inches (30 cm), and place one seed every 2 inches (5 cm), ¾ inch (2 cm) deep.

LATE SPRING

In colder areas, start sowing now, ready to plant out in early summer.

EARLY SUMMER

Keep watering your plants when beans start to form to encourage pods to fill out. Start picking when beans are 4 inches (10 cm) long.

MIDSUMMER

Sow another crop of beans direct into the soil, as above. Beans should start cropping in early fall, when the earlier beans have finished.

LATE SUMMER

Keep watering and picking your beans.

Fava beans

Fava beans are delicious and easy to grow too.

○○○○○ VALUE FOR MONEY
○○○○○ MAINTENANCE
○○○○○ FREEZE/STORE
CROPPING SEASON: EARLY SUMMER–LATE SUMMER

Expensive in the supermarkets and often not as sweet as you'd like, fortunately fava beans are an easy crop to grow, and unlike bush and runner beans, they are hardy. Where winters are mild (zone 8 and above), they're planted in early fall, to give one of the earliest crops in the spring. From a further spring sowing, you can extend the harvest from around four weeks to seven or eight weeks. In the kitchen, they combine well with early summer vegetables, such as young carrots, peas and asparagus. If you're feeling adventurous, pick them young and eat them whole — pods and all!

Perfect for picking
Whether you sow in spring or fall, it's important to pick fava beans when they're still young to ensure you get great-tasting, tender beans.

Where to grow Fava beans fit with other beans in a rotation (see pages 22–23). They take up a fair amount of space, and each plant will produce only a couple of handfuls of beans, so they are not ideal for growing in pots. They're best grown in blocks or as a series of rows. Fava beans can get fairly tall too, and if you do grow them in a block, there is a simple way to help the beans stand upright (see right).

Types and varieties Often, fava beans are categorized into spring-sowing varieties and fall-sowing varieties. In reality, they are all hardy, and so all varieties will grow in the fall too. More recent breeding has produced many small-podded fava beans, which are easier for agricultural machines to pick. Generally, these are meant to be sweeter than some of the older varieties and they can be picked young and eaten whole.

Pests and diseases Fava beans are fairly trouble-free, except for black bean aphid. These cluster around the growing tip — nipping these out in early summer will help to control the pests. You could try spraying with an organic pesticide if the pests persist.

Mice can also be a problem if you sow direct into the soil — if they are eating your seeds, consider starting the beans off in pots and plant out after a few weeks.

Harvesting and storage Pick over the beans each week, selecting those that have filled out the pods.

You can pick beans when they're very young and tender, or just 2 inches (5 cm) or so long. These can be eaten whole, including the pods. They are best eaten fresh from the garden.

In the kitchen The skins, which can be tough, are easily slipped off. Fava beans are

SUPPORTING FAVA BEANS

1 When the plants reach a height of 12 inches (30 cm), they can be damaged in strong winds.

2 Insert canes around the edge of the crop.

CONTROLLING BLACK BEAN APHID

1 Keep an eye out for aphids on the tips of your beans. If left, they'll spread down the plant and spoil your crop.

2 Nipping out the growing tips of fava beans helps minimize the damage caused by aphids. Pinch out the top 4 inches (10 cm) or so.

fantastic lightly steamed with other early-summer vegetables. If you're eating the beans and the pods, steam lightly and add butter.

VARIETY SELECTOR
- **'Windsor'**: 5–6 inch (13–15 cm) pods, which contain 3–5 large 1-inch (2.5-cm) shell beans (see below).
- **'Egyptian'**: small-seeded type.

3 Tie string around the canes, keeping the beans inside the support.

CALENDAR

EARLY FALL

In mild winter areas, sow blocks of beans 2 inches (5 cm) deep, with 8 inches (20 cm) between seeds. Sow a short row of extra beans close together that you can use to fill any gaps.

EARLY WINTER

Order more beans now for planting in the spring.

EARLY SPRING

Provide supports to growing crop (see opposite).

MID-SPRING

Sow another block of seed now, which will produce a harvest later in the summer.

LATE SPRING

Watch out for black bean aphid and pick off the tips of plants where they congregate.

EARLY SUMMER

Provide supports to your spring-sown crop.

MIDSUMMER

Your fall crop should be ready for picking. Pick over the crop each week, squeezing the beans to see if they've filled out.

LATE SUMMER

Check the spring-sown crop. Pick when ready.

EARLY FALL

Clear away your spent plants and place on the compost heap.

Peas

Universally popular, fresh, super-sweet peas rarely make it from garden to kitchen without a few being eaten on the way.

⬤⬤⬤⬤⬤ VALUE FOR MONEY
⬤⬤⬤⬤◯ MAINTENANCE
⬤⬤⬤⬤⬤ FREEZE/STORE
CROPPING SEASON: LATE SPRING–MID-FALL

One of the earliest crops to sow, peas are quick and easy to grow. Provide them with a little support and they'll scramble up some strategically placed twigs or floating row covers, and produce a welcome crop in early summer. Peas have been bred to be so tender and sweet that it isn't really necessary to cook them any more. In fact, if you have children in your house, you'll be lucky to see any at all!

Where to grow Peas fit in with the other peas and beans, and should be part of your crop rotation (see pages 22–23). Like fava beans, they take up a fair amount of room, so you need to make sure your garden can accommodate them. Best sown in rows, most require some support as some can reach well over 5 ft. (1.5 m) high.

Types and varieties Peas are often separated into earlies and maincrops.

In the garden Peas are generally sown in late winter/early spring before the last spring frost date. From a single sowing you'll get around a month when peas can be picked. If you sow a succession, say, every two weeks right through early and mid-spring, then the supply of peas for the kitchen will be much greater and more sustained.

Pests and diseases Plants can suffer from powdery mildew — keeping plants well mulched and watered during dry spells should help.

Harvesting and storage When the pods start to fill out, pick a few peas. If they're not quite ready, leave them a few more days. You'll need to pick over your peas every few days to avoid the peas over-maturing and becoming dry and tough.

GERMINATING PEAS

1 Buy (or scavenge) some plastic eavestrough and cut it into 3 ft. 2-in. (1-m) lengths (or the length of your rows).

2 Block the ends with a brick or any other suitably sized object and fill with multipurpose potting mix.

3 Sow the seeds about 2 inches (5 cm) apart (you'll get a couple of rows). Cover the seed with a dusting of potting mix.

STAR PLANT
SWEET TASTE
SUMMER CROP

Sweet treats
There is nothing more rewarding than picking fresh peas from your garden. Make sure you keep picking every few days to ensure your crop is especially sweet.

In the kitchen Fresh peas can be eaten raw, straight from the pod. If you can manage to shell some without eating them all, steam lightly and add butter — they'll be so much tastier than the frozen versions.

Note: Pea tendrils are the curly leaf-like structures used to help the plant to grow and climb — these can be eaten. Pea shoots are basically very young plants — you can eat leaves, stem and all.

VARIETY SELECTOR

- 'Green Arrow': 3–4 ft. (90–100 cm) tall vines with well-filled pods.

- 'Eclipse': holds sweetness. Don't plant too early.

CALENDAR

LATE WINTER
Make your first sowing toward the end of winter. Peas tolerate frost and snow. Create a trench and sow a double row 1 inch (2.5 cm) deep and around 2–4 inches (5–10 cm) apart.

EARLY SPRING–LATE SPRING
Keep sowing rows every two weeks. Create some supports for your peas, either using sticks from the garden or canes and netting.

EARLY SUMMER
Keep watering plants. Start harvesting now.

4 Water and leave to grow in a sheltered spot, such as a greenhouse, a polytunnel, or even in the shelter of a wall or fence.

5 When plants have germinated, create a shallow trench in your plot and carefully push the peas out of the eavestrough and into the trench.

6 Once the peas are planted, water them in well and use twiggy stems or a series of canes and netting to support the peas as they grow.

Snow peas and Snap peas

If you tire of shelling peas but love the flavor, these two alternatives fit the bill perfectly.

✪✪✪✪✪ VALUE FOR MONEY
✪✪✪✪✪ MAINTENANCE
✪✪✪✪✪ FREEZE/STORE
CROPPING SEASON: LATE SPRING–MID-FALL

Time your harvest
Pick snow peas as soon as the pods are formed, since these will provide the sweetest pods.

Young pods taste as sweet and juicy as the peas themselves. Snow peas produce flat pods, while snap pea pods are rounded, often with peas just starting to grow inside. At the grocery store, both command premium prices. At home, they're just as easy to grow as peas, and as you eat both the peas and pods you'll get even more edible crop for the same amount of space. In fact, from a 3 ft. 2-in. (1-m) row of either snaps or snow peas, you can expect to harvest around 4½ lb (2 kg) of good-quality pods — if you manage to keep up with the picking, that is. In the kitchen, both can be used fresh, in stir-fries or lightly cooked as a summer vegetable.

Where to grow Just like peas, varieties of snow peas and snaps differ in height. Some shorter varieties can be self-supporting, while others definitely need support for their tendrils to cling on to. Grow snaps and snow peas alongside other peas and beans, but as with

PEA TENDRILS

One other part of the pea plant is perfectly edible and tasty — the tendrils. They can be picked and eaten in salads. There are semi-leafless types of peas, which produce more tendrils than most. A good semi-leafless variety of snow peas is 'Sugar Crystal'. Start picking the tendrils when the plant is young, but be sure to leave enough to allow the plant to cling while it climbs.

VARIETY SELECTOR

Snow peas

• **'Dwarf Grey Sugar'**: purple flowers, 30 inch (75 cm) tall vines, 2 ½–3 inch (6.5–7.5 cm) pods.

Snap pea

• **'Sugar Snap'**: 5–7 ft. (1.5–2.1 m) tall vines, excellent flavor, 3-inch (7.5-cm) pods.

• **'Sugar Ann'**: 2 ft. (60 cm) tall vines, early croppers, 2 ½-inch (6.5-cm) pods.

peas, a few sowings through late winter and early spring will provide a continual supply of pods through early summer.

All peas prefer an open site, with fertile soil that has plenty of organic matter dug in. The soil also needs to drain freely. As with other vegetables, it's a good idea to work over the soil before sowing direct. This way, you remove any unwanted weeds and allow the seeds to get off to a good start. If you struggle to get peas germinated in the soil direct, consider sowing in pots. Place two or three seeds in each small pot, and keep in a cool greenhouse or on a sunny windowsill until big enough to plant out. Plant out in their clumps around a wigwam or other support. Once the peas start to flower, it's a good idea to make sure they don't go short of water. Watering at this stage will really boost your harvest.

Pests and diseases As with peas (see page 74).

Harvesting and storage You can start to pick snow peas as soon as they form on the plant. If left too long they can become stringy, tough and bitter — it's a good idea to pick the pods a couple of times a week during the harvest period. Snaps are generally sweeter than snow peas and will need to be harvested when mature. Pick as soon as they plump out — pods make a characteristically pleasing snap when bent.

In the kitchen Both can be used raw in salads or very lightly steamed or stir-fried. If left to mature, they can be shelled like ordinary peas, but often the taste is dry and unpleasant so eat fresh for best results.

CALENDAR

LATE WINTER
Make your first sowing now. If still cold, either plant under cloches or start off in pots in a cool greenhouse or on a sunny windowsill.

EARLY–MID-SPRING
Continue sowing outside. Sow 2 inches (5 cm) deep and about 4 inches (10 cm) apart. You can sow in bands — double rows — as shown on page 74 when sowing into eavestrough.

LATE SPRING
Insert supports around the plants to allow the peas to climb.

EARLY SUMMER
Pick over peas regularly. Be sure to pick over-mature peas, even if you are not going to eat them.

MAKING PLANT SUPPORTS FOR PEAS

PEA STICKS
Use pea sticks — twiggy sticks scavenged from around the garden. They can be used on their own for shorter varieties to clamber up, or used on a wigwam to give young plants a head start.

WIGWAMS
These are a series of canes tied at the top to create a wigwam shape. Either tie string around or use large-gauge netting to provide support for the peas.

PLANTING PEAS
Wherever you plant, give the peas a helping hand and encourage them to grow up the supports.

Zucchini

Just one or two zucchini plants will provide plenty of zucchini through the summer and into fall.

○○○○○ VALUE FOR MONEY
○○○○○ MAINTENANCE
○○○○○ FREEZE/STORE
CROPPING SEASON: EARLY SUMMER–MID-FALL

Zucchini are tender plants, but as they are such quick growers, they'll be successful in all but the coldest of climates. They crop readily too: in midsummer you'll need to pick over your plants every other day to keep up with production. Left on the plant, a zucchini fruit will just keep on growing at the expense of any other zucchini, so it's worth picking them even if you're not going to eat them. With a zucchini produced every other day, just one or two plants are plenty for any household. While the green, long zucchini are most widely grown, it's also worth trying a more colorful yellow variety, or even one of the unusual-shaped summer squashes. These are grown and cooked in the same way as zucchini and should also be picked regularly.

Where to grow Zucchini are attractive plants with broad green leaves. They grow as a small bush, so even though they get pretty big, they don't get out of control. You'll need around 10 square feet (1 sq m) for each plant in the ground, or alternatively, an individual plant can be grown in a large container — one that holds at least 8 gallons (30 L) of potting mix.

Set out plants or seeds only after the last chance of frost has passed. Once in the ground, they grow rapidly and are greedy feeders. They require deep, fertile and moisture-retentive soil, so it's worth digging in plenty of organic matter before you plant. Zucchini are part of the cucumber — or curcurbit — family, which also includes pumpkins and cucumbers. It's best to keep all of these plants together in the garden and rotate them with your potatoes and onions

Types and varieties The most popular and well-known zucchini are the long, green

PREPARING FOR AND PLANTING ZUCCHINI

1 Before planting, dig in plenty of organic matter and create a small mound.

2 To prevent the stem rotting off, push down a piece of tubing next to where the plant will go. Water once a week down the tubing to get the water straight to the roots.

Patty pan squash
As well as traditionally shaped zucchini, why not try growing some of the more unusual patty pan, such as the kind that carry "flying-saucer" fruits.

The mighty zucchini
Zucchini grow into huge plants. They're productive too, so you'll only need a couple of plants to keep your family in good supply.

3 Plant an individual zucchini on top of each mound. While they like plenty of moisture, this will prevent the stem from rotting off.

varieties. More recently, spherical green zucchini have been developed, but the yields aren't as great. The yellow varieties are a colorful choice, producing bright yellow fruit.

Zucchini and other summer squashes don't store well, so should be used as close to picking as possible. There are some unusual-looking squashes, such as the knobbly crooknecks or the patty pan squashes, which look attractive in the garden as well as on the plate.

Pests and diseases Zucchini need plenty of water. When the soil runs dry, a powdery mildew can develop, forming white patches across the leaves, which weakens and can even kill plants. Pick off the leaves where it develops. Prevent mildew by keeping plants well watered.

Insect pests that target zucchini are cucumber beetle (see page 85), squash bug (see page 85) and vine borer.

Harvesting and storage Zucchini grow prolifically given a decent summer and plenty of water. Pick over plants every other day — small zucchini are definitely tastier than if left to grow too big. Flowers can be picked and eaten too. Pick them just as they're about to open and before any fruit has developed. If you're going away for a few days, it's a good idea to pick over any developing flower buds and young fruit to prevent massive zucchini developing while you're away.

In the kitchen Flowers can be dipped in batter and deep-fried as a delicacy. Young zucchini are a delicacy and can be grated or chopped and eaten raw in salads. Larger zucchini are best cooked. For best results, fry in a pan or on a griddle to take on a slightly smoky flavor, and add to Mediterranean-style dishes.

VARIETY SELECTOR

Best green zucchini variety
• 'Costata Romanesco'.
Best yellow zucchini variety
• 'Soleil'.
Best spherical zucchini variety
• 'Eight Ball'.
Crookneck squash
• 'Yellow Crookneck'.
Patty pan squash
• 'Scallop Mixed'.

CALENDAR

MID-SPRING

There is no point starting any earlier than this as zucchini are rapid growers but sensitive to frost. Start off seeds in individual small pots. Place the seeds on their side and cover with ½ inch (1 cm) of potting mix. Plants need a temperature of around 65°F (18°C), but at this time of year seeds will quickly grow in a greenhouse or on a windowsill.

LATE SPRING

Keep plants well watered, and when the threat of frost has passed, plant out in the garden, giving each plant at least 10 square feet (1 sq m).

You can also plant individually in large 8-gallon (30-L) containers filled with multipurpose potting mix and slow-release fertilizer.

MIDSUMMER

Start picking fruit once they start to form. Keep plants well watered.

LATE SUMMER

Remove any leaves that look affected by powdery mildew. Keep watering plants if the weather is dry, and keep picking the fruit.

EARLY FALL

Plants should continue producing fruit.

Squash and Pumpkin

If you've got plenty of space but not much time, low-maintenance winter squashes and pumpkins are a rewarding crop to grow.

> ✪✪✪✪✪ VALUE FOR MONEY
> ✪✪✪✪✪ MAINTENANCE
> ✪✪✪✪✪ FREEZE/STORE
> CROPPING SEASON: MIDSUMMER–MID FALL

Winter squashes are different from summer squashes in that they take all summer to grow and are ready for harvest at the beginning of winter. The same is true of pumpkins, but while the flesh of pumpkin is wetter and less tasty than that of winter squash, they can't be beaten when it comes to carving them for Halloween!

The only downside to winter squashes and pumpkins is the space they require. They grow into huge trailing plants, each plant easily covering several square yards. Each plant will give only a handful of fruit at most. Winter squashes do store well, right through the winter, but pumpkins with their thinner skins don't last much beyond Christmas.

Halloween treats
Orange pumpkins are great for carving, but if you select your variety carefully, winter squashes and pumpkins can also be extremely productive for the kitchen.

Where to grow If you have a very large garden it would be sensible to rotate your winter squashes and pumpkins around it (see pages 22–23). If you've also decided to grow melons, outdoor cucumbers and zucchini, it's best to try to keep them all together. In reality, since they take up so much space, they may not fit into your vegetable-growing plot, and you may need to find a corner of the garden in which to grow a couple. Many people plant direct into an old compost heap because they like plenty of nutrients and moisture. Otherwise, you'll need to enrich the soil with organic matter and select a sunny spot. Because they take up a lot of ground space, many people interplant (see page 226).

Types and varieties The large, orange winter pumpkins are an obvious choice to grow, but they don't taste that great. It's worth growing one or two for carving, but for eating, it's best to stick to winter squashes. Winter squashes come in all shapes and sizes — many are incredibly beautiful with their bumps and nobbles. There is also a wonderful diversity

GROWING SQUASH AND PUMPKIN

1 Dig in plenty of organic matter. Plant young plants once all threat of frost has passed. Plant an inverted large plastic bottle with the end cut off next to the squash.

2 During the summer, the bottle can be topped up with water — an easy way to make sure water reaches the roots.

of colors, ranging from orange and yellow, to green, multicolored and even blue!

Pests and diseases Squashes and pumpkins are generally trouble-free.

Harvesting and storage Pumpkin and squash fruits should be left outside until they take on their full color. If the weather is fine, leave them outside. But as soon as frost is forecast, bring them inside. Leave the skins to harden and the stalks to dry to prolong the storage period (this is known as "curing").

Pumpkins don't store so well, so it's best to carve these by Halloween or eat by Christmas.

Squashes, however, can last much longer and since they're generally tastier can last right into the new year. Store them in a cold, dry and light place such as a garden shed or greenhouse.

In the kitchen Most squashes and pumpkins typically have orange or yellow flesh. Once peeled and the seeds removed, the flesh can be roasted with other winter vegetables. The sweet and smooth flesh is also fantastic puréed and made into hearty winter soups. The seeds are edible and can be roasted.

VARIETY SELECTOR

Pumpkin
- **'New England Pie'**: weighs between 5–7 lbs (2–3 kg).

Buttercup
- **'Sweet Mama'**: sweet orange flesh.

Butternut
- **'Waltham'**: small seed cavity.

Others
- **'Delicata'**: sweet, nutty flavor and creamy texture.
- **'Spaghetti'**: once cooked, strands resemble spaghetti.

CALENDAR

MID-SPRING
Sow seeds individually in small pots. Place the flat seed on its side and cover with ½ inch (1 cm) of potting mix. Keep in a well-lit and warm place (above 65°F/18°C).

LATE SPRING
Pot on into larger pots if frosts are still likely. When all chance of frost has passed, plant outside with at least 3 ft. 2 in. (1 m) between plants, or sow seeds directly into the ground.

EARLY SUMMER
Keep unruly plants under control by moving their long, winding stems back into their allotted space.

MIDSUMMER
Water if very dry — a couple of really good soaks should do.

LATE SUMMER
Fruit should be set and starting to ripen.

EARLY FALL
Once fruits start to ripen and reach their full size, start to harvest from now on.

The prince of pumpkins
Varieties such as 'Crown Prince' (left) and butternut squashes can be harvested in late fall and stored for use right through the winter.

Marrow

Too large to be a zucchini and not sweet enough for a squash, marrows make attractive plants and provide plenty of fruit for the kitchen.

⬡⬡⬡⬡⬡ VALUE FOR MONEY
⬡⬡⬡⬡⬡ MAINTENANCE
⬡⬡⬡⬡⬡ FREEZE/STORE
CROPPING SEASON: MIDSUMMER–MID-FALL

Marrows may look just like large zucchini, but they are in fact a vegetable in their own right. The fruit grow much bigger than zucchini and often have an unusual stripy appearance. They are similar to zucchini in that they produce fruit throughout the summer, which you can pick as they grow. However, the last fruits of the year, harvested just before the first frosts, should store for several months.

Where to grow
Grow marrows with your other zucchini and squash. Marrows either come as bush varieties — making growing in a relatively small space possible — or as trailing varieties — more like the squashes that send out long shoots reaching well beyond their original space.

Bush varieties are good for small spaces but trailing varieties can be trained — when tied into a wigwam or trellis, they look attractive when the fruits form and hang down.

Types and varieties
Mainly split into bush or trailing types, some types store better than others.

Pests and diseases
As with zucchini (see page 79).

Harvesting and storage
Fruits can be picked throughout the summer when they reach the size suggested on the seed packet — usually around 12 inches (30 cm). Keep picking until the first frosts. These last fruits should be left outside (or in a greenhouse) to cure and for the skins to harden, but make sure all are collected before any severe frosts.

Store in a dry, cool place — a shed or garage is fine. Either store individually in boxes or hang in nets to allow air to circulate.

In the kitchen
Marrow can be used like zucchini. Once the skins have gone hard, peel or cut the flesh lengthwise. They can then be stuffed and roasted.

Mammoth marrow
An overlooked vegetable, the humble marrow doesn't store well and can lack flavor. However, it can look impressive when the large fruit forms in the summer and fall.

TRAINING A CLIMBING MARROW

1 Plant against a sunny trellis.

2 As the plant grows, tie in stems up the trellis. Ensure plants are well supported when large fruits form.

CALENDAR

LATE SPRING
Sow seeds individually on their side in small pots. Cover with ½ inch (1 cm) of potting mix. Keep somewhere bright and warm (at least 65°F/18°C).

EARLY SUMMER
Wait until any threat of frost has passed and plant out into rich, fertile soil with plenty of organic matter. Allow 10 square feet (1 sq m) for each plant.

MIDSUMMER
Water the plants during dry spells — a couple of really good soaks. Fruits can be protected from damp by placing an old plate, brick or tile underneath them as they form.

LATE SUMMER
Keep picking fruit.

EARLY FALL
At the first sign of frosts, the mature fruit can be picked, cured and put into storage.

Cucumber

This summer salad mainstay
is easy to grow outdoors and
under cover.

⬡⬡⬡⬡	VALUE FOR MONEY
⬡⬡⬡⬡	MAINTENANCE
⬡⬡⬡⬡	FREEZE/STORE

CROPPING SEASON: MIDSUMMER–MID-FALL

Cucumbers are one of the most popular salad
crops, and they're also one of the easiest to
grow. You don't need too many plants as just
one can produce over 22 pounds (10 kg) of
cucumbers — more than enough to feed a
family every week throughout the summer
months. In cooler climates (zone 7 and below),
if you have a greenhouse, you'll probably opt
for a variety that has been bred specifically
for growing under glass, in the same way
as a cordon tomato. If you don't have a
greenhouse, some cucumbers (and gherkins)
can easily be grown outside. If they are left to
trail over the ground, much like squashes and
melons, you'll have to hunt for the cucumbers
under the plants' large, hairy leaves.

Prolific croppers
Cucumbers can be extremely productive — expect a couple every day during
the summer months.

GROWING CUCUMBERS IN GROWING BAGS

1 Place a pot over the growing
bag and cut out a circular hole
the size of the pot.

2 Repeat this twice more, so
that the holes are spaced
evenly along the length of the bag.

3 Once all threat of frost has
passed, gently remove your
young cucumber from the small
container it has been raised in.

4 Plant one cucumber into each
hole, making sure the plant
is level with the growing bag.
Water well.

Where to grow In the greenhouse, it is best to grow cucumbers in either growing bags or 4-gallon (15-L) pots filled with multipurpose potting mix. Plants grow very large and require lots of watering and feeding in the summer. This is ideal if you have a greenhouse packed with tomatoes, eggplants and peppers, since they can be cared for together.

Outside, cucumbers need a sunny spot and rich, fertile soil. It's worth adding some homemade compost to the soil before you plant. Grow in an area with your other curcurbits — squashes, pumpkins and zucchini — rotating around the garden each year (see pages 22–23).

All cucumbers are sensitive to frost, so you'll need to be careful when planting outside, waiting until late spring or early summer in most parts. Even in the greenhouse it's not worth starting seeds too early, unless your greenhouse is heated — greenhouse cucumbers like a temperature of around 68°F (20°C).

Types and varieties Cucumbers are mainly separated according to where they are grown.

Outdoor cucumbers
Growing cucumbers outside is really easy, and recent breeding has meant that these new varieties can be just as sweet and tender as greenhouse varieties.

Greenhouse types Cucumbers grown under glass generally have very smooth skins and are similar to the ones found in the supermarkets. Their taste, however, fresh from the greenhouse, far surpasses anything you'll find wrapped in plastic in your local greengrocer. Modern greenhouse varieties are bred to produce only female flowers and don't need to be pollinated to set fruit. You'll need to train this type up a cane or string. As they produce only female flowers, their seeds cannot be kept to produce new plants each year because there are no male flowers to pollinate them.

Outdoor types Typically, outdoor types were renowned for having thicker skins and spikes or prickles, as well as a more distinctive flavor.

Typical cucumbers reach about 16 inches (40 cm) in length but there are lots of smaller-fruiting varieties that reach about half that size. More recent breeding has developed varieties that produce fruit that measure just 4 inches (10 cm) — perfect for snacking on.

Pests and diseases In a greenhouse, cucumbers can succumb to the typical greenhouse pests of spider mites and whitefly. Try an organic pesticide on outdoor crops, or alternatively go for a biological control — but this will work only for greenhouse crops

TRAINING GREENHOUSE CUCUMBERS

1 Position a supporting cane or string attached to a high horizontal wire down next to the plant.

2 Wind the plant around the support as it grows. Tie in loosely a couple of times.

3 Shoots that appear from the leaf joint of the main stem need to be removed on a regular basis to create a thin cordon plant. These can be nipped out with the fingertips, leaving just the main stem growing.

4 When the leading shoot reaches the top of the support, tie it in. Pinch out the growing tip and allow the last two side shoots to hang down.

because the insects released to devour the spider mite and whitefly will be lost if placed outdoors. Keeping a greenhouse humid will also help to deter spider mite — try "damping down," which is basically watering the floor of your greenhouse every day during the summer to allow a humid atmosphere to develop.

Other cucumber pests include the cucumber beetle — resistant varieties are available but the beetle can be controlled by applying kaolin spray — and squash bugs, which can be picked off the plants or trapped under boards placed on the soil.

Powdery mildew also affects cucumbers. In hot, dry conditions, white powdery patches develop across the leaves. The best way to avoid powdery mildew outdoors is to ensure the soil is rich, fertile and moisture-retentive, and water (at the base of the plant, not on the leaves) when the weather is dry. Planting through black polythene or any other type of mulch is also said to help. In the greenhouse, you just need to ensure your plants don't dry out and keep the windows open on hot days.

Other diseases affecting cucumbers are bacterial wilt, which can be combatted through the use of control aphids, and cucumber mosaic virus, which has no cure. Plants should be removed and destroyed to prevent the virus spreading.

Harvesting and storage Cucumbers are ready for harvesting toward the end of midsummer, and in a good year should continue through late summer and well into early fall. Check your plants as cucumbers can easily blend in with their surroundings or hide behind large leaves! You'll need to pick cucumbers at least twice a week. They should keep for a week or so in the fridge.

In the kitchen Well loved in salads and sandwiches, cucumbers, particularly the smaller varieties, are a good choice for children who can munch on them whole.

CALENDAR

GREENHOUSE CUCUMBERS

MID-SPRING

Sow seeds singly in small pots. Keep pots somewhere warm — preferably around 77°F (25°C). They should germinate quickly and grow rapidly. Pot seedlings into larger pots after a couple of weeks.

LATE SPRING

Plant up in a growing bag — three per bag — or in large containers filled with multipurpose potting mix. Place in the greenhouse.

EARLY SUMMER

In colder areas, plant in your greenhouse now, as above. You'll need to start training the plants up a support (see opposite). Keep watering.

MIDSUMMER

Water well, and when the first fruits start to form, also start watering with a tomato fertilizer. You'll need to water every day during this time. Start picking your first cucumbers.

LATE SUMMER

Keep watering and feeding, as well as damping down the greenhouse floor to deter spider mite.

EARLY FALL

Cucumbers should still be producing. Pick over twice a week at least, even if you're not going to eat them all — the plant will stop fruiting otherwise.

OUTDOOR CUCUMBERS

MID-SPRING

Sow in small individual pots about ½ inch (1 cm) deep, keeping the pots in a warm place — preferably a heated propagator, or outdoors if chance of frost is past.

LATE SPRING

Pot plants on into larger pots, but don't consider planting outside until all threat of frost has passed.

EARLY SUMMER

It should now be safe to plant outdoors. Give each plant at least 1 square yard (1 sq m) of enriched fertile soil to grow in. If possible cover the ground with black polythene, burying the edges — cut a slit in the middle and plant through.

MIDSUMMER

Water the plants and feed regularly with a tomato fertilizer once plants start to flower. Fruit should be ready for picking about 60 days from sowing — check seed packet details for ideal fruit size.

LATE SUMMER

Keep picking and feeding. Keep a watch for pests and diseases. When watering, avoid getting the leaves wet and remove any damaged or diseased-looking leaves.

EARLY FALL

Picking should start to slow down. When it finally stops, put all the old plants on the compost heap.

TIP

Seed is expensive — you can raise just a couple of plants, keeping the rest of the seed you bought for next year. Alternatively, visit your plant store in early summer for ready-grown young plants.

VARIETY SELECTOR

Large greenhouse cucumber
- 'Telegraph', 'Holland'.

Small-fruiting outdoor cucumbers
- 'Little Leaf H-19'.

Very small-fruiting outdoor cucumbers
- 'Mexican Sour Gherkin'.

Outdoor gherkin
- 'Sooyow', 'Marketmore 76'.

Majestic corn
Corn needs plenty of space and is not the most productive crop, but once you've tasted the sweetest corn fresh from your garden, you'll be sure to find a gap for a few plants each year.

Corn

With new super-sweet varieties, corn has got to be one of the most child-friendly vegetables.

✪✪✪✪✪	VALUE FOR MONEY
✪✪✪✪✪	MAINTENANCE
✪✪✪✪✪	FREEZE/STORE

CROPPING SEASON: LATE SUMMER–EARLY FALL

Corn looks fantastic in the garden. It is ornamental in its own right, with tall grass-like stems producing large, arching tassels in midsummer. Each plant will provide you with a single cob — two if you're lucky. As each plant needs around 12 inches (30 cm) square they're not the most economical of plants in terms of space. However, because they grow almost vertically, it is possible to plant in between. A crop of lettuce, spring onions or turnips is a possibility, as is planting with your winter brassicas or winter squashes, which will continue to grow well after your corn has been harvested and eaten.

Where to grow Corn is a wind-pollinated plant and needs to be fertilized from the pollen produced on its tassels.

To ensure this happens, it is best to plant corn in blocks (3 x 3 or 5 x 5) rather than in rows, or hills (clumps) of three to four plants, with the clumps 2 ft. (60 cm) apart.

VARIETY SELECTOR
- 'Spring Treat': super-sweet variety.
- 'Luscious': bicolored super-sweet — a combination of white and yellow kernels.
- 'Golden Bantam': an unusual variety — yellow kernels that are sweet but not super-sweet, with a rich flavor.

Corn plants like plenty of sunshine so you'll need to select a sunny spot, and as they grow tall, nowhere too windy either. And because they become large plants, they'll need plenty of organic matter worked into the soil before you plant.

As they are tender plants, they are usually started late in the garden. You can get the crop growing, and therefore harvesting earlier, by starting plants off in pots, or growing under floating row covers. However, for a simple life, you can sow direct from the last frost through early summer.

One word of warning: corn can be pollinated by different varieties of corn — if your neighbor is growing an unusual variety, watch out for some rogue-colored kernels!

Types and varieties Intense breeding has now produced many varieties with a super-sweet taste — so sweet that the cobs can be eaten fresh off the plant! There is also a range of unusual-colored varieties — often heritage or old varieties that, while they aren't as sweet as the super-sweets, make an interesting display on the plate and have a rich flavor.

Pests and diseases Mice, raccoons and groundhogs can eat the seeds if sown direct — if this is a problem, start your seeds off in pots indoors. Corn borers can also attack the cobs — either ignore, cut off the affected cobs or put a drop of mineral oil on the tassels after pollination (when the tassels lose their sheen) as a preventative measure.

Harvesting and storage When the tassels on the cob start to shrivel and go brown, the corn inside should be almost ripe. Check by peeling away one of the leaves around the cob and push your thumbnail into a kernel. If the liquid is creamy, the corn is ready; if it's watery leave for a few more days. New varieties of corn keep their sweetness for longer after they've been picked, but they're still best eaten fresh off the plant.

In the kitchen Throw onto a late-summer barbecue, seasoned with olive oil, salt and pepper. Alternatively, they can be boiled.

CALENDAR

MID-SPRING
Plant individually in small pots. Use long, narrow pots such as Rootrainers if possible. Corn needs a temperature of at least 59°F (15°C) to germinate and does not like very cold conditions.

LATE SPRING
In warmer areas, you can consider sowing corn direct into the ground. Plant seeds ½ inch (1 cm) deep and cover with floating row covers to help keep the warmth in.

Once any threat of frost has passed, plant out your corn grown in pots or remove the floating row covers. Space plants about 14 inches (35 cm) apart.

MIDSUMMER
Tap the tassels gently, which helps the pollen to drop down, pollinate the flowers, and form the cobs.

MID–LATE SUMMER
Check cobs for maturity and harvest as and when ready.

INTERCROPPING CORN

1 Once you've raised your corn plants, plant them direct in the soil 20 inches (50 cm) apart each way in early summer.

2 Sow a row of bush beans or lettuce in between each row of corn, or plant out a couple of young winter squash plants.

Eggplant

With their large purple flowers and brightly colored fruit, eggplants look just as good on the patio as they do on the plate.

✪✪✪✪✪	VALUE FOR MONEY
✪✪✪✪✪	MAINTENANCE
✪✪✪✪✪	FREEZE/STORE

CROPPING SEASON: LATE SUMMER–MID-FALL

These egg-shaped fruits, which are related to tomatoes, hail from the warmer climes of India and China, and are a staple vegetable in their cuisines. With a little care and attention it's possible to grow eggplants anywhere.

Traditionally, in cooler climates, eggplants were grown in greenhouses, with constant warm temperatures ensuring that the large, purple fruits swell to maturity before the weather turns cool. With the breeding of eggplants creating more and more varieties, most are now perfectly happy sitting on a patio in a pot or growing in a bed. Grown well, a single pot can produce around 50 fruit of the smaller-fruiting types. Choose a large-fruiting variety, and you'll get between five and 10.

Regal vegetable
Eggplants are one of the most ornate vegetable plants, with downy silver foliage, delicate purple flowers and impressive white or purple fruits.

EGGPLANTS MADE EASY

1 Grow in a frost-free area until any threat of frost has passed. A windowsill or greenhouse will do fine.

2 Plant out — one plant per container at least 12 inches (30 cm) in diameter or three to a growing bag. Plant deeply to help prevent the plant from toppling over once covered in fruit.

3 Pinch out the growing tip, feed and water regularly.

4 Once the plant starts to flower, feed it with a tomato fertilizer. Your first eggplants should start to form in a matter of a few days.

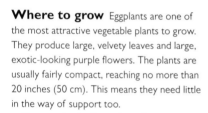

VARIETY SELECTOR

- 'Ichiban Hybrid': tender skin and delicate flavor.
- 'Cloud Nine': compact plants, 6 inch (15 cm) white fruit.
- 'Orient Express': long, slender, glossy black fruit.

Small and sweet
The flesh of small eggplants varieties is usually sweeter than the larger fruiting kinds.

CALENDAR

EARLY SPRING

For the best choice of varieties, raise from seed. Start seeds off in small pots. Sow in multipurpose potting mix and keep plants somewhere warm (a propagator if you have one, see page 201) — they need a constant temperature of 68°F (20°C).

MID-SPRING

Keep plants somewhere warm and in good light. If you don't want to raise plants from seed, plant stores will be selling young plants at this time, but the choice of varieties won't be as good as with seed.

LATE SPRING

Pot on into larger pots if you're keeping in the greenhouse. Plant out either in the garden or into large 1½-gallon (5-L) pots containing potting mix and slow-release fertilizer.

EARLY SUMMER

If your plants are destined for the patio and you haven't done so already, plant into large containers now or plant in the garden once all threat of frost has passed. Pinch out the growing tip when the plant reaches around 8 inches (20 cm) to encourage the plant to bush out.

MIDSUMMER

Keep watering well and start including a tomato feed. Watch out for pests.

LATE SUMMER

Pick over the plants every week. They should keep producing fruit for up to six weeks until early fall.

Where to grow Eggplants are one of the most attractive vegetable plants to grow. They produce large, velvety leaves and large, exotic-looking purple flowers. The plants are usually fairly compact, reaching no more than 20 inches (50 cm). This means they need little in the way of support too.

Because they're fussy about the temperature, eggplants are often grown in a greenhouse in cooler climates. If you have some greenhouse shelves available, it's definitely worth adding a pot or two of eggplants. If you don't have a greenhouse, a large pot on the patio is the best option. Choose a pot that holds around 1½ gallons (5 L) of potting mix. Use general multipurpose potting mix and add a handful of slow-release fertilizer. This will give it a good start, but when the plant starts to flower, begin feeding with a tomato fertilizer to encourage flower and fruit production.

Types and varieties Any variety will succeed in a greenhouse. Outdoors, your choice is more limited, but it's better to go for the smaller-fruiting types. As well as dark purple, you can also find white-fruiting eggplants, as well as many with pretty speckles and flecks of color. If you really want to try something unusual, then there are orange, yellow and green varieties, such as 'N'Goya', 'Toga', and 'Kermit'.

Pests and diseases Outside eggplants are usually fairly trouble-free, although flea beetles are sometimes a problem. To avoid an attack, protect your plants with floating row covers. In the greenhouse, however, where temperatures and humidity are much higher, they can be a magnet to pests. Like other greenhouse crops, they can suffer from spider mite, whitefly and aphids. You can use an organic pesticide to try to control these pests, or use biological controls (see page 217). These are natural enemies of the pests that can be introduced into your greenhouse to devour the pests.

Harvesting and storage Eggplants should start to ripen in late summer. You'll need to harvest the fruits regularly rather than in one go. Refer to the packet instructions to find out how big the fruits are meant to be, and pick once they've reached this size. Don't leave too long as seeds will start to grow inside, making them inedible.

In the kitchen In the past, eggplants were salted before cooking — chopping up, sprinkling them with salt and leaving for an hour removed the bitterness sometimes found in the fruit. With better breeding, new varieties don't have this problem. Chop, slice and fry. Eggplants can be used in Mediterranean and Asian cuisines. They are fantastic grilled on the barbecue, or roasted whole, with the inside scooped out and made into a dip.

Sweet pepper

Sweet, juicy and colorful, these Mediterranean vegetables look fantastic growing on the patio.

⬡⬡⬡⬢⬢	VALUE FOR MONEY
⬡⬡⬡⬢⬢	MAINTENANCE
⬡⬡⬡⬢⬢	FREEZE/STORE
CROPPING SEASON: MIDSUMMER–MID-FALL	

If you're growing tomatoes, it's definitely worth having a go with sweet peppers too. They can be tricky to grow in cooler climates, only in that they need a long, hot summer to fruit well. If you have a greenhouse you can easily cheat, but many varieties also do well on the patio in large containers. They look stunning too, with large red, yellow, and orange fruits.

Where to grow It is possible to grow peppers outdoors in the ground in mild climates (zone 8 and above). There is nothing more disheartening than nurturing a plant from seed only to find that you've run out of summer and the small green fruits are never going to ripen. If you're keen on success, it's definitely worth growing in a greenhouse if you have one. Even if you don't, peppers grown in a container on a hot, sunny patio will also do well. They're beautiful plants too, so even if you're growing in a greenhouse, make sure they are easily visible to enjoy when you are walking by.

Like eggplants, peppers don't grow particularly large — up to around 20 inches (50 cm). Some varieties naturally bush out, creating attractive-shaped plants. Others have a tendency to grow straight up. If your plant is more like the latter, pinch out the growing tips when the plant is around 8 inches (20 cm) high. This will encourage the plant to bush out. Peppers are generally self-supporting, but when laden with large fruits they can sometimes struggle to keep upright. It is a good idea therefore to insert a short cane and tie the main stem in, ensuring the plant doesn't flop.

They can also be grown in a large container — choose one that holds around 1½ gallons (5 L) of potting mix. Alternatively, they can be grown in a growing bag — three per bag — or outside in the garden in milder areas (zone 8 and above).

Types and varieties Sweet peppers come in a variety of shapes, and not just the typical bell shape, but there are now much longer, chili-like varieties too. Then of course there are the colors. Red is most common, but orange and yellow varieties are available to gardeners, as well as dark purple and brown too.

GETTING THE MOST OUT OF YOUR PEPPERS

1 When plants are about 8 inches (20 cm) tall, pinch out the growing tip using your thumb and finger. Be careful not to damage the rest of the plant.

2 Remove the first fruits that form in early summer to encourage plants to bush out and fruit more heavily.

Vibrant peppers
Sweet peppers come in all shapes, colors and sizes and can bring some bright colors to your patio.

VARIETY SELECTOR
- **'Chocolate'**: great-tasting fruits that go brown in color when ripe.
- **'New Ace'**: a pointy, early variety that has been widely adapted.
- **'Sweet Italia'**: a long, red early variety that has been widely adapted.
- **'Gypsy Hybrid'**: an early variety that has orange-red fruits.

All varieties prefer long, hot summers with plenty of sun, in a greenhouse in cooler climates. They do all right on the patio, too, in warmer climates.

Pests and diseases Peppers are likely to suffer from the same pests as tomatoes, cucumbers and eggplants when growing in the greenhouse — namely whitefly, red spider mite and aphids. If you're growing in a greenhouse keep a close eye on your plants, and if necessary, reach for an organic spray.

Fruits can also be affected by sunscald. To avoid this problem, stake the plants at the beginning of the season so the fruits are better shaded from the sun's rays.

Outdoor plants can be attacked by the corn borer. Protect your plants with floating row covers and use BT spray if affected.

Harvesting and storage Make sure you know the color of your peppers and pick them when ripe — usually in late summer and early fall. Green, unripe peppers can be picked off the plant at the end of the season. Leave on a sunny windowsill and they may ripen up, otherwise use them green. Once ripe, the fruits will be much sweeter.

Keep picking fruits as they ripen as this will encourage more fruit to develop. You can store them in the fridge until you need them but once picked they'll last only a couple of weeks.

In the kitchen Sweet peppers can be used in Asian and Mediterranean cooking. They can be enjoyed raw in salads or roasted. You can blacken the skins on the barbecue or under the grill. They will peel off easily, leaving sweet, succulent flesh underneath.

CALENDAR

EARLY SPRING
Sow a couple of seeds in a small pot of multipurpose potting mix. You'll need a propagator or warm windowsill to maintain the required temperature of 68°F (20°C). Once germinated, remove the weaker seedling.

MID-SPRING
Once the seeds have germinated, the pots can be moved to a cooler place — between 53 and 64°F (12 and 18°C).

LATE SPRING
Pot on to a larger 1½-gallon (5-L) pot or plant in a growing bag, or plant outside in a bed in milder areas (zone 8 and above). They'll still need to be kept under cover or indoors if there is a threat of cold weather. If you didn't get round to growing from seed, buy from your local plant store now.

EARLY SUMMER
Place in the sunniest spot available. If plants are becoming leggy, pinch out the growing tips to encourage them to bush out.

It's hard to do, but removing some of the earlier fruit that develop now will encourage the plant to develop a lot more.

MIDSUMMER
Start watering more frequently as the weather warms up, keeping the potting mix just moist. Also, start feeding with a tomato feed to encourage more flowers and fruit.

LATE SUMMER
Pick off your fruit as they ripen.

EARLY FALL
Fruiting should be plentiful at this time, so keep picking and watering.

MID-FALL
If the weather is starting to turn cooler, bring any outdoor plants indoors if you can to encourage ripening.

LATE FALL
Pick off any existing fruit and use in the kitchen.

Chili

Cousins of the sweet peppers, chilies add fire to your food and color to your kitchen garden.

STAR PLANT
★ GREAT FUN, BRIGHT COLORS ★

◉◉◉◉◎ VALUE FOR MONEY
◉◉◎◎◎ MAINTENANCE
◉◉◉◉◎ FREEZE/STORE
CROPPING SEASON: MIDSUMMER–MID-FALL

Originating from Central and South America, chilies were first spread to the rest of the Americas then on to Asia. Popular in Mexican and Asian cuisines, chili peppers are similar to sweet peppers in looks and growing requirements, the only difference being the heat of the fruit! The small bushy plants produce green, variegated and even black glossy leaves that look attractive in any garden, greenhouse or even on a windowsill. But it's the color of the small chili peppers themselves that provide a real show. Even if you don't use chilies much in your cooking, a chili pepper plant can be as ornamental as any flowering plant.

Chilies have become extremely popular with gardeners in recent years. Intense breeding has created hotter and hotter chilies and gardeners like to outdo each other with the varieties they grow — and eat. The hotness is due to the chemical capsaicin held in the flesh and seeds. The more capsaicin, the hotter the chili. This heat can be measured and is reported in Scoville heat units. One of the hottest so far is the 'Dorset Naga', which has a heat-rating of over 900,000 Scoville units! Chili festivals have become really popular in recent years. Usually taking place in late summer, they offer a chance to look at the huge range of chili plants available to gardeners and to taste how hot they really get.

Where to grow In the garden the growing requirements of chili peppers are exactly the same as sweet peppers — hot and sunny conditions over a long season. But again, while some varieties do well only in a greenhouse in cooler climates, others will be happy on a sunny patio. They're tender plants, so you can only grow them outside during the seasons that are free from frost. For some gardeners it won't be worth growing in the

Fiery characters
Brightly colored chilies look fabulous in the garden, greenhouse and on the windowsill. Dry the fruits and they'll provide heat to your food for the whole year.

ground and in any case, these small, highly attractive plants suit being grown in a pot, to allow you to appreciate their attractive fruit close-up. If you select one of the smaller varieties, you can even grow them on a windowsill in the kitchen.

Types and varieties Ranging in height between 10 and 20 inches (25 and 50 cm), chili peppers are rather compact. Chilies come from the capsicum family and are actually short-lived perennials — meaning they would, if the weather permitted, last more than a year. In the garden it's more usual to treat them like an annual — growing from seed and fruiting all in

a single year. There are thousands of varieties of chili to choose from, varying in color from green, yellow, and orange, to red and purple. All also vary in their hotness too, but this depends on the exact growing conditions — it's not uncommon to find two chilies on the same plant with different levels of heat.

Harvesting and storage Chilies should be harvested when ripe. You can store fresh chilies in the fridge or freeze whole and use individually when required. Chilies often ripen together. You can cut off the whole plant, and leave it hanging upside down to dry. Alternatively, pick off chillies individually and leave in the sun or in a very low oven to dry off. These can be crushed and sprinkled into the cooking pot when required. Be careful when handling chilies — their hotness can easily transfer to your fingers, so make sure you wash your hands after handling.

In the kitchen Chilies are a common ingredient in Mexican and other Central American dishes. They are also used regularly in Asian and Mediterranean cooking to add hotness to dishes and are usually fried at the beginning of cooking, along with onions and garlic. Inner ribs of chilies are usually hottest — if you prefer a milder taste, cut away the ribs. Otherwise chop finely and add the whole chili, including the seeds.

VARIETY SELECTOR

Hot chilies

- 'Habanero'.

Milder chilies

- 'Hungarian Wax': starting sweet, the heat intensifies.

Best for a patio

- 'Filius Blue', 'Mirasol', 'Purple Tiger', 'Numex Twilight'.

Best for a windowsill or greenhouse

- 'Explosive Blast', 'Paper Lantern'.

CALENDAR

EARLY SPRING

Sow seeds individually in small pots to a depth of around ½ inch (1 cm) six to eight weeks before the last frost date. You'll need somewhere with a constant temperature of 68°F (20°C) — use a heated propagator if you have one.

MID-SPRING

Seeds should germinate in a fortnight. Once germinated, the temperature can be cooler, with a minimum of 54°F (12°C). Pot on into slightly larger pots and keep well watered and in a sunny, warm spot.

LATE SPRING

Plant out into the final pots of up to 1½-gallon (5-L) capacity if the varieties are quite large, or in the garden one week after the last frost date. Smaller varieties should cope with a ½-gallon (2-L) pot, but they will require more attention to keep them well watered. Pinch out the growing tips if the plants are looking leggy.

EARLY SUMMER

If you are growing them outside, place the plants on the hottest part of your patio. Make sure the plants are protected or taken back indoors if there is any chance of frost at night.

MIDSUMMER

If plants are becoming top heavy, stake using a short cane, and tie in with string. If the flowers don't seem to be setting fruit, give the plants a little tap to distribute the pollen, or even try using a small paintbrush.

LATE SUMMER

Start to harvest your chilies as they ripen.

CHILI VARIETIES

'Explosive Blast' is an ornamental chili with clusters of different colored fruits.

'Filius Blue' carries purple-blue, egg-shaped fruits that ripen to red, losing their pungency in the process.

'Numex Twilight', an attractive, drought-resistant plant, yielding medium-hot fruits.

'Mirasol', the name means "looking at the sun" and the plant carries an abundance of upward-pointing chilies.

Tomato

Whether you have a windowsill, patio or greenhouse, there are varieties of sweet, succulent tomatoes suitable for all situations.

✪✪✪✪✪	VALUE FOR MONEY
✪✪✪✪✪	MAINTENANCE
✪✪✪✪✪	FREEZE/STORE

CROPPING SEASON: MIDSUMMER–MID-FALL

Tomatoes have got to be the most well-loved and popular salad fruit. And home-grown tomatoes taste so much better than store-bought, so this is definitely one crop that's worth growing year after year.

It's no wonder they're so popular: inch for inch, tomato plants are one of the most bountiful and space-worthy crops to grow. Rich in vitamins and antioxidants, they are best enjoyed fresh from the garden through the summer and early fall, and in salads and Mediterranean-style dishes. The excess at the end of the season can be dried, frozen, puréed or turned into chutney.

Container tomatoes
Recent breeding means that tomatoes can now be grown in small containers and baskets, producing a plentiful supply of small and extremely sweet fruit.

Where to grow There are tomatoes for almost all situations of the garden (and house!). New breeds mean that small-fruiting varieties can be grown in pots small enough to fit on a windowsill. Although they won't give you a huge supply of tomatoes, there may be enough to throw into a salad every week or so.

For larger harvests and milder climates (zones 8 and above), opt for growing in the garden. On the patio or in the greenhouse, tomatoes can be grown in growing bags or containers. Some trailing or bush varieties also look decorative and are perfect for a hanging basket. Whichever container you choose, potting mix from a growing bag is ideal, preferably peat-free.

Types and varieties Intense breeding has produced a huge range of tomato varieties suitable for all tastes and growing situations.
Color Red is still the favorite. Nowadays there is a range of oranges, yellows and even striped varieties.
Size Ranges from fruits measuring less than ½ inch (1 cm) in diameter to much larger "beefsteak" types.
Flavor Think about what you want the tomatoes for before you choose the variety to grow — cherry tomatoes are great for salads, plum varieties are ideal for cooking and full-size tomatoes are good for slicing in sandwiches. For the biggest croppers, go for a salad variety.
Climate Tomatoes are tender plants, but can be grown outdoors as long as the temperature stays above 70°F (21°C).

In the garden
Planting and training When planting out tomatoes, plant deep. Roots will grow out from the stem and provide greater ➡

Ripe for picking
Tomatoes come in all shapes and colors. It's worth trying a few types such as cherry, plum and salad types, to provide contrasting tastes and colors to your dishes.

TOMATOES IN FOUR EASY STEPS

1 In late spring, buy three young tomato plants, or raise three plants from seed — a good place to start is with the cherry tomato cordon varieties, such as 'Sungold'. Also, get a growing bag and a bottle of tomato feed — that's all you need.

2 Once all threat of frost has passed, cut three evenly spaced holes in the growing bag, push the potting mix out of the way and carefully plant the tomatoes into the bag. Gently press down the soil around the base of each plant, and water.

3 Insert and secure three 6 ft. 5-in. (2-m) high canes next to each plant, being careful not to damage the plants. After four weeks, start to feed as instructed with the liquid tomato food. As the plants grow, tie them to the canes. As side shoots develop, remove them from the plant, as shown here.

4 Leave the fruits on the plant until they are really ripe — they taste even better when they're allowed to ripen on the plant. Take into the kitchen and enjoy!

Ripen on the vine
Leaving the fruit on the plants until they're really ripe will produce the best flavor.

support for the plant above. For bush varieties, these can be left to sprawl on the ground — you can always use a plastic or permeable fabric to keep the fruits clean, or alternatively use a loose wire cage made of chicken wire wrapped around the plant as a means of support.

Cordon varieties need more maintenance. Train the leading shoot up a sturdy stake. Nip out side shoots as they grow (see page 95). Nip out the tip of the leading stem toward the end of summer. That way all the energy will go into ripening the fruits already on the plant and not into producing new fruits that are unlikely to ripen before the end of the season.

Feeding If you are growing your tomatoes in a pot or growing bag, feeding is essential. You'll need to start feeding your plants around four to six weeks after planting out. You can use a regular plant food until the fruits start to form, then switch to a liquid tomato food. High in phosphate, this feed will ensure a bumper crop.

Mulching If you are growing in the ground, add a good, deep layer of garden compost or other bulky organic matter (see pages 218–223) in the spring. Start to feed with a liquid tomato feed in summer.

Watering Tomatoes hate to dry out, and doing so can lead to blossom end rot (see below). Watering during dry spells is therefore essential in the ground. In a container, watering up to twice a day may be necessary at the height of summer. Think about setting up an automatic irrigation system (see page 215).

Pests and diseases Blossom end rot is a problem caused by fluctuating temperatures, insufficient water, excessive heat or calcium deficiency. Water your tomatoes regularly to decrease the chances of them developing this problem.

One major problem that affects tomatoes is blight — a fungal disease that spreads on the wind. You can use a preventative fungicide spray, but you'll need to use it through the whole season.

There are a number of diseases that affect tomatoes. The fungal disease septoria leaf spot can be avoided by mulching your tomatoes

GROWING TOMATOES FROM SEED

1 Sow seeds individually in seed modules in mid-spring.

2 Prick out the seedlings into small pots and keep indoors until after the last frost date.

3 When the seedlings are around 6 inches (15 cm) high, it is time to transfer them to growing bags in the greenhouse or plant outside.

SEEDS OR PLANTS?

Tomatoes have got to be one of the easiest plants to grow. Throw a tomato onto a compost heap and seedlings will soon emerge. However, if you want to grow a range of varieties, it may be cheaper (and easier) to buy a few young plants from your local plant store than several packets of seed, although the range of varieties bought this way may be limited. Stored properly, tomato seed can last many years, but if you've missed sowing time (see Calendar), then head for the plant store to see what you can pick up.

(see left), making sure air can circulate around your plants and cleaning up properly at the end of the season.

Two more fungal diseases, anthracnose and fusarium, can be problematic. Resistant varieties are now available.

Harvesting and storage Tomatoes should be picked when they're as juicy and ripe as possible. If you're only making weekly trips down to your plot, picking tomatoes that are just turning pink is still fine. Just leave them on a sunny windowsill to ripen up. Tomatoes in the greenhouse may need to be picked a couple of times a week from late summer right into fall. Expect tomatoes right into late fall if the weather stays mild. However, once the weather turns, you'll need to collect everything that's left. Try ripening in a paper bag with a banana to speed the process up. Alternatively just use green tomatoes either fried or in a pickle.

In the kitchen Tomatoes are delicious in salads, soups or puréed. If there's a glut, you can make salsas, chutneys, jams and pickles, or dry them in the sun (in hot areas) or in the oven (see pages 240–241). Excess tomatoes can be frozen whole or puréed for winter use.

VARIETY SELECTOR

- 'Sungold': best cherry variety.
- 'Carmello': best salad variety.
- 'San Marzano': best plum variety.
- 'Brandywine': best full-size variety.
- 'Tumbling Tom': best basket variety.
- 'Sub Arctic Cherry': best for a windowsill.

CALENDAR

LATE WINTER

If you have a heated greenhouse, you'll be able to start seed off now in a propagator — they'll need 64°F (18°C) to germinate.

MID-SPRING

For growing in an unheated greenhouse or outside, sow indoors in small pots.

Prick out individually into small pots once plants have germinated, and keep indoors until after the last frost date.

LATE SPRING

Plant out tomatoes in their final positions — in pots, baskets or in the ground. Plant no more than three plants per growing bag, aim for a pot size of 3.5 gallons (15 L) for pot grown, and as big a basket as you can manage to cut down on watering.

In the ground, set a plant every 17–23 inches (45–60 cm).

EARLY SUMMER

Start feeding with a specialist tomato feed once the first fruits have formed.

Nip off all side shoots from cordon varieties.

Start to water every day.

MIDSUMMER

Keep nipping out side shoots and feeding plants. Start to harvest tomatoes as the first fruits ripen. Watch out for pests such as spider mite and whitefly.

LATE SUMMER–EARLY FALL

Nip out the leading shoot on cordon varieties.

Pinch out side shoots and remove any yellowing leaves.

LATE FALL

Pick the last of the ripe fruit and any unripe fruit before the first frosts hit.

STEM AND FLOWER CROPS

These stem and flower crops include some of those that are more tricky to grow. However, if you just love broccoli and have a real addiction to Florence fennel, they're worthy of space in any vegetable garden. For those of you who have less time, why not try some of the perennial vegetables such as asparagus and globe artichokes?

Broccoli

If you decide to grow only one member of the cabbage family, make it broccoli. The tender, sweet flower buds and stems are well used in the kitchen.

✿✿✿✿✿ VALUE FOR MONEY
✿✿✿✿✿ MAINTENANCE
✿✿✿✿✿ FREEZE/STORE
CROPPING SEASON: LATE SUMMER–MID-SPRING

Ready for harvest
The Calabrese broccoli is similar to other broccoli but it produces a single head.

Broccoli stems
When the main head has been harvested, the plant will produce side stems for later harvest.

A real superfood, broccoli is one of the most popular brassicas to grow. It's meant to help prevent cancer as well as heart disease, and it's also rich in vitamins and folic acid. And best of all, most children will at least give it a go! In the garden, you can grow broccoli almost all year round.

Where to grow Broccoli needs plenty of space. It can become a large plant, needing around 16–24 inches (40–60 cm) between plants, depending on the variety. Grow with the rest of your brassicas, or intercrop overwintering purple-sprouting broccoli, which really does grow quite large, with corn (see page 86). Here you may need to stake as with Brussels sprouts, pushing in a

cane and tying in (see page 56). Like other brassicas, broccoli is a greedy crop so sprinkle over a general-purpose fertilizer before you plant.

Types and varieties Traditional broccoli produces lots of side shoots with small heads of flowers. Stems and flowers are picked when the buds are still tight, traditionally in early spring when there's not much else available from the garden. Often these flowers are purple or white.

Calabrese broccoli, originating from Calabria in Italy, is similar, but instead produces a single large stem with a large flowerhead. Picked before the flowers open, this gives a single large head of broccoli.

Recently, new varieties of broccoli have become available, which allow you to pick broccoli in the fall from a spring sowing.

Pests and diseases Broccoli suffers from all the same pests and diseases as cabbages (see page 55). Grow and protect with the other members of the cabbage family.

Harvesting and storage Broccoli can be picked in midsummer from a spring sowing. If you space the plants fairly wide apart, once you've cut the main stem, leave the plants to grow. Further side shoots will keep growing, and these can be picked continuously right into winter. The main season is fall. Broccoli is worth picking over every week to

VARIETY SELECTOR

Crops for summer and fall

- 'Calabrese', 'Tendergreen', 'Marathon': big head.
- 'Waltham 29', 'De Cicco': many side shoots.
- 'Cheddar': orange.

ensure you pick before the flowers open, and it should be eaten straight away. Alternatively, you can blanch for a minute or two, drain, then freeze, making sure the stems don't freeze together.

In the kitchen Young broccoli and calabrese can be tender enough to eat raw as a crudité. Otherwise, broccoli and calabrese can be steamed, stir-fried or added to soups.

TIP

Space large-heading types wide apart for large main heads, or close together for smaller main heads and lots of side shoots.

CALENDAR

EARLY SPRING

This is a good time to start off broccoli. Sow seeds individually in small pots, about ½ inch (1 cm) deep.

MID-SPRING

Prepare your vegetable bed by digging over and adding some fertilizer.

LATE SPRING

Once the plants have grown on, plant out in the garden. Spacing will depend on the variety. Cover the crop with floating row covers to protect it from birds and other pests.

EARLY SUMMER

Make sure all your plants are planted out. Firm in well and provide a cane for support for tall varieties. Sow plants for a fall crop.

MIDSUMMER

Water plants well during dry spells and while they're becoming established. Add another sprinkling of fertilizer over the surface. Start to pick heads when the heads are formed.

LATE SUMMER

Keep picking side shoots.

MID-FALL

Pick over the plants.

LATE FALL

In many areas, broccoli will finish around now.

HOW TO MAXIMIZE YOUR BROCCOLI CROP

1 Plant out the seedlings at least 18 inches (45 cm) apart.

2 Cut off the main head when the tight flower buds have formed.

3 Leave the plant to produce side shoots and keep picking these as they grow.

Cauliflower

This is a difficult vegetable to grow, but new growing techniques make it just a little easier.

○○○○○ VALUE FOR MONEY
○○○○○ MAINTENANCE
○○○○○ FREEZE/STORE
CROPPING SEASON: ALL YEAR ROUND

Cauliflowers are one of the trickiest vegetables to grow. Not only do they suffer from every brassica-family pest and disease imaginable, but they're also liable to bolt. They also need harvesting as soon as they're ready — if left outside their curds can spoil. In spite of that, cauliflowers are a rewarding crop to grow — in addition to the traditional white types, there are purple and green, as well as the pointy romanesco types.

Where to grow Grow cauliflowers with your other cabbage-family crops, preferably under a floating row cover to try to keep many of their pests at bay. Enrich the soil with compost, and add a general-purpose fertilizer just before you plant out. Traditionally cauliflowers should be planted about 18 inches (45 cm) apart each way, giving the plants plenty of space to grow and produce large curds. However, grow them much closer together and you'll be rewarded with smaller, but a larger overall weight of curds from the same space. A large cauliflower can sometimes be too big for a single meal, so these smaller ones are perfect.

Cauliflowers are often split into summer, fall and winter varieties. Winter varieties are generally very hardy and will survive through a long period of cold. The summer and fall varieties are generally harvested the year they are planted — from late summer right through to early winter.

For a bit of interest, it's worth trying a colored variety, and especially some of the new romanesco types.

Pests and diseases As troublesome as any other cabbage-family crop (see page 55). Flea beetle, slugs, snails, caterpillar, aphids and cabbage root fly can all be a problem. (See pages 226–227 for controls.)

Creamy curd
A popular winter vegetable, cauliflowers are now available in a variety of colors.

Harvesting and storage The outer leaves protect the cauliflower curds, but you'll need to pull them back to check their progress. When ready, curds should be colored as expected, and the individual flower buds should not be distinguishable. Cut below the curd using a sharp knife. They can be kept in a cool, dark place for a week or so, or alternatively, broken up into pieces and frozen.

In the kitchen Use in soups, stews or even turn into a pickle, such as piccalilli.

VARIETY SELECTOR
Summer and fall cauliflowers
• 'Snow Crown': white.
• 'Violet Queen': purple.
• 'Cheddar': orange.
• 'Veronica': Romanesco.

CALENDAR

EARLY SPRING
Start sowing now for an early summer crop. Sow seeds individually in small pots in a cool greenhouse or cold frame.

MID-SPRING
Plant out your first sowing. For mini cauliflowers, space out 10 inches (25 cm) each way between plants. For regular-sized cauliflowers, go for around 18 inches (45 cm) each way. Water well at planting, but not after.

MIDSUMMER
Sow for a fall crop.

LATE SUMMER
If the soil becomes dry, give your plants a really good soaking once or twice a week to prevent bolting.

EARLY FALL ONWARD
Keep a look out for pests and harvest when ready.

Kohlrabi

An unusual vegetable, where the swollen stem makes for an interesting crop.

○○○○○ VALUE FOR MONEY
○○○○○ MAINTENANCE
○○○○○ FREEZE/STORE
CROPPING SEASON: LATE SPRING–EARLY WINTER

Kohlrabi is part of the brassica family, but this is the only member where the stem is the edible part. Plants grow to around 12 inches (30 cm) high, but around halfway up the stem, it starts to swell into a ball. This swollen part of the stem is the edible part, making a tasty, tender (if picked at the right time) and sweet treat.

Where to grow Kohlrabi can be quick-growing, reaching an edible size within eight weeks. To avoid problems with pests, it is best grown with your other brassicas, under a floating row cover. However, it can also be grown as a quick-growing crop among some other slower-growing plants such as corn, or grown quickly once another crop has been taken out, say, after fava beans.

Because it's quick-growing, you can also make several sowings through the spring and summer, which spreads out the harvest well. Sow in early spring for a summer crop in

Red kohlrabi
Red forms of kohlrabi look almost alien-like, but they taste just as good as the other colors.

northern regions. In the south, plant in early summer for a fall and winter harvest.

Types and varieties There is not much in the way of breeding of new kohlrabi varieties, but there are still some interesting forms available in purple, green or white. All have creamy white flesh with a turnip-like flavor.

Pests and diseases As with other brassicas, kohlrabi can suffer from a variety of pests (see page 55). However, they are said to be a bit tougher than other brassicas, and so may be worth a go even if you've failed with others. They are also supposedly more heat- and drought-tolerant than other types too.

Harvesting and storage Harvest on a regular basis when the stems reach golf ball size. Left to grow to the size of a tennis ball, the flesh turns woody. They are also fairly tough and will survive some of the cold weather if not harvested in time.

They're not worth storing for very long, so eat when they're fresh.

In the kitchen Picked young and tender, they can be peeled and chopped into salads. They can also be steamed.

Exotic vegetable
The swollen stems of kohlrabi are delicious both raw and lightly cooked.

CALENDAR

EARLY SPRING
Sow individually in small pots or modules in a cool greenhouse or cold frame.

MID-SPRING
You can start to sow direct into the soil — make a shallow drill and go for a couple of seeds every 4 inches (10 cm) or so in rows 12 inches (30 cm) apart. Take out the weakest seedling if two come up at each place.

LATE SPRING
Plant out your early harvest 4 inches (10 cm) apart. Keep sowing direct into the soil, as above.

EARLY SUMMER
Sow seed of long-season storage types.

EARLY FALL
In southern regions, sow six weeks before the first fall frost date for a fall and winter harvest.

Florence fennel

The aniseed-flavored fleshy stem of this plant is perfect in salads and fish dishes.

⬡⬡⬡⬡⬡ VALUE FOR MONEY
⬡⬡⬡⬡⬡ MAINTENANCE
⬡⬡⬡⬡⬡ FREEZE/STORE
CROPPING SEASON: LATE SPRING–EARLY FALL

VARIETY SELECTOR
- 'Zefa Fino': bolt-resistant variety.
- 'Orion': large, thick, rounded bulbs.

Fennel is a rather unusual vegetable in the garden, but is becoming more popular in the grocery store. Despite it being a bit tricky to grow, there's little reason not to give this plant a try. Florence fennel produces fine, feathery foliage, much like the herb however, this plant is grown to produce a swollen fleshy base to its stem. It has juicy, crunchy stems, a bit like celery, and a fine aniseed flavor.

Where to grow Fennel prefers deep, rich soil. It will grow on sandy and heavy clay soil, provided that the soil is kept constantly moist. It also doesn't like the cold. Because of this it's best not to sow fennel too early in the season because it is liable to bolt. Fennel sometimes bolts when it has been disturbed when being grown. It's a good idea to start fennel off in small pots, then plant out individually. This way the roots are not disturbed.

Types and varieties There aren't many varieties of fennel; however, some do claim to resist the urge to bolt.

Pests and diseases Slugs can be a problem, particularly early on in the plant's growth. Other than this, Florence fennel has few problems.

Harvesting and storage Plants can mature in as little as 10 weeks after sowing. Cut off the bulbous stem an inch (2.5 cm) above the soil level. Leaving the root in the ground encourages the plant to reshoot. Don't leave the plants standing for too long as, again, they may bolt.

In the kitchen The fine aniseed flavor of fennel goes well with fish of all types and works well braised in the oven.

CALENDAR

MID-SPRING
Sow a couple of seeds in small individual pots or modules.

LATE SPRING
Keep the strongest seedling going (thin out the weakest) and plant out in the garden after a few weeks of growing. Give plants plenty of space — around 12 inches (30 cm) each way.

EARLY SUMMER
You could still sow a row or two directly in the soil now — around ⅝ inch (1.5 cm) deep. Sow a few seeds every 12 inches (30 cm) and thin out if more than one comes up at each point.

MIDSUMMER
Water your plants well through any dry spells. Start to harvest early crops.

LATE SUMMER
Keep watering and harvesting.

Feathery fennel
Florence fennel is tricky to grow, but if you succeed, you'll be rewarded with crunchy, sweet and tender stems perfect for salads.

TIP
Use the feathery foliage in the kitchen as well as the bulbous stems. Cut off the foliage with scissors as required.

Leek

Leeks are one of the few vegetables you can continue to harvest right through winter.

✪✪✪✪✪	VALUE FOR MONEY
✪✪✪✪✪	MAINTENANCE
✪✪✪✪✪	FREEZE/STORE
CROPPING SEASON: LATE SUMMER–EARLY SPRING	

Just like their cousin, the onion, leeks are an incredibly versatile crop. They are well known for standing through the cold of winter, allowing you to pull a stem or two any time you need. They're also a good summer crop. Grown close together, "baby leeks" can be picked when they resemble spring onions, or left to become larger. Baby leeks are expensive in the supermarket, but very easy to grow at home.

Hardy crop
When there is little else to harvest in mid-winter, you'll be pleased that you planted a couple of rows of leeks.

GROWING BABY LEEKS

1 Sow several seeds in small pots in spring.

2 Once they've germinated, plant these clumps out in the garden, spaced 12 inches (30 cm) apart.

3 The young plants will push each other apart and produce a fine crop of young baby leeks.

Where to grow Leeks should be grown alongside your other onion-family members and moved around the garden every year (see pages 22–23). If you don't have much space in your garden, they can be grown in a pot on the patio. Here, sow seeds 1 inch (2.5 cm) apart and cover with a dusting of potting mix. Keep watering well and you'll be able to pull leeks when they reach pencil thickness. Leave a few to grow even bigger.

Types and varieties There is little difference in color and flavor between varieties. If you're growing as baby leeks you'll need plenty of seed.

Pests and diseases Leeks are relatively trouble-free.

Harvesting and storage Harvesting of leeks can span from midsummer right into the following spring. If you've planted them close together, you can start pulling very small leeks in the summer and use them like spring onions. Left a little longer, more can be harvested when the stems are around ¾–1¼ inches (2–3 cm) in diameter. By this time there should be a plant every 8–12 inches (20–30 cm). These can be left in the ground and pulled whenever they're needed in the kitchen. Because they're happy left standing outside, there is no need to harvest and store. In northern areas, cover with a thick mulch in winter to keep severest cold and snow off leeks and soil.

How to get leeks all year In late winter or early spring, sow leeks direct into the ground. Sow seeds thickly, aiming for a seed every ½–¾ inch (1–2 cm). Once the seeds have come up, thin out to every inch (2.5 cm). Leeks can start to be pulled after around 10 weeks. Be careful not to disturb the neighboring plants, which will continue to grow. Keep pulling until you have a plant every 8–12 inches (20–30 cm). These can be left to mature to full size and pulled through the winter right up to next spring.

In the kitchen Leeks have a mild oniony flavor and can be used as an onion replacement. Their tender stems are popular steamed or used in soups and stir-fries.

TIP

Grow your own seed
Leave one or two plants in the garden and they'll run to seed. The white flowers become so tall they may need some support, but they should produce a good crop of small, black seeds that can be used to grow more leeks.

CALENDAR

LATE WINTER–EARLY SPRING
Sow in small pots or modular trays. Plant one seed in each and cover with potting mix. Leave in a cool greenhouse, cold frame or sunny window.

MID-SPRING
Water seedlings and feed if necessary with a liquid fertilizer.

LATE SPRING
Transplant into the ground. Make a hole with a dibber around 4 inches (10 cm) deep and drop the young leek into the hole. Water. Keep around 12 inches (30 cm) between rows and space 6 inches (15 cm) apart.

EARLY SUMMER
Water well and keep weeds down.

MIDSUMMER
Keep watering if it's dry.

LATE SUMMER
You can start to harvest baby leeks now, or leave to grow on in the ground right up to next spring.

VARIETY SELECTOR
- **'King Richard'**: early leek, 1 inch (2.5 cm) shanks, long variety, which is not winter hardy in northern areas.
- **'Lincoln'**: baby leeks or 2½-inch (6.5-cm) giants.
- **'Bleu de Solaize'**: of French origin, very cold hardy.

High-return crop
Leeks are a valuable winter crop, which are perfect for adding to hearty winter casseroles or soups.

Spring onion

This onion crop is a good vegetable for those eager for a quick crop.

✪✪✪✪✪	VALUE FOR MONEY
✪✪✪✪✪	MAINTENANCE
✪✪✪✪✪	FREEZE/STORE

CROPPING SEASON: LATE SPRING–LATE FALL

Spring onions, or scallions, are a fast-growing crop, perfect for using in salads or stir-fries. If you're new to gardening and new to onion-growing, this is a good place to start, since it's both a quick crop to mature and one that can be sown any time between early spring and early fall.

Where to grow It's a good idea to keep spring onions with any other onions you have, rotating them around the garden each year (see pages 22–23). However, as spring onions take up such a small amount of space and can be sown right through the growing season, they're a good choice for any patch of spare ground you have. For example, a short row can be sown between larger brassicas early in the season, or sown in place of a crop of fava beans or peas, which finish in summer.

GROWING SPRING ONIONS IN A CONTAINER

1 Select a container 12 inches (30 cm) in diameter or 1½ gallons (5 L) in volume and fill with multipurpose potting mix.

2 Scatter seed individually every inch (2.5 cm) across the surface of the pot.

3 Cover with a layer of potting mix and water with a fine rose.

Quick croppers
A quick-growing crop, you can start harvesting spring onions in just six to eight weeks.

If you are short of space, spring onions are brilliant in containers. You can sow fairly thickly and you'll have plenty of onions for pulling.

Whether you're growing in containers or in the ground, they can be sown outside from early spring onward. Sowing every few weeks through the growing season will provide you with fresh spring onions up to and, in warm winter regions, right through winter.

Types and varieties Most traditional spring onions tend to produce a small bulb at the end. Japanese bunching onions are similar, except for the fact that they're much straighter without a bulb. Some varieties are crosses of the two types. For a bit of interest, there are now even red spring onions, which look good both in the garden and on the plate.

Pests and diseases These quick-growing onions are relatively trouble-free, but can still suffer from white rot and downy mildew, which affect all members of the onion family. If your crops are affected by this problem, it's best to destroy the harvest and don't grow onions in this part of the garden again.

Harvesting and storage Spring onions can grow in as little as 10 weeks. As soon as they're pencil thickness, start to harvest, gently pulling the stems. If the soil is firm, loosen with a garden fork.

Spring onions taste best fresh from the garden. It's therefore not worth storing them in the fridge for more than a week. They'll stand well enough in the ground — just pull a few at a time as you need them in the kitchen.

In the kitchen Spring onions are traditionally used as a garnish, but their milder flavor means they're good in salads too. They are often used in Asian stir-fries, or to replace onions in cooked dishes, particularly when you want a milder flavor.

CALENDAR

LATE WINTER
Prepare your soil by digging over well and removing any perennial weeds.

EARLY SPRING
Start to make your first sowings. Make a shallow trench, about ½–¾ inch (1–2 cm) deep and around 4 inches (10 cm) wide, and sprinkle seeds along it, aiming for a seed every inch (2.5 cm). Cover with soil.

MID-SPRING
You can still sow now, as above.

LATE SPRING
It's worth making another sowing, even if you made one last month, to spread out the season.

EARLY SUMMER
Continue to sow now, as above, or think about sowing into small gaps as they open up in the rest of the vegetable garden.

MIDSUMMER
Start to water if your soil is dry. Your early sowings can start to be harvested.

LATE SUMMER
You can keep sowing, and watering as necessary to keep the plants growing. Keep harvesting your earlier crops through the fall.

4 Young onions will start to swell at the base after just a few weeks.

5 Start to pull spring onions when they're pencil thickness. Leave others to grow a little more.

VARIETY SELECTOR
• 'Nabechan': excellent, complex flavor when cooked.
• 'Evergreen Hardy White': a perennial, develops clumps to eat, divide and replant.
• 'Deep Purple', 'Rossa Lunga di Firenze': red spring onions.

Celery

An extremely popular salad vegetable in the kitchen, but one that is tricky to grow in the garden.

✪✪✪✪✪ VALUE FOR MONEY
✪✪✪✪✪ MAINTENANCE
✪✪✪✪✪ FREEZE/STORE
CROPPING SEASON: EARLY SUMMER–LATE FALL

Celery, like Florence fennel, prefers warm but moist conditions. These can be difficult to sustain in a vegetable patch when crops often dry out in the summer. So, celery is really only worth a go if you've got time to devote to this crop. Given the right conditions, you'll be rewarded with long, distinctively flavored crunchy stems that are fantastic eaten raw as well as used in soups and stews.

Where to grow Celery seed is slow to germinate. Seeds need light to grow, so sow on the surface of a small pot or tray of potting mix. Cover either with a thin layer of vermiculite, which allows light through, or place some plastic wrap or a piece of glass over the top to keep the surface of the

GERMINATING CELERY SEED

1 Fill a small pot with potting mix and sow a few seeds on the surface.

2 Cover with a thin layer of vermiculite, and mist with a fine spray. Alternatively, after watering, you could cover the pots with plastic wrap.

3 Mist regularly with water and keep at a constant temperature of 59°F (15°C). Keep the pots in a propagator to ensure the humidity is kept high, and the temperature constant.

Crunchy celery
New varieties of self-blanching celery means that they're much easier to grow in the garden — as long as you keep them well watered.

potting mix moist. The seeds also need a temperature of around 59°F (15°C).

It's worth growing celery in the vegetable garden only if you can devote some time and effort to these plants, making sure they're well watered. They prefer rich, moisture-retentive soil, with a pH of around 7 (see page 219).

Types and varieties
Celery used to need trenching up, where soil was pushed against the stems as they grew to preserve their pale color and tender stems. Now there are new varieties called "self-blanching" — meaning that you don't need to keep pushing soil against the stems every couple of weeks. Self-blanching celery produces long-stemmed plants that reach up to 18 inches (45 cm) high. They don't like the weather too cold, so are best grown in the summer. Blanched celery is also no longer as popular as green celery. You can find celery in a range of colors, not just green: there are varieties with creamy-yellow stems as well as ones with pinkish-red stems.

Pests and diseases
Slugs can be a problem because the soil is kept constantly wet. Use appropriate controls to keep them at bay.

Leaf blights can affect celery. If this happens, rotate the crop around the garden next season (see pages 22–23). Celery mosaic virus can also be a problem, although resistant varieties are available. If your crop is hit, destroy the infected plants and use control aphids.

Harvesting and storage
Once the celery looks ready for harvesting, use a garden fork to ease the plant out of the ground and cut off the root. Once cut, it will only remain fresh for a week or so. Plants may bolt or be damaged by frost if left in the ground as the weather turns cool, so it's worth harvesting all plants before the weather turns too cold.

In the kitchen
The unusual flavor of celery works well with onion and carrot as a base for all sorts of stews. It also works well in soups. French crunchy celery is popular with children and great eaten as a crudité.

CALENDAR

MID-WINTER
With a minimum temperature of 59°F (15°C) (use a propagator), sow seed on the surface of a tray of multipurpose potting mix 12 weeks before the last frost date. Keep moist and at a constant temperature.

LATE SPRING
Once germinated and grown on, start acclimatizing the plants to cooler conditions.

Plant the seedlings out in the garden around the last frost date when they have several true leaves. Plant in rich, moisture-retentive soil, with around 10 inches (25 cm) of space each way. Water the plants well and cover with floating row covers.

MIDSUMMER
Keep watering the plants at least twice a week.

LATE SUMMER
Keep watering. Plants should be ready to start harvesting now.

EARLY FALL
Keep watering and harvesting.

VARIETY SELECTOR
- 'Giant Red': red stems.
- 'Golden Self-Blanching': yellow stems.
- 'Ventura': easier to grow, tasty.

Tasty crop
If you get the watering right, celery can be a productive and rewarding crop to grow.

Asparagus

One of the most expensive vegetables to buy in the supermarket but probably one of the easiest to grow — however, you will have to wait a year or two for a crop.

STAR PLANT
GOURMET VEG
LOW EFFORT

✪✪✪✪✪ VALUE FOR MONEY
✪✪✪✪✪ MAINTENANCE
✪✪✪✪✪ FREEZE/STORE
CROPPING SEASON: MID-SPRING–LATE SPRING

Asparagus is a perennial vegetable, which means that you need to plant it only once and it keeps coming back year after year. The first two years you should not harvest as the plant settles in and bulks up. However, after this period you'll be able to pick spears of asparagus from mid-spring to early summer. Plants are either male or female. Males produce larger spears; females produce seed and smaller spears. You don't need to grow males and females together to produce a crop.

Zone 4–9.

Succulent stems
Once the plants are established, you'll be able to pick fresh asparagus from the garden for at least six weeks.

Where to grow Unlike many other vegetables that move around the garden each year, you'll have to find a spot to keep your asparagus permanently. Find an open site with well-cultivated ground, which is free from any weeds. Enrich the soil with some homemade compost. You'll have to order plants (known as crowns) in the winter, and these will be

PLANTING NEW CROWNS

1 Dig a trench around 16 inches (40 cm) wide.

2 Lay the crowns on a mound in the center of the trench, spreading the roots on either side. The top of the crown should be around 4 inches (10 cm) below the surface of the soil.

3 Aim for a plant every 18 inches (45 cm) along the trench, and leave 3 feet (90 cm) between trenches if you're planting a block.

4 Cover with soil and a layer of homemade compost.

VARIETY SELECTOR

- **'Jersey Giant'**: all male — male varieties are more productive than female.
- **'Jersey Knight'**: all male.
- **'Purple Passion'**: purple spears.

CALENDAR

MID-SPRING

Create your new asparagus bed. Established plants should start producing spears for cutting now.

LATE SPRING

Keep cutting established plants, but stop cutting now if your plants are only two years old.

MIDSUMMER

Stop cutting established plants now. Apply a fertilizer and add a thick layer of homemade compost.

LATE FALL

Cut the dead foliage down to the ground.

delivered in mid-spring. After planting out, keep the plants well watered and the plots weed-free. Don't consider picking any spears in the first year, and in the second, just pick for three to four weeks in late spring, to encourage the plants to develop even further. After the second year, you should be rewarded with well-established plants that produce ferny-like foliage through the summer.

Types and varieties Modern hybrids produce only male plants, which means they yield more spears than female plants. You'll need to order crowns (one-year-old plants) in the winter for delivery in the spring.

Pests and diseases Asparagus succumbs to only one main pest, which is the asparagus beetle. This serious pest is easy to identify — the yellow and black beetles cover the spears in early spring. The easiest solution is to try to pick off the beetles as you see them

— otherwise they will damage the spears. Also, after your second-year harvest, harvest all stalks during the harvest period.

Harvesting and storage After the second year, you can start to harvest from mid-spring for around six to seven weeks. Wait until the spears reach around 4 inches (10 cm) in height with a tight bud. Using a sharp knife, cut the spear around 1–2 inches (2.5–5 cm) below the surface of the soil. You'll need to check the plants almost every day, since they can grow very quickly. Asparagus doesn't store well, so should be used as you harvest it. Alternatively, it can be frozen — blanch for a couple of minutes before doing so.

In the kitchen Asparagus is best eaten lightly steamed or stir-fried to appreciate its subtle flavor. Tender asparagus is also good raw in salads, grilled or barbecued, or cooked in risottos.

Globe artichoke and Cardoon

Globe artichokes are statuesque plants. They are
worth growing if you have plenty of space and enjoy
the unique flavor of this perennial vegetable.

Cardoon bud
Artichokes and cardoons may not be the most
productive crop for the space they take up, but
they do make for interesting looking plants.

○○○○○	VALUE FOR MONEY
○○○○○	MAINTENANCE
○○○○○	FREEZE/STORE
CROPPING SEASON: LATE SPRING–EARLY SUMMER	

Globe artichokes are elegant, silver-leafed
plants with beautiful thistle-like flowers that can
look good in an ornamental border as well as
the kitchen garden. They require a lot of space,
reaching 3 ft. 9 in. (1.2 m) high and around 3 ft.
2 in. (1 m) wide, and since they are perennial
(only where the temperature stays above 49°F
[9.5°C]), you'll need to devote part of your
garden to them for at least two or three years.

You can buy young plants from the plant
store, but they're also fairly straightforward to
raise from seed. You won't get a huge crop in
your first year, but look after them well and
they'll return the favor by producing a good
crop of fleshy edible buds year after year.

Zone 7 and above.

Where to grow Artichokes prefer
rich, moisture-retentive soil and a fairly sunny
spot. They don't like strong winds or cold
conditions, so avoid areas that suffer badly
from frost.

Types and varieties There are few
named varieties of artichoke, and often plants
from the same packet vary in vigor and
performance. It's a good idea to discard the
weaker plants and concentrate your efforts on
the stronger performers. There is some choice
when it comes to color. As well as green, there
are also artichokes with a purple tinge.

In the garden As they are perennial
plants they'll slowly grow larger each year,
producing more edible buds. Keep the plot
weed-free and mulch in spring with a good dose
of homemade compost or equivalent. After
four years or so the yield may reduce, and it is
probably a good time to either take cuttings
from original plants or start again from seed.

Globe artichokes
There are not many varieties to choose from, but it's worth trying both green and purple versions, if you have the space.

Pests and diseases Globe artichokes and cardoons are generally trouble-free.

Harvesting and storage The edible part of the globe artichoke is the immature bud and the stem just below. The whole bud can be eaten when very young and the bud is very tight. However, artichokes are most commonly picked when the bud is larger, just before it starts to open into flower. In the first year you'll get only a single bud. But in further years, side shoots will produce many more, often up to 12 per plant. These are produced over the summer. Cut with around 4 inches (10 cm) of stalk.

In the kitchen Young buds can be eaten whole. Larger buds will need to be prepared. This usually means boiling for 20 minutes or so, then cutting out the fleshy bottom of the bud, leaving the bristly developing flower or "choke." You can also eat the fleshy base of each scale — a favorite way is dipping in melted butter or French dressing and running it against your teeth to remove the flesh.

Flowering artichoke
Once flowered, it's not worth trying to harvest. Just enjoy the plant for its architectural beauty.

CALENDAR

LATE WINTER
Sow seeds in a seed tray, cover with a dusting of potting mix and germinate in a brightly lit place indoors.

EARLY SPRING
Select the strongest seedlings and plant into larger pots. Grow on in a sunny window or cold frame.

MID-SPRING
Feed plants with a general fertilizer if necessary.

LATE SPRING
Plant out into the garden, leaving around 3 feet (90 cm) between plants. Mulch well.

EARLY SUMMER
Water plants and as buds form, harvest for the kitchen.

LATE FALL
Cut dead stems back to the ground and keep the plot weed-free. Mulch each spring.

VARIETY SELECTOR
- **'Green Globe'**: this variety produces elegant plants, good enough to plant in the flower border.
- **'Purple Italian Globe'**: good for cooler regions and makes attractive purple-colored artichokes.
- **'Imperial Star'**: good for growing as an annual.

Sprouting seeds

Grown on the kitchen windowsill, this is definitely one crop you can succeed with right through the year.

○○○○○ VALUE FOR MONEY
○○○○○ MAINTENANCE
○○○○○ FREEZE/STORE
CROPPING SEASON: ALL YEAR ROUND

Tasty morsels
Sprouting seeds are quick and easy to grow and are a great way to keep you eating healthily right through the year.

Sprouting seeds have been popular for some years, and are a mainstay in vegetarian and vegan diets. However, even if you're not a vegetarian, these healthy and nutritious sprouts are simple to grow and tasty to eat. They're a good choice for growing in the winter when very little else is available in the garden and can provide you and your family with some fresh salad right through the year.

Seed companies have caught on to their popularity and have been extending the range of the seeds available for sprouting. You'll need to buy seed especially for sprouting — not because the seed is any different to those you grow in your garden, but just that you need lots more. Also, you need to make sure that the seed has not been treated with pesticides.

Where to grow To grow sprouting seeds all you need is a jar; however, there are plenty of specialist sprouting kits that you can buy. The best of these are tiered, allowing you to sprout several different seed types on separate tiers of the sprouter. These are ideal and take up little space in the kitchen. Alternatively, if you're trying sprouting seeds for the first time and want to see whether they're for you, just use an old jam jar, and instead of the lid, use plastic wrap.

Next get hold of the seed. You can buy it from your regular seed supplier, or alternatively, health food stores often stock seed for sprouting.

Each seed will require slightly different growing requirements, so consult the seed packet, but the basics are essentially the same. First, soak your seed for the specified length of time — usually overnight — in fresh water. Then rinse the seed and transfer into the sprouter or jar. The seed will need to be rinsed through, preferably twice a day. Using a sprouter with holes to allow for rinsing is best and easier than using a jar. Leave on a windowsill, covered and out of direct sunlight. After anything between three and 10 days the seed will have sprouted and be ready for eating.

You can store the sprouted seed in the fridge for a few days, but it will need to be rinsed each day.

Types and varieties There are lots of seeds that are sold for sprouting — some are quicker to sprout than others, while some are tastier. Here's a quick guide to what's around.
Alfalfa Five days to harvest.
Crunchy stalks with a nutty flavor.
Fenugreek Five days to harvest.
Crispy stalks, with a mild curry taste.
Mung bean Three days to harvest.
Large beans that produce chewy, fat sprouts.
Radish Four days to harvest.
A strong radish flavor, with a hot aftertaste.
Sunflower Five days to harvest.
Crunchy sprouts with a slight pea flavor.

In the kitchen Sprouted seeds are great in stir-fries, and the bigger seeded types, such as mung bean and fenugreek, are perfect for this. The smaller seeds, such as alfalfa and radish, are great in salads and sandwiches.

Sprout variety
There are lots of different sprouting seeds to choose from. All have a different texture and taste so it's worth trying a few before you decide on your favorite.

Microgreens

A cross between sprouting seeds and baby-leaf salads, microgreens make a pretty garnish and add zing.

✪✪✪✧✧ VALUE FOR MONEY
✪✪✧✧✧ MAINTENANCE
✪✪✧✧✧ FREEZE/STORE
CROPPING SEASON: ALL YEAR ROUND

Microgreens are essentially very young leafy plants. Unlike sprouting seeds which get eaten before the leaves have grown and developed (see opposite), microgreens are picked and eaten when the first young leaves start to grow. While mustard and cress are a favorite among children, microgreens are becoming fashionable in restaurants too. Adding a sprinkling of young seedlings to salads can really pack a punch. There are all sorts of seeds you can use for growing microgreens — basil, celery, coriander, fennel, radish, sorrel, and watercress are all popular, as are those mentioned below. While very little of the plant is actually used, you'll still be able to taste its intense flavor.

Where to grow Microgreens can be grown almost all through the year, but you'll need either a bright windowsill, or ideally a greenhouse or polytunnel. Because you're picking the plants when they're very young you do end up harvesting very little. For this reason, it is quite labor-intensive and requires a fair amount of space to get decent amounts. It's worth growing just a tray or two to begin with, to see whether this crop works for you.

You'll need some large seed trays to grow microgreens, filled with multipurpose potting mix. Seeds are sown thickly onto the potting mix, and kept moist and somewhere light and warm. In a matter of a week or so, the seeds should have germinated. Microgreens are harvested by just snipping off at the base when the seed leaves have opened out.

Types and varieties You'll need to buy seed especially for growing as microgreens because you'll need a lot more seed than if you were growing full-size plants. Seed suppliers are tapping into this new area of gardening and are quickly increasing their ranges.

Miniature salads
Microgreens are essentially baby leaves that are harvested early on in their lives.

Broccoli Six days to harvest. Crunchy stalks with a mild, but slightly spicy broccoli flavor.
Chervil Ten days to harvest. Usually grown as a herb, these microgreens have a slight aniseed flavor.
Red mustard Six days to harvest. A popular choice with schools, but worth growing at home too for their spicy crunchy stems.

Harvesting and storage Microgreens won't store, so you'll need to time your growing to perfection. Once harvested, use immediately.

In the kitchen Add a sprinkling onto meals at dinner parties to give that restaurant-style presentation, or add a handful to salads.

Chervil
Use chervil as a microgreen to add a hint of aniseed to your dishes.

Red mustard
Attractive mottled red leaves will bring a dash of color to a salad bowl.

Edible flowers

For gardeners who want to show off
their skills, adding a few edible flowers
to a dish can really brighten up a meal.

✪✪✪✪✪ VALUE FOR MONEY
✪✪✪✪✪ MAINTENANCE
✪✪✪✪✪ FREEZE/STORE
CROPPING SEASON: ALL YEAR ROUND

There are hundreds of plants that produce
edible flowers, but some are more tasty than
others. Most are used fresh, added to salads
or drinks. Some are used in hot food to
provide color, while others are sometimes used
in preserves. Many edible flowers also make
attractive garden plants. It's certainly worth
growing a few in your kitchen garden or patio
to brighten up the area, while providing a bit of
color to your food too. Saffron and elderflower
are common flowers used in supermarket
products, but to really show off, why not try
growing violets, nasturtiums or borage?

Where to grow Edible flowers come in
all shapes, sizes and colors. You'll need to think
about the final size of your plant and decide
where it can fit in before you grow it. Many
people grow their edible flowers at the
entrance to their vegetable plot, along a
pathway or in between herbs. This makes an
attractive and colorful entrance to your garden,

Sweet violets
Edible flowers, such as sweet violets, can look
stunning in the garden as well as being a useful
addition in the kitchen.

while also ensuring that you can eat everything
that you grow. Because the flowers vary widely
in their cultivation it's not possible to list every
site, situation and growing method for each
one. Try selecting a few, follow the seed packet
instructions, and see how you get on. Don't
expect hundreds of flowers, but appreciate the
few you do get, and enjoy their color in the
garden and flavor in the kitchen.

Harvesting and storage Pick flowers
early in the day. Handle them gently as they can
quickly bruise. If flowers have insects nestling
inside, gently tap to remove or just leave to
one side until they leave. It's best not to wash
the flowers if you can help it, but you can dip
the flowers in ice-cold water to refresh them

just before serving in a salad. Some flowers,
such as zucchini and nasturtiums, can be used
whole, while others, such as pot marigolds and
daisies, will need their petals tearing off.

In the kitchen Sprinkle petals of
daisy-like flowers over salads just before
serving, or add larger flowers, such as
nasturtiums, in with baby leaves. Fry lightly
battered zucchini flowers, and try violet and
sweet bergamot in tea. Stronger flavors of
lavender and sweet William are reserved for
using in small amounts in baking. Use basil and
oregano flowers just as you would their leaves.
Borage, with its bright blue flowers, looks great
added to summer drinks.

Daylily
In some Asian cuisines, all parts of the daylily
are eaten: flowers, buds and leaf shoots.

VARIETY SELECTOR

The list of edible flowers is lengthy. Some of them you may have growing in your garden already, and you can pick a few flowers as you need them, leaving the rest to enjoy in the garden. Others you'll need to grow specially, particularly those raised from seed.

PERENNIALS

You should be able to buy these from plant stores as plants.

Pinks (Dianthus)
The flower of this popular garden plant, which you may have growing in your garden already, can have a heady scent of cloves with a sweet flavor. Add petals to ice cream and fruit salads.

Chives (Allium schoenoprasum)
This common garden plant produces pretty pink flower heads. Sprinkle these onto salads or use as a garnish in soups and stews.

Rose (Rosa)
Rose petals can be added to salads. Some have an unpalatable taste so try before you harvest.

Lavender (Lavandula)
These strongly flavored flowers can be added in small quantities to cakes. You can even add some to ice cream.

Daylily (Hemerocallis)
Flavors of this common garden herbaceous perennial vary. It is thought that the lighter the color of flower, the sweeter the flavor. Try before you eat and add to salads.

Sweet violet (Viola odorata)
These can provide color to salads, but their taste is nothing special, with just a hint of perfume. Violets can be dried and used in tea.

Daisy (Bellis perennis)
A common plant found in the lawn or growing as a weed. The flowers are perfectly edible. There are cultivated forms too, with larger, sometimes more colorful, flowers. All are edible — just pick off the petals and add to salads.

Daisy
As well as looking great in the garden, with their tangy flavor, daisies make an interesting and unusual addition to salads.

Borage
Borage is a pretty plant and a useful nectar-rich species to encourage bees into your garden.

Nasturtium
Nasturtiums are easy to grow from seed and, given a sunny, dry spot, will grow and flower well all summer long.

FLOWERS TO GROW FROM SEED

These flowers won't last more than a year, but are easy to raise from seed and can be great for filling space in your garden or patio.

Pot marigold (Calendula officinalis)
These easy-to-grow annuals can be sown direct to produce their bright orange flowers throughout the summer. They have a faint peppery taste and are a good choice for adding color to cakes and salads.

Sweet arugula (Hesperis matronalis)
This pretty plant produces spires of pale purple flowers. They have a slight perfumery flavor. Add them to salads.

Nasturtium
Probably the most well-used edible flower because the plant flowers so prolifically. This plant is easy to grow from seed each year, and there is a wide selection of colors and varieties to choose from. The flowers are often used in salads.

Borage (Borago officinalis)
This large plant is easy to grow and will reach up to 3 ft. 2 in. (1 m) in height. It produces lots of pretty blue flowers during the summer. The flowers are sweet and can be added to puddings and ice creams, and also look great added to a summer punch.

Zucchini
If you've got too many zucchini, pick the flowers before they set fruit. These buttery yellow flowers are delicious battered then lightly fried, or alternatively they can be eaten in salads.

Basil
If your basil plants start flowering, don't fear, just pick the flowers and add them to your Mediterranean dishes instead.

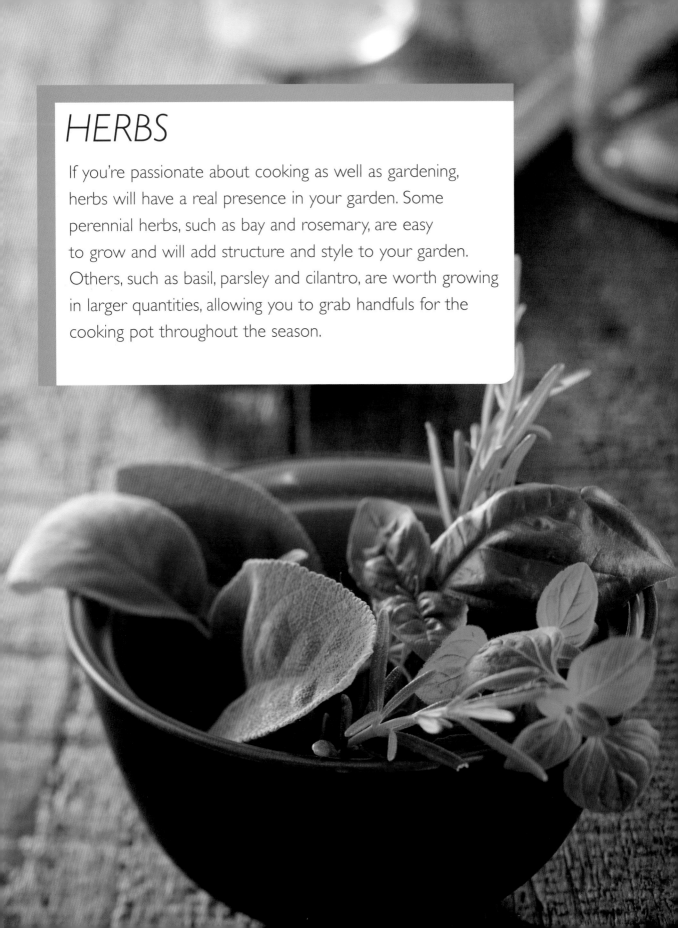

HERBS

If you're passionate about cooking as well as gardening, herbs will have a real presence in your garden. Some perennial herbs, such as bay and rosemary, are easy to grow and will add structure and style to your garden. Others, such as basil, parsley and cilantro, are worth growing in larger quantities, allowing you to grab handfuls for the cooking pot throughout the season.

Bay

Bay leaves bring flavor and depth to sauces and stews.

⭘⭘⭘⭘⭘	VALUE FOR MONEY
⭘⭘⭘⭘⭘	MAINTENANCE
⭘⭘⭘⭘⭘	FREEZE/STORE
CROPPING SEASON: ALL YEAR ROUND	

Bay trees are often grown for their elegant appearance and are a good choice for any garden — not one used just for growing food. They can be grown as standard trees and survive well in containers, and for that reason are often found on patios or terraces all over the world. However, it's their aromatic leaves that are also used in cooking that really make this plant worth keeping on the patio. Step outside at any time of year and your plant will yield fragrant leaves that can be used in Italian sauces, soups and even desserts.

Zone Hardy to zone 7.

Where to grow Bay trees are often grown in the ground, and while they can be damaged by extreme cold or wet conditions, they'll come through most winters unscathed.

If you are planting in the garden, select a spot that gets some sun and is sheltered from strong winds and out of any frost pockets.

You'll most often see bay grown in a container. Bay trees trained into tall standards with a ball-shaped head have become popular in plant stores. They survive well in containers and require little attention — except for regular watering. Plants in containers can be brought indoors to a cool, sunny room in winter.

Types and varieties You'll mostly just see the species *Laurus nobilis* with its bright, shiny green leaves.

Pests and diseases Bay can suffer from scale insects. They attach themselves to the leaves and bark and encourage the growth of sooty mold. The best way to get rid of these insects is by scrubbing the leaves and stems with soapy water. Then rinse.

Harvesting and storage Pick leaves as required. When pruning in midsummer,

Year-round seasoning
Bay trees look stunning in the garden and their leaves, either fresh or dried, can be used in the kitchen all year round.

leave prunings to dry and store dried leaves for use later in the year.

In the kitchen Tear leaves in two to release the flavor and add to soups, sauces and stews.

CALENDAR

MID-SPRING
If you have a container-grown tree, add a sprinkling of slow-release fertilizer in the spring. If necessary, repot into a larger container — this is a good time to do this.

LATE SPRING
Keep watering the plant through the rest of spring and summer.

EARLY SUMMER
The plant should have put on some new growth. Now is the time to clip the plant back into its original shape — or consider trying some topiary shapes.

MIDSUMMER
Keep watering and pick leaves as required for the kitchen.

LATE FALL
Move the container-grown plant to a more sheltered spot out of any direct wind.

BAY PRUNING AND MAINTENANCE

1 By early summer you can cut back your bay tree. If it is already pruned into a ball or other shape, keep stepping back to take a look as you work slowly around the shrub.

2 Scale insects often attack bay trees — use a bowl of warm soapy water and a sponge scourer to gently remove the scale and mold by rubbing the leaves and stems.

Basil

Basil is probably one of the most rewarding herbs to grow and the most useful in the kitchen.

⬤⬤⬤⬤⬤ VALUE FOR MONEY
⬤⬤⬤○○ MAINTENANCE
⬤⬤⬤⬤○ FREEZE/STORE
CROPPING SEASON: EARLY SUMMER–MID-FALL

Basil is used in lots of cuisines, but most famous is its use in Italian and Asian cooking. Each style of cooking uses one of the two distinct types of basil. Sweet basil is used in Italian cooking to make pesto and add flavor to pasta sauces. "Thai" basils, with their stronger, spicier flavor and thicker, hairy leaves, are used in Asian cooking.

Whichever types you go for, their growing requirements remain the same — they prefer hot conditions, and if not continually picked, will quickly run to seed.

Where to grow Basil can be sown direct and grown in the garden anytime in the summer months. Sometimes it's grown in pots on the patio or even on the windowsill. Watered and fed often enough, a single pot will give a continual supply. If you want to make pesto, it's worth growing a much larger amount in the garden, then freezing the fresh leaves for making pesto at a later date.

Grocery stores often sell basil, and other herbs, growing in a small pot. You can use these as young plants and encourage them to carry on growing through the season.

Genovese basil
The leaves of Genovese basil are perfect for growing in bulk — collect all in one go to make pesto, then freeze for later use.

Pests and diseases Basil is generally trouble-free.

Harvesting and storage Basil can be frozen then used in cooking or for making pesto. Otherwise just add leaves straight from the garden to the pan.

In the kitchen Used widely in both Asian and Italian cooking, the chopped leaves are often added to dishes in small amounts just before they're served to add flavor.

MAKING THE MOST OF STORE-GROWN BASIL

1 Buy a pot of grocery-store basil. Remove the plastic and soak the pot in water.

2 Plant in a larger pot, with multipurpose potting mix and a sprinkling of slow-release fertilizer.

3 Keep the basil on a sunny windowsill and pick as required.

CALENDAR

EARLY SPRING

Start sowing now in small pots indoors. Sprinkle a few seeds on the surface of a small pot filled with potting mix and cover with a dusting of potting mix. Keep moist. The seed may take a couple of weeks to germinate.

MID-SPRING

Once the seedlings have grown to around 6 inches (15 cm), pinch out the tip to encourage them to bush out. Pot them into larger containers, or, if frost is past, plant out in the garden.

MIDSUMMER

Start to harvest the leaves and pick off any developing flowers, as after flowering the plant will start to decline.

EARLY FALL

If you have space, move your containers to a sunny, warm windowsill to keep the plants growing.

VARIETY SELECTOR

Italian or sweet basil
- 'Greek': a small-leafed version.

Genovese basil
- 'Sweet Green', 'Neapolitan'.
- 'Red': a red leafed basil.

Thai basil
- 'Siam Queen': pretty purple flowers.
- 'Lime Mrs. Burns': lime scented.
- 'Holy': purple stems, pink flowers.

BASIL VARIETIES

'Greek' basil
Used in Greek cuisine, this is a compact form with tiny leaves less than ½ inch (1 cm) long.

'Siam Queen' basil
An attractive form of Thai basil, 'Siam Queen' has an excellent aroma and flavor.

Holy basil
Native to India, holy basil is used in ayurvedic medicine as well as the kitchen. It is a great container plant.

'Lime Mrs. Burns' basil
Lime-scented leaves that can be used in cooking, chopped in salads or used to make fresh herbal tea.

Chervil

With its parsley-like flavor, chervil is a favorite winter herb.

○○○○○ VALUE FOR MONEY
○○○○○ MAINTENANCE
○○○○○ FREEZE/STORE
CROPPING SEASON: MID-SPRING–LATE FALL

This hardy annual is often used in French cooking. It has a parsley flavor, but with a hint of aniseed. The leaves are rich in vitamin C and iron and can be used to make a refreshing tea. In the garden, it's an easy herb to grow, but should be sown regularly for a constant supply of fresh leaves.

Types and varieties Stick to the species *Anthriscus cerefolium*.

Where to grow Plants reach around 2 feet (60 cm) in height and around 12 inches (30 cm) across. It can be a scruffy-looking plant, so it's best kept in the vegetable garden. It grows quickly and can soon set seed, after which it will die. Therefore, sowing seed every two to four weeks will provide you with a regular supply. Chervil grows best in semishade as full sun will encourage it to bloom and die. You could try growing it in between other taller and longer-growing crops such as corn or some brassicas.

Pests and diseases Chervil is generally trouble-free.

Harvesting and storage To keep its fresh, aniseed flavor, chervil is best picked and used immediately. If you have too many leaves all ready for picking, they can be chopped and frozen immediately.

In the kitchen Chervil leaves can be chopped and used in soups and sauces, and go particularly well with vegetable, fish and chicken dishes. Adding the herb toward the end of cooking will help to retain its flavor.

Attractive foliage
The delicate leaves of chervil can look attractive in their own right.

CALENDAR

EARLY SPRING
Start to sow chervil direct in the ground. Draw out a drill about ⅝ inch (1.5 cm) deep and add a few seeds every 8 inches (20 cm). Cover with soil.

MID-SPRING
Thin out seedlings if more than one comes up at each station. Sow another row of seeds now.

LATE SPRING
Start to pick leaves as they become ready.

SUMMER
Continue to sow chervil for another harvest in eight weeks or so.

EARLY FALL
Make a final sowing now for herbs through the winter. Although chervil is hardy, you may want to protect it with a cloche or floating row cover to keep the leaves in good shape.

GROWING CHERVIL IN CONTAINERS

1 Fill a pot with multipurpose potting mix.

2 Sow a seed every 2 inches (5 cm) and cover with a dusting of potting mix. Water.

3 Cut chervil 2 inches (5 cm) from the base — young leaves should start to grow again from the base.

Chives

A relative of the onion, this perennial herb is both pretty and productive in kitchen gardens.

✪✪✪✪✪	VALUE FOR MONEY
✪✪✪✪○	MAINTENANCE
✪✪✪✪○	FREEZE/STORE
CROPPING SEASON: EARLY SPRING–LATE FALL	

The pinky flowers of chives make this one of the most attractive herbs to grow. It can be grown in a pot on the patio or even in an ornamental border. It is often used as edging too, down the side of a path or along the front of fruit trees, for example. The leaves can be picked all through the summer and well into fall.

Zone 3–9.

Where to grow Chives can be grown from seed, or bought as young plants from the plant store. It's pretty simple to grow from seed, and once established will last for many years. In fact, after a couple of years' growth, an established clump can be dug up, split and replanted around the garden. It's a worthwhile herb to grow as it's so productive.

Chives can be grown in a pot, and as long as they are kept watered, will keep producing new stems for picking all through the summer. Alternatively, just grow it around your garden either in rows or in small clumps and enjoy the pretty flowers that will be covered with bees in early summer.

Types and varieties There's little to choose from, but as well as the common pink flowering type, you may also come across white-flowering chives. All grow to around 10 inches (25 cm) in height.

Pests and diseases In theory, chives will suffer from the same diseases as onions, garlic and leeks (see page 46), but in reality they are usually trouble-free.

Harvesting and storage Snip off leaves at the base of the plant as required.

Tasty seasoning
Chives can be used as a border plant. What's more they're extremely productive too.

In the kitchen Chives can be used to add a delicate onion flavor to almost anything, but is often chopped finely and added as a garnish on soups and stews.

CALENDAR

MID-SPRING
Seed can be sown now either direct in the ground or in pots. Sow around ½–¾ inch (1–2cm) deep.

LATE SPRING
Young leaves will be starting to emerge. If you sowed into pots, make sure plants are kept well watered.

EARLY SUMMER
Start cutting leaves as you need them in the kitchen. Cutting off at the base of the plant will encourage more stems to be produced.

LATE FALL
Tidy up plants now by removing any dead or dying foliage.

DIVIDING CHIVE PLANTS

1 Dig up a whole plant using a spade.

2 Gently pull it apart with your fingers into smaller clumps with roots.

3 Replant these small clumps around the garden.

Cilantro

Another favorite in the kitchen, cilantro is a must for anyone who enjoys cooking Indian or Middle Eastern dishes.

✪✪✪✪✪ VALUE FOR MONEY
✪✪✪✪○ MAINTENANCE
✪✪✪✪○ FREEZE/STORE
CROPPING SEASON: EARLY SUMMER–MID-FALL

Productive herb
Regular sowing of cilantro through the spring and summer will provide a plentiful supply.

Cilantro is a well-loved herb, but its reputation is one of a tricky-to-grow plant that often sends up flowers before you've had a chance to pick any leaves. However, sow at the right times and there's a good chance you can harvest fresh bunches of herbs for much of the year.

Where to grow Cilantro grows well in a pot, as well as in the ground. A large container is ideal on the patio where you can keep an eye on it and you can pick leaves as often as you like. Traditionally, cilantro was sown in the spring; however, it does just as well when sown in the fall. Considering it originates in southern Europe and Asia, it's actually a pretty hardy plant and will survive winters outside if temperatures are not too cold. For best results, make repeated sowings through spring and summer. When the finer, feathery leaves start to grow, the plant is about to set seed. Either leave the plant to flower and collect what seeds are produced for use in the kitchen or just start again.

Types and varieties Varieties are now being bred that are less likely to bolt and produce more leaves.

Pests and diseases Generally trouble-free, but slugs and snails can be a problem.

Harvesting and storage Wait until the plants are around 6 inches (15 cm) high, then snip the leaves with a pair of scissors around 2 inches (5 cm) from the base of the plant as required. Leaves should regrow. Use immediately in the kitchen. Seeds can be collected and dried in a paper bag. Store in the kitchen in an airtight container. They can be crushed with a pestle and mortar when needed. Seed is known as coriander.

In the kitchen Fresh cilantro leaves are often added to Indian dishes just before serving. They're also added to South American, Caribbean and Middle Eastern dishes. Small amounts can be added to salads.

CALENDAR

LATE SPRING/EARLY SUMMER
Fill a large container with multipurpose potting mix and add some slow-release fertilizer. Sprinkle a seed every 2 inches (5 cm) on the surface. Cover with a dusting of potting mix and water. Alternatively, sow a row of seed ¼ inch (0.5 cm) deep, and thin plants to around 4 inches (10 cm).

MIDSUMMER
Keep watering, and don't let the plant dry out, both in the ground and in a pot. Pick leaves as required. Picking leaves can help to prevent the plant from running to seed. Make repeated sowings through summer, every two weeks.

LATE SUMMER
Plant in the same way as above. Your spring sowing is probably finished by now so wait to collect the edible seeds.

FALL/WINTER
You can keep your summer/fall-sown container outside, but place it in a sheltered spot. Bring indoors where winter temperatures fall below 30°F (1°C).

EARLY SPRING
Start to harvest the leaves from the pot you sowed last year. Harvest quickly because plants will bolt soon.

VARIETY SELECTOR

- **'Cilantro'**: good for both leaves and seed.
- **'Calypso'**: slowest to bolt of all the varieties.
- **'Santo'**: slow to bolt, Mexican variety.

GROWING CILANTRO IN CONTAINERS IN WINTER

1 Choose a small pot, and in early fall, fill with multipurpose potting mix.

2 Add a sprinkling of seed, cover with a dusting of potting mix and water. Cover with plastic wrap.

3 Remove the plastic wrap when the seeds have germinated and place on the windowsill for herbs into winter.

Dill and Fennel

These pretty herbs produce a fine feathery foliage with large saucer-shaped flowers.

✪✪✪○○	VALUE FOR MONEY
✪✪✪✪○	MAINTENANCE
✪✪✪○○	FREEZE/STORE
CROPPING SEASON: LATE SPRING–MID-FALL	

The leaves of dill and fennel are often used in fish and potato dishes. Dill has a subtle aniseed flavor, whereas the flavor of fennel is slightly stronger. While dill is an annual, its larger cousin, fennel, will survive in the garden for some years. If you're going to grow just one of these, go for fennel. The plant is much more attractive — especially the bronze-leafed version — and it's much easier to grow.

Zone Fennel: 5–10.

Where to grow Dill is a fairly small herb and it's worth growing a few plants from seed for your herb garden. Fennel is a much larger plant, often reaching 6 ft. 5 in. (2 m) high. It's an attractive plant too, and often found in ornamental borders as well as in kitchen gardens. Because it grows so big, it's not worth trying it in a pot.

If plants dry out, they can quickly run to seed, so plant in an area that won't go short of water.

Types and varieties There are a few varieties of dill. 'Fernleaf' is often grown for its leaves, whereas 'Bouquet' is usually grown for seed, which can be collected and dried.

There are just two choices of fennel — either green- or bronze-leafed. Both reach up to 6 ft. 5 in. (2 m) in height.

Pests and diseases Dill and fennel are generally trouble-free.

Alluring blooms
The ethereal flowers and foliage of dill and fennel is a common sight in kitchen gardens.

Harvesting and storage Cut leaves as required. For dill seed production, use a variety such as 'Bouquet' with its huge seed heads. These can be cut and dried in a large paper bag to collect the seed.

In the kitchen Leaves can be added to yogurt and cucumber, and eaten with fish, often smoked salmon. Seeds can be added to soups, pickles and potato salads.

CALENDAR

EARLY SPRING
You can start to make sowings now, but germination may be sporadic. Create a ⅝-inch (1.5-cm) drill and sprinkle seeds thinly along it. Aim for a seed every inch (2.5 cm). Cover the drill with soil.

MID-SPRING
Sow the seed of dill direct in the ground in short rows, about ¾ inch (2 cm) deep.

LATE SPRING
Thin out seedlings so there's a plant every 6 inches (15 cm) or so. If you're growing fennel, buy just one or two plants from the plant store and plant out immediately into rich, fertile and moisture-retentive soil.

EARLY SUMMER
Keep plants well watered and start to cut as a herb.

MID TO LATE SUMMER
Cut off flower heads and save the seed if required either for cooking or regrowing next year.

Feathery fronds
The feathery, green fronds of dill can be used in a wide variety of dishes in the kitchen.

Lovage

This giant of a herb gives a hearty, meaty flavor to soups and stews.

✪✪✪✪✪	VALUE FOR MONEY
✪✪✪✪✪	MAINTENANCE
✪✪✪✪✪	FREEZE/STORE

CROPPING SEASON: MID-SPRING–LATE FALL

As a perennial, lovage will last for a long time in the garden but as it can reach up to 5 feet (1.5 m) in height when in flower, it needs plenty of space. You'll need only a single plant as each one grows into a large clump. It's an attractive plant, with shiny, green leaves and long, tall stems. It was originally used by the ancient Greeks who believed chewing the stems would aid digestion. The leaves are also believed to have an antiseptic effect on the skin.

Zone Hardy to zone 3.

Where to grow Lovage prefers deep, rich, moist soil. It is happy in semishade or full sun, but does need a plentiful supply of water to keep it going in the summer. It's a good idea to add plenty of well-rotted organic matter to the site before planting, and another bucketful or two each spring around the plant. As it's a perennial, it will look after itself, coming back each year. To stop the plant getting too big, consider dividing the plant every few years. Spring is a good time to do this.

Types and varieties *Levisticum officinale* is the species that is normally grown; it produces tiny yellow flower clusters in summer.

Pests and diseases Relatively trouble-free, but leafminers can often spoil the leaves. If this becomes a big problem, cut down and put the leaves in a garbage bag. Water well and the plant should return. Slugs and snails can also be troublesome.

Harvesting and storage Leaves are worth picking fresh, which are available all through the growing season. If you do want to store some leaves, they can be frozen whole, then crushed before use.

Giant of the herb garden
Reminiscent of celery in looks and taste, this sturdy but attractive herb is easy to grow.

In the kitchen Lovage has a particular flavor, somewhat similar to celery. The leaves can be used to add robust flavors to soups and stews, and it's also a good choice to add when making stock. The root and stem can also be used in cooking as a vegetable, but it can be somewhat bitter.

DIVIDING AN ESTABLISHED LOVAGE CLUMP

1 Use a garden fork to dig out a large clump of lovage.

2 Using a spade, cut the clump into smaller, more manageable pieces and replant.

Oregano

Also known as marjoram, this herb picked fresh is so much tastier than the stuff you get dried in the supermarket.

✪✪✪✪✪	VALUE FOR MONEY
✪✪✪✪✪	MAINTENANCE
✪✪✪✪✪	FREEZE/STORE
CROPPING SEASON: ALL YEAR ROUND	

Used in Mediterranean dishes, oregano adds flavor to sauces. It's fantastic used fresh, but it can also be dried and stored for winter use.

Zone 5–10.

Where to grow This plant is very well behaved in the garden. It reaches around 12 inches (30 cm) high, and in midsummer produces pretty pink flowers. These can be cut down at the end of summer and the plant will regrow the following year. It's also a great-smelling plant, and for that reason is a good one to plant around the edges of permanent beds and borders, particularly in sunny, dry spots where the aromatic foliage can be enjoyed as you brush past.

Types and varieties The wild type of oregano, *Origanum vulgare*, is the one often found in plant stores, but there are other versions too. There's a yellow form, *Aureum*, which produces a brightly colored carpet of leaves in the spring. Whereas most species will keep coming back year after year, there are some varieties which aren't hardy, such as 'Sweet Marjoram', and these will have to be grown from seed each year.

Pests and diseases Oregano is trouble-free.

Harvesting and storage Leaves can be picked throughout the growing season. For drying, pick in the summer and dry by hanging upside down in the greenhouse. Dried leaves can be stored in airtight containers.

In the kitchen Use fresh leaves in marinades for meat and fish or add to pasta sauces. Dried leaves can be used through the winter in tomato sauces or sprinkled onto pizzas.

Mediterranean gem
This aromatic herb is a must for any lover of Mediterranean food.

CALENDAR

MID-SPRING
Buy one or two young plants from the plant store.

LATE SPRING
Plant out in the garden. Choose a dry, sunny spot. Oregano prefers dry, sandy soils so if necessary, add some coarse sand to heavy soil.

EARLY SUMMER TO EARLY FALL
Keep picking fresh leaves.

EARLY FALL
Cut back flowering stems to the base.

HOW TO DRY OREGANO

1 Cut long stems of oregano in early to midsummer.

2 Tie stems together at the base and hang upside down to dry in a greenhouse or bright kitchen.

Versatile herb
Fresh mint can be used both in cooking and
in tea to provide a refreshing drink.

Mint

STAR PLANT
CHEF'S FAVE,
FRESH OR
DRIED

This refreshing herb is simple to
grow — just make sure it doesn't
take over your garden!

✪✪✪✪✪ VALUE FOR MONEY
✪✪✪✪✪ MAINTENANCE
✪✪✪✪✪ FREEZE/STORE
CROPPING SEASON: EARLY SPRING–MID-FALL

Mint is a shade-loving, moisture-requiring plant.
It grows in rich, moist soil and, with the aid of
its roots, can be rampant in the garden.

In the kitchen and elsewhere, mint is widely
used. Food, cosmetics and aromatherapy all
make use of this herb. It's used in medicines
too, to aid digestion, and as an antiseptic and
a decongestant.

MINT VARIETIES

Black peppermint
Dark green-purple leaves and stems,
with blue flowers in summer. This
variety is also great for the pot.

Ginger mint
A pretty spicy-scented, variegated-
leaved variety. This variety has pink
flowers through summer.

There are hundreds of varieties of mint. All differ slightly in their growth habit but markedly in their scent and taste. From peppermint, with its strong, minty flavor, to lemon mint, spicy Moroccan mint, pineapple mint and even chocolate mint — all give an extra dimension to the minty flavor.

Zone 4–9.

Where to grow All mints are easy to grow in the garden, but need to be restrained. If left on their own, they'll quickly spread through the soil, taking over large swatches of garden and reach into the smallest of cracks.

Often mint is planted into a sunken large pot or container, with the lip of the container ½ inch (1 cm) or so above the soil level. This helps to keep the mint in check. Alternatively, just grow in a raised pot.

If you are going to plant mint directly into the soil, then at least every couple of years you'll need to dig it out and replant it where it came from!

Types and varieties Mint is a perennial, and if cut down at the end of fall, it will come back again in the spring with fresh leaves. There are around 30 species of mint, and many, many named varieties, often with unusual tastes. It's a good idea to have a variety growing in your garden with a good, plain minty flavor, which is great for making tea and using in food. It's also a nice idea to select a couple of more unusual-smelling and -tasting varieties (see below). It's easiest to buy mint as plants from plant stores or specialist herb suppliers — this way you'll be sure of getting the variety you want.

Pests and diseases Trouble-free but can suffer from rust. Just cut down any affected foliage. Water well and feed with a fertilizer to encourage new shoots.

Harvesting and storage Cut fresh stems of mint when required. Mint can be dried, or chopped finely then frozen for use throughout winter when there is little available in the garden.

In the kitchen Drop whole stems into boiling water for refreshing mint tea. Use to make traditional mint sauce to go with lamb, or try in Greek, Moroccan and Middle Eastern dishes.

Chocolate mint
Incredible chocolate flavors are released when this variety is crushed. Also a stunning plant in the garden.

Lemon mint
A useful aromatic plant. When crushed the leaves release a wonderful lemon scent.

Peppermint
Another good culinary choice, the fresh taste of peppermint is also wonderful used fresh in tea.

Spearmint
Has the strongest minty flavor. Spearmint extract is used in all sorts of products from toothpaste to drinks.

CALENDAR

EARLY SPRING
Order young plants from a specialist nursery, or buy plants from a plant store.

MID-SPRING
Plant out in the garden, giving each plant plenty of room — at least 12 inches (30 cm) square. Alternatively, plant in a large container and sink into the ground. Use multipurpose potting mix with a slow-release fertilizer added.

LATE SPRING ONWARD
However you've planted your mint, it prefers rich soil and plenty of moisture. If the weather turns dry, give your plant a good watering. Start to pick stems as they grow. Keep watering and feeding to encourage new growth.

FALL
If your plant is overcrowded, consider digging up, splitting and replanting smaller, thriving sections.

Parsley

This well-used herb is a must for any gardener and cook.

⊙⊙⊙⊙⊙	VALUE FOR MONEY
⊙⊙⊙⊙⊙	MAINTENANCE
⊙⊙⊙⊙⊙	FREEZE/STORE
CROPPING SEASON: ALL YEAR ROUND	

Parsley is probably the most well-used herb in the kitchen — certainly in quantity. It can be used in abundance in all sorts of food, adding flavor and a certain freshness. Parsley is also very easy to grow. It's available in plant stores as young plants, but as you'll probably need a few plants to keep you going for most of the year, it's worth growing this herb from seed. It doesn't grow well in the winter, but it will produce leaves throughout the spring, summer and fall months. If you do want parsley in the winter too, then either growing in the greenhouse, or growing under cloches or floating row covers is the way to go.

Zone 3–9.

Where to grow If you're short of space, parsley will grow happily in a container. It also looks extremely attractive too, and many people grow parsley for its ornamental value — its fresh, green leaves can look attractive in containers mixed with flowers or on the edge of a path or border. But if your aim is to produce a really good supply of leaves for the kitchen, it's best to devote a bit of the herb or vegetable plot to this plant.

Parsley will happily grow in full sun or partial shade. It prefers a good, rich soil and, given the right conditions, can produce large plants. You can keep the plants small, however, by picking leaves regularly through the season. While some advocate chopping the plant right down in one go, parsley will keep growing if you just pick one or two stems at a time.

Types and varieties Parsley can be split into two main groups, based on the leaf shape. Curly-leafed varieties were once the most commonly grown and are thought to

Perfect with fish
Parsley is easy to grow from seed, and is worth making regular sowings to provide for your kitchen all through the year.

stand up well to cold, unfavorable weather. Nowadays though, the flat-leafed parsleys are becoming more popular. Their taste is thought to be a bit stronger, but their texture is less coarse and good enough to be used in salads. Flat-leafed parsley is a common ingredient in many Mediterranean dishes, but it is in fact just as hardy as the curly types.

Within these two groups there are a few varieties — selected for their vigor and resistance to bolting (see Variety selector).

Pests and diseases Parsley is trouble-free.

Harvesting and storage Cut down whole plants about ¾ inch (2 cm) from their base and the plants should regrow.

Alternatively, just pick leaves when required. Parsley is biennial so once flower shoots start to form, either leave to enjoy the flowers or dig up and start again.

If you have lots of parsley it can be picked, chopped and frozen in a zip-lock plastic bag.

In the kitchen Use whole leaves in salads or as a garnish. Chop leaves finely and add to sauces, salads, soups and stews.

CALENDAR

MID-SPRING
Sow seeds in small pots or modular trays. Sow just one or two seeds per pot and cover with a dusting of potting mix.

LATE SPRING
Seeds can be slow to germinate, but once grown, plant out in the garden about 6 inches (15 cm) apart. Alternatively, plant individually in mixed containers.

EARLY SUMMER
Start harvesting leaves.

MIDSUMMER
It's worth making another sowing now, either in pots or direct in the ground, for leaves throughout fall and into spring next year.

LATE SUMMER
Plant out young plants sown last month. Keep all plants, particularly young seedlings, well watered. Keep picking leaves.

FALL
Pick leaves throughout the season.

EARLY WINTER
Cover plants with cloches or floating row covers to keep leaves looking good for picking over winter. Don't pick too much during this time to allow the plant to survive into spring.

PARSLEY VARIETIES

Curly-leaved parsley
Tends to have slightly tougher leaves, and is often used in a kitchen garden as an ornamental edging plant.

Flat-leaved parsley
Flat-leaved varieties tend to have softer leaves and can be just as productive as the curly types.

VARIETY SELECTOR
Curly-leafed parsley
• 'Champion Moss Curled', 'Rosette'.
Flat-leafed parsley
• 'Plain Leaved 2'.

Rosemary

This useful culinary herb makes an elegant, attractive, and aromatic plant to grow in any garden.

○○○○○ VALUE FOR MONEY
○○○○○ MAINTENANCE
○○○○○ FREEZE/STORE
CROPPING SEASON: ALL YEAR ROUND

Pretty flowers
Rosemary is a beautiful plant in its own right, and worthy of a spot or pot in every garden.

The scent of rosemary is enough to make you think of Mediterranean holidays. This shrubby plant is now cultivated almost everywhere and is a useful herb both in the garden and in the kitchen. It's an evergreen, so looks good almost all year with its pine needle-like leaves and pretty blue, white or pink flowers. Despite heralding from the Med, it's pretty tough too. It will survive in most gardens, but can be damaged by long periods of cold weather. It has a habit of flowering not just in the summer, but in winter too, making it a useful plant for pollinating insects such as bees toward the end of fall.

Zone Zone 7 and warmer.

Where to grow Because it's a shrubby perennial, once planted it will happily stay there for many years. Choose a sunny, sheltered spot with well-drained soil. You could plant a single specimen, or grow them into a hedge, by

planting several plants together, 2 feet (60 cm) apart. Others have a prostrate growing habit — perfect for growing over walls or on a gravel path. Usually the plant will reach around 3 ft. 2 in. (1 m) or so in height, but it can be pruned to keep it much smaller.

Types and varieties There are a number of varieties and types of rosemary. All essentially taste similar but their growth habit and flower color vary.

Pests and diseases Rosemary is trouble-free.

Harvesting and storage Rosemary can be picked whenever it's required. The main growing season is spring and summer, and a mass of foliage will be available for harvesting as required during these seasons. A little can be harvested outside this time.

In the kitchen Rosemary combines well with lamb. Whole sprigs can be pushed into roasts and the flavor infused. It also works well with chicken, roast potatoes and sauces. Fresh sprigs can also be added to salad dressings, but be careful as the flavor can sometimes be overpowering.

CALENDAR

MID-SPRING
Buy individual plants from the plant store.

LATE SPRING
Dig over the soil well, add some coarse sand if the soil is heavy, and plant.

EARLY SUMMER
Once the plant has flowered, it can be pruned back into shape. Take cuttings from early to midsummer to propagate new plants.

PROPAGATING ROSEMARY

1 In midsummer, select side shoots that are about 4 inches (10 cm) long. Pull down on these individually, tearing them off the parent stem. These are known as heel cuttings. Remove all the lower leaves and pinch out the tip.

2 Push individual cuttings into small pots filled with gritty potting mix. Water and cover pots with a clear plastic bag and leave somewhere cool and out of direct sun.

VARIETY SELECTOR
Ground-hugging rosemary
• The Prostratus Group grows 12 inches (30 cm) high and spreads along the ground. Usually light blue flowers in summer.
White-flowering rosemary
• *Rosmarinus officinalis var. albiflorus.*
Pink-flowering rosemary
• 'Roseus'.
Blue-flowering rosemary
• *Rosmarinus officinalis.*
Good for hedging
• 'Miss Jessopp's Upright' reaches 6 ft. 5 in. (2 m) in height.

Sage

This pretty Mediterranean herb is popular in the herb garden. Easy to grow, it will look good for most of the year.

ooooo VALUE FOR MONEY
ooooo MAINTENANCE
ooooo FREEZE/STORE
CROPPING SEASON: EARLY SPRING–EARLY WINTER

Aromatic leaves
The slightly furry evergreen leaves of sage make this herb an essential for the winter kitchen garden.

This shrubby plant is often used in Mediterranean cooking. It produces thick, downy leaves that provide a rich flavor when cooked with meat. You don't need much to impart their flavor, so you'll only need a single plant in the garden. Because it's an evergreen perennial, it's easiest to buy plants from the plant store rather than growing from seed.

In the garden, sage is a pretty plant, and grown next to other Mediterranean herbs, such as rosemary and thyme, it will continue to look good throughout the year. Because it's perennial, you'll be able to keep picking leaves all year round too.

Zone 5–9.

Where to grow This plant likes fairly well-drained soil and a sunny spot. It prefers alkaline soil, but would grow in most soils. If your soil is heavy, consider digging in some gravel or coarse sand to improve the drainage.

Plants are well behaved in the garden and don't reach more than 2 feet (60 cm) in height and spread. Place just one or two plants in your perennial herb garden and it will provide you with leaves for years to come.

If the plant becomes straggly, consider taking some cuttings in the summer and propagate your plant to produce new ones for the following year.

Types and varieties The most common sage used in cooking is plain garden sage (*Salvia officinalis*). There are others, particularly with purple or variegated leaves. Try 'Purpurescens' for colorful purple foliage, or 'Tricolor' with leaves in pink, cream and green. One to try in containers is pineapple sage (*Salvia elegans* 'Scarlet Pineapple'). It's not hardy like the other sages, so you'll either have to move it somewhere frost-free during the winter months or start again the following year. It has striking red flowers and pineapple-

scented leaves, but is not necessarily the best for cooking.

Pests and diseases Sage is trouble-free.

Harvesting and storage Pick leaves as you need them. Leaves can be dried but as you should be able to pick leaves for most of the year, it isn't usually necessary. In mild winter areas, you can continue to pick leaves, but covering the plant with a cloche or floating row cover will help to protect the plant and keep the leaves looking good.

In the kitchen Add to meat such as pork or lamb when roasting. It's often used in stuffings or you can add it to oil to impart its flavor.

PROPAGATING SAGE

1 Remove some stems from this year's growth and remove the lower leaves.

2 Insert individual stems into small pots filled with multipurpose potting mix.

3 Water well and cover with a plastic bag. Keep somewhere in good light but out of direct sun.

CALENDAR

EARLY–MID-SPRING
Buy plants from the plant store. You'll need only one, but try some different forms to add color to your garden.

LATE SPRING
Grow on in a pot in a sheltered spot until all threat of frost has passed, then plant in a well-drained, sunny spot in your garden. Sage can also be grown in a container.

EARLY SPRING YEAR 2 ONWARD
Each year in early spring, cut back plants to around 6 inches (15 cm) above the ground to prevent the plant going leggy.

Tarragon

This somewhat leggy perennial herb is an attractive, productive plant for the herb garden.

✿✿✿✿✿ VALUE FOR MONEY
✿✿✿✿✿ MAINTENANCE
✿✿✿✿✿ FREEZE/STORE
CROPPING SEASON: LATE SPRING–EARLY FALL

Tarragon is a pretty plant and a good choice along a path or entrance. It grows fairly tall for a culinary herb, to around 3 feet (90 cm), but its feathery leaves do look attractive. Tarragon is often used to complement fish and chicken, particularly cold dishes. With its faintly aniseed flavor, it works well with delicately flavored foods, and is the main herb used in sauce béarnaise.

Zone 3–8.

Where to grow
Grow tarragon in a warm, dry spot. Go for direct sun if you have it and make sure the soil is well drained. It can be a fussy herb to grow and will die off if the soil remains cold and wet for a long period. It's a slow grower, but does get quite big, so give it plenty of space and this perennial will keep coming back year after year.

Types and varieties
There are just a couple of types to choose from. Russian tarragon is sharp in flavor but disliked by many. French tarragon (*Artemisia dracunculus*) is considered to be far superior with a much more subtle aniseed flavor.

Pests and diseases
Generally trouble-free, but can suffer from rust — reddish spots appearing on the leaves. If this poses a problem, just cut the plants right down to the ground and remove any infected foliage. Water and feed, and the plant should return.

Temperamental tarragon
A tall plant, tarragon can be fussy and won't do well in every garden.

Harvesting and storage
Harvest stems around halfway up the plant throughout the growing season as you need them. Tarragon can be chopped and frozen to be used in winter months.

In the kitchen
Look out for tarragon in recipes using chicken and fish.

DIVIDING TARRAGON PLANTS

1 Once the weather and soil start to warm up, dig up the clump of tarragon with a garden fork.

2 Using another fork, insert both into the middle of the root clump and pull the forks apart. This splits the plant without damaging too much root.

3 Replant the smaller clumps immediately and water in well.

CALENDAR

SPRING
Buy plants from the plant store. Make sure you look for French tarragon and avoid Russian tarragon. Plant in a sunny, well-drained spot. You'll only need one or two plants, but leave plenty of space around them.

SUMMER
Cut leaves as required in the kitchen. If you have plenty, consider freezing some in a zip-lock plastic bag.

FALL
If the plant gets too big after a year or two, consider lifting the plant and splitting it. Sections can be planted up around the garden.

Thyme

This small, shrubby plant is a must for any herb garden. It grows well in a container or window box too.

⦿⦿⦿⦿⦿	VALUE FOR MONEY
⦿⦿⦿⦿⦿	MAINTENANCE
⦿⦿⦿⦿⦿	FREEZE/STORE
CROPPING SEASON: ALL YEAR ROUND	

A variety of varieties
There are lots of varieties of thyme to choose from, and it may be worth selecting a few to grow.

Thyme plants rarely reach higher than 12 inches (30 cm). Many are ground-hugging plants that produce an aromatic carpet of leaves; others are taller and produce short spires of pink or purple flowers. Whichever of the many varieties you go for, thyme is useful in the kitchen too.

Zone 4–9.

Where to grow Like the other Mediterranean herbs, thyme prefers a dry, sunny spot. If the soil isn't well drained, consider digging in some coarse sand, and where the soil is acid, think about adding some garden lime in the spring before planting. Because the plants remain small, thyme grows well in containers too, as well as in small crevices in walls or in cracks in paving. A bit like lavender, thyme plants don't last too long, becoming straggly and leafless after a few years:

replace plants when they get to this stage. Plants are best bought at the plant store or by mail order. They're tricky to grow from seed but it is possible if you want a lot of plants. To make more of your plants, you can propagate thyme from cuttings in early summer.

Types and varieties There are hundreds of varieties of thyme. The most common culinary herb is common thyme (*Thymus vulgaris*). This is the one you're likely to find if you want to grow thyme from seed. There are plenty of other thymes as well, often varying in habit, flower color and flavor.

Pests and diseases Trouble-free.

CALENDAR

SPRING

Prepare the soil in spring by digging over and adding coarse sand to improve drainage. Buy plants from the plant store, and plant out in the garden. Varieties vary in height and spread, so consider this when planting.

SUMMER

Leaves can be picked throughout the season. Once the plant has finished flowering, trim it back to neaten. Cuttings can be taken in late summer to propagate plants for next year.

Harvesting and storage In theory, this evergreen plant can be picked all year, but during winter the plant becomes very straggly. Cut whole stems and either pull off leaves to use, or throw in whole stems.

In the kitchen Whole stems can be used in stocks and when roasting meat and potatoes. Remove the leaves from the stems and chop finely to add directly to sauces or stuffings.

GROWING COMMON THYME FROM SEED

1 Sow seed in mid-spring in multipurpose potting mix in small pots.

2 Place the pots in a propagator and ensure the temperature remains fairly constant and above 59°F (15°C).

VARIETY SELECTOR

- *Thymus vulgaris*: a good choice if you're growing from seed and want plenty of plants.
- 'Archers Gold': a ground-hugging variety, which produces golden leaves and has a mild flavor.
- **Lemon thyme**: reaching up to 12 inches (30 cm) in height, this lemon-scented thyme produces pink flowers in the summer.
- **Caraway thyme**: reaches just a few inches in height. Produces dark green leaves with a smell of caraway. Good with meat.

FRUIT CROPS

Fruit can be even easier to grow than vegetables. Just an annual prune and a mulch of compost and your fruit crops will reward you for years to come. Berries require little space and can be grown in a pot if necessary, while some tree fruit reach much loftier proportions suitable only for larger gardens. Select your varieties carefully for both suitability to your garden and your palate — once they're planted, you'll have to keep harvesting, year after year.

TREE FRUIT

The first fruits worth considering for a place in your garden are tree fruits. While some varieties and rootstocks need to be planted in open ground and are liable to cast shade, others can be grown alongside paths or even in containers.

Apples, pears, plums and other tree fruit are incredibly rewarding to have in your garden and are a simple way of growing food.

Apple

Whatever size garden you have, there'll be an apple tree that looks good and produces delicious fruit.

⬤⬤⬤⬤⬤	VALUE FOR MONEY
⬤⬤⬤⬤⬤	MAINTENANCE
⬤⬤⬤⬤⬤	FREEZE/STORE

CROPPING SEASON: LATE SUMMER–MID-FALL

When you think about an apple tree from your childhood it's probably a big one, with a swing hanging off it or branches low enough to climb. Although a tree of this size will certainly be productive, there are smaller apple trees that can bear just as many fruit.

If your garden is big enough, an orchard is the traditional place to grow apples. Set among a wildflower meadow, orchards are havens for wildlife. The blossom provides nectar for bees and other pollinating insects, while the trees themselves provide food and shelter for all manner of invertebrates. And in the winter, the windfall of apples provides food for garden birds.

But even in a small garden, an apple tree can be a useful plant, not just for wildlife but for your garden too. Apples can be trained into all sorts of shapes and, if you get the right rootstock, sizes too. They can be placed along paths, in front gardens, at the back of an ornamental border, against walls and fences, as well as in the productive part of the garden.

Zone 3 to 9.

Where to grow Apples do best in sunny spots, out of any harsh winds. They prefer rich, fertile soil that doesn't easily dry out. Saying this, apples (particularly the culinary types) also do well in semi-shade, and if you improve your soil with plenty of organic matter will survive in most soil types. If the ground is really unsuitable or winters are particularly harsh, you can even grow apples in containers and move them undercover in winter.

The position you have in mind will determine the variety you finally go for when buying a new tree. While some varieties are more vigorous than others, it's the rootstock that will ultimately determine the final size of the tree.

Productive apple trees
Low-maintenance apple trees will supply you with plenty of fruit in the fall, which can be stored through the winter too.

Rootstocks All apple trees are grafted. This means the stem of the selected variety has been grown onto the root of another variety. These rootstocks, as they are known, have specific characteristics that will ultimately determine the vigor and final size of your selected apple variety. Your choice of rootstock can also be decided by the ➔

PLANTING A BARE-ROOT APPLE TREE

1 Clear the area around where you are going to plant the tree, removing any perennial weeds. Dig a good-sized plant hole (much larger than the roots), and ensure the tree goes in at the same depth as it has been originally grown.

2 Drive a stake vertically into the ground. This will support the tree as it grows.

3 Spread the roots of the bare-rooted tree out well over a low mound and push back the original soil.

4 Use a tree tie to ensure the tree remains secured to the stake, and if rabbits are a problem, consider adding a trunk protector, which wraps around the base of the stem, preventing rabbits and other pests from nibbling at the bark.

5 Fill the planting hole in with the original soil and add a sprinkling of a general-purpose fertilizer on top of the soil. If you are planting by a wall, ensure the tree isn't too close to it. Aim to plant it about 10–14 inches (25–35 cm) away from the foot of the wall.

6 The tree will need regular watering in its first year. Give it a watering can-full every week during the spring and summer. If it's really hot, a couple of times a week will be necessary. In subsequent springs, ensure the base of the tree is well mulched. Add a sprinkling of fertilizer and loosen the tree tie as the trunk widens.

quality of the site you have in mind. More vigorous rootstocks will do better on poor soils than a dwarfing rootstock, for example.

There are around six main rootstocks you can choose from. Sometimes you won't get a choice of rootstock, but if you go to a specialist fruit nursery, the selection of combinations of rootstock and varieties will be much greater. Here are a few listed:

M27 This is an extremely dwarfing rootstock with plants reaching from 5–5 ft. 9 in. (1.5–1.8 m). Needs good soil and can also be grown in a container.

M9 This is known as very dwarfing, with a mature height of 7 ft. 8 in.–9 ft. 8 in. (2.4–3 m). Needs good soil and is useful for training into small cordons and espaliers.

M26 This dwarfing rootstock will create a tree from 9 ft. 8 in.–11 ft. 4 in. (3–3.5 m). Needs good soil. You should use this rootstock for small trees, as well as cordons and espaliers.

MM106 This semi-dwarfing rootstock produces a tree from 13–18 ft. (4–5.5 m). A good choice for a medium-sized garden, and can be used on poorer soils for cordons and espaliers.

MM25 Known as a vigorous rootstock, the mature height will reach from 13–16 ft. 4 in. (4–5.5 m). A good choice if you want a larger tree or if you want to train it into more elaborate shapes. A good choice for poor soil.

M2, MM111 These very vigorous rootstocks can produce trees up to 29 ft. 5 in. (9 m) in height and should be used only for orchards.

Types and varieties Once you've worked out the ultimate size of the tree you want, you'll need to decide what sort of apples you'd like in your garden.

Apple trees need at least one other apple tree nearby to pollinate the fruit. This can be a crabapple or other edible apple. If your garden is small, your neighbors' apple trees may also help.

Apples can be separated into dessert apples (for eating fresh) and culinary/cooking apples (for cooking). While dessert apples are often crunchy, sweet and juicy, culinary apples have a much sharper taste and turn readily into a purée. Additionally, apples start to ripen in midsummer, with early varieties being ready to be picked first. Later-ripening varieties will be ready as late as mid-fall, and often these store much better over the winter months too.

Tree forms and growing methods

Bush and standard The most common shape of apple tree grown in gardens is a bush type or standard. This basically means having a stem or trunk of anything from 2–6 ft. 5 in. (60 cm–2 m). The top part of the tree is pruned in the winter to produce a compact round or goblet shape.

The other tree shapes are used where space is short. There are a number of shapes you can attempt.

Cordon The most common shape is the cordon. It is usually grown at an angle of around 45 degrees, against a wall or fence. Growing at an angle allows you to get a longer trunk for a given height, and so maximizes your crop. Because the side branches are kept very short, you can plant trees close together — up to 2 feet (60 cm) apart.

Espalier Another common shape is the espalier. This is also commonly grown against a wall or fence, where the longer side branches are trained in a two-dimensional form, often horizontally along the wall.

Step-over The other type of espalier is a step-over, where a single stem is trained horizontally as low as 6 inches (15 cm) to allow you to step over it — perfect for edging a path.

Pests and diseases and other problems When apples grow well, they grow in abundance. However, they do suffer from their fair share of ➡

TREE FORMS AND GROWING METHODS
(FOR PRUNING AND TRAINING FRUIT TREES SEE PAGES 206–209)

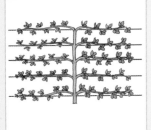

Bush or standard
The most common apple-tree shape with the highest yield, this form should be pruned in winter to maintain its round shape.

Cordon
A compact form useful for small spaces. Cordons are grown at an angle of 45 degrees. Regular pruning is essential.

Espalier
An attractive compact form, the high-yielding espalier works well grown against boundary walls or fences.

Step-over
A step-over is a single-armed espalier, and is useful for when space is limited. They are pruned in the same way as espaliers.

problems. This shouldn't put you off growing apples though, but there are some things to watch out for.

Sometimes trees underperform, simply because they're short of food. This is especially true if they're growing in the lawn or meadow. Adding around 3½ ounces per square yard (100 g per sq m) of general-purpose fertilizer each spring, applying a mulch, and removing a circle of grass 3 ft. 2 in. (1 m) around the base of the tree will all help. If fruit are small or you are only getting fruit every other year, you need to remove some fruit in the spring. This thinning out of fruit will help the fruit that are left to grow on and ripen. The tree should also have enough energy to repeat fruiting the following year.

Caterpillars can damage the leaves of apple trees but most are not a problem. Codling

Apple orchard
It's unlikely you'll be growing trees on a commercial scale — just one or two trees, well-spaced in your garden, should be plenty.

REJUVENATING A NEGLECTED APPLE TREE

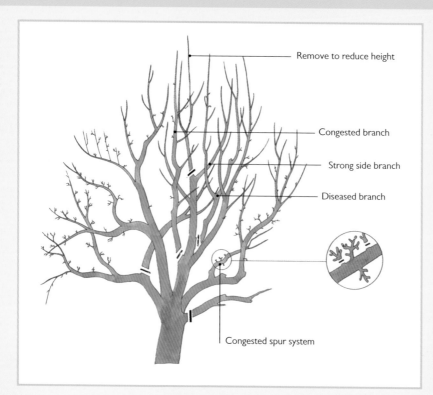

Remove to reduce height

Congested branch

Strong side branch

Diseased branch

Congested spur system

You can encourage a neglected apple tree to crop well again and improve the fruit quality by pruning. Renovation work should be carried out during the dormant season.

1 Cut out any diseased, split or otherwise damaged branches. Cut well back into healthy wood, or remove the branch completely if badly affected.

2 If the tree is very congested, cut out some branches to let in more light, especially in the center of the tree. Remove crossing or badly placed branches, cutting them right back to the point of origin.

3 If the tree is too tall, cut back the tallest branches to strong side branches.

4 Thin out the spurs drastically (see page 207). It may be necessary to remove some entirely, cutting them flush with the stem. Avoid leaving clusters of spurs closer than 9 inches (23 cm) apart.

5 Clean up any major pruning wounds and seal with a specialist wound paint, available from plant stores.

moths, however, are. You can get traps that can be hung in the trees in spring to catch them or spray them with kaolin. Apple maggot can also be controlled through the use of traps — hang them in the trees five weeks after the trees bloom.

Powdery mildew can also be a problem. Make sure the tree has been pruned appropriately, and ensure that it isn't suffering from a lack of water. Scab — where the fruits are damaged — is caused by a fungus. Again, the best advice is to try to keep the tree healthy through regular pruning, mulching and watering where necessary, and clear away fallen leaves and fruit in the fall.

Trees can also be affected by plum curculio. If this insect strikes, spray with kaolin from just before bloom to six weeks after bloom.

Apples can also be affected by diseases, such as fireblight, which is controlled by pruning and destroying the diseased branches or sourcing resistant varieties. Cedar apple rust can also be a problem, but resistant varieties are available.

Harvesting and storage As apples can ripen any time between midsummer and late fall, it's a good idea to know what variety you have. However, once apples start dropping to the ground, you know it's time to start picking. It's a good idea to pick over a number of weeks, harvesting the most ripe fruit first. The fruit should be stored somewhere cool, dark, and if possible, slightly damp. A cellar, cool shed or garage would be fine. Store on trays and check over fruit regularly, removing any that start to rot. Those harvested later in the season generally store for longer.

In the kitchen Ripe fruit can be eaten straight off the tree — at least those varieties that are sufficiently sweet. Culinary varieties tend to be sharper in flavor, and whether you're making an applesauce to go with your Sunday roast pork, or creating an apple pie or crumble, adding sugar is a necessity.

Storing apples
Apples can be stored in boxes in a cool dark place, but preferably not piled up, since one rotten apple will spoil the whole box.

VARIETY SELECTOR

Dessert apples

• **'Golden Delicious'**: heavy cropping, stores well.

• **'Macoun'**: soft flesh, tart flavor.

• **'Honeycrisp'**: exceptionally crisp with a juicy flavor.

• **'Liberty'**: scab-resistant variety.

Culinary (cooking) apples

• **'Cortland'**: sweet flavor; browns slowly when cut.

CALENDAR

EARLY SPRING
A good time to plant your apple trees. Plant at least two trees to ensure good pollination.

MID-SPRING
Make sure your trees are well mulched and fed with fertilizer.

LATE SPRING
Hang up your codling moth traps.

EARLY SUMMER
Ensure all perennial weeds have been removed and are not growing back. Thin out the number of fruit.

MIDSUMMER
Ensure your tree doesn't go short of water.

LATE SUMMER
Trees grown in a restricted form, such as cordons and espaliers, need to be pruned back now.

EARLY FALL
Start to pick fruit as they ripen.

MID-FALL
Clear up fallen fruit and diseased leaves.

LATE FALL
Finish harvesting the fruit.

WINTER
Prune all your trees now. Go for an open goblet shape for trees, or cut back to keep the original shape of espaliers and cordons, ensuring you don't cut off the larger buds likely to turn into flowers.

Pear

Delicious pears taste good both cooked and ripened off the tree.

✪✪✪✪✪	VALUE FOR MONEY
✪✪✪✪✪	MAINTENANCE
✪✪✪✪✪	FREEZE/STORE

CROPPING SEASON: LATE SUMMER–MID-FALL

Ripe pears
The heavy cropping and juicy, sweet texture of pears means it's worth making space in any fruit garden.

Pear trees are renowned for being slow to fruit. And it's true that a newly planted tree will take a couple of years to really start to bear fruit. However, if you've ever been rewarded with moving into a new house and finding a pear tree in the garden, you'll know that every garden should have one.

Pears can be grown like apples, either as standard trees, often shaped into an open goblet shape, or trained as cordons or espaliers.

Because pears are a bit more fussy about the weather and prefer warmer conditions, particularly early in the season, training them against a sunny wall or fence is ideal. That way, they take up little room. Just an annual prune and a little care and attention through the season, and you'll have a productive tree for many years to come.

Zone 4 to 9.

VARIETY SELECTOR

- **'Barlett':** sweet musky flesh, grainy texture.
- **'Comice':** largest and sweetest variety, known as "Queen of the Pears."
- **'Seckel':** delicate flavor, smallish fruit.
- **'Highland':** melting, juicy flesh, smooth texture.
- **'Aurora':** bright yellow and russet, sweet flavor.

Where to grow Pear blossom comes out in early spring, and needs pollinating and protecting from frosts. In cooler areas, it's safest to grow pears against a wall or fence. This way, the flowers and fruit are provided with some protection against potential harsh weather. In warmer areas, growing in an open garden will allow you to grow a large tree.

Pears are fairly unfussy when it comes to soil, so long as it's not very chalky or overly wet. It's worth mulching your soil with well-rotted compost each year, but apart from that, and annual pruning, they need little other care.

Pears, like apples, are grafted onto rootstocks. This ensures they grow to a specified size and helps them be vigorous enough to produce plenty of fruit. Once you've selected a spot for your pear tree, selecting your rootstock is crucial to making sure it fits into its allotted space.

Rootstocks Most pears are sold on rootstocks from quince trees. They're named either Quince A or Quince C. Quince C produces a smaller tree of around 9 ft. 8 in. (3 m) and should be used where you want to keep a tree small. Quince A can produce a tree of 13 feet (4 m) or more — ideal if you want a large tree, or if your soil is very poor. When it comes to espaliers, cordons and step-overs, you won't have a choice: the supplier will use the most appropriate rootstock. They are also sold on one of a series of OX×F rootstocks of various sizes.

Types and varieties Most pears need another tree in the vicinity to cross-pollinate with, and these should flower at the same time. A few varieties, such as 'Magness', do not produce good pollen. Some varieties, such as 'Bartlett' and 'Seckel' cannot cross-pollinate.

Growing methods and pruning

The size of tree you wish to grow and the shape you train it into will all depend on your garden and the space you have within it. Pears, on the whole, can be trained exactly the same way as apples, as either stand-alone trees or as cordons or espaliers, usually trained against a fence or wall (see page 141).

Once grown into the desired shape, the pear tree will need regular pruning (see pages 206–209). Over-grown trees can be cut down to size too. Here, the best time to prune is in mid-winter.

Pests, diseases and other
problems One problem with pear trees can be a lack of fruit. This is often caused by a cold spring affecting the blossom. If frosts are predicted when in bloom, try covering with a floating row cover during the night, making sure you remove it in the morning.

Fruit can often be affected by scab (where black spots appear on the fruit). The only treatment is to rake up affected leaves and fruit and burn them, as well as ensuring your tree is well pruned, with any cracked or damaged shoots cut out. Fireblight is a disease that affects whole branches, where they can turn black and appear to be burned. The best option is to cut out diseased branches well below where they have been affected.

Birds and wasps can also damage fruit, but there isn't much you can do about it, apart from drape a floating row cover over the tree.

Harvesting and storage The best time to pick pears is just before they ripen — that way they'll store for longer. It can be tricky to know exactly when to pick them, and often the best way is to start picking individual pears and try them. Another way is to twist the stem — if the pear comes off easily, it's ready.

Pears are best stored at around 41°F (5°C) in a tray, laid out separately. Try a cold cellar or garage during winter. Most pears don't keep too well, so look to eat them within a couple of months.

In the kitchen Fresh pears picked from the garden often don't even make it into the kitchen, but if they do, there are plenty of recipes that use pears. Poaching pears in wine is a classic way of cooking them. Otherwise, use fresh in salads. They also work particularly well with strong cheese.

REJUVENATING AN OLD PEAR TREE

A very old pear tree is often best replaced with a new one, but a tree that has simply been neglected can often be rejuvenated. Do this during the dormant season.

1 If the tree is large, it is a good idea to mark the branches to be removed with chalk or string, then stand back to check that you've picked the right ones. If the tree is large or complex, remove dead or diseased wood before continuing, so that you can assess the remaining branches more clearly.

2 Next remove crossing and badly placed branches. Where there is a choice, retain the branch with the most or the fattest buds.

3 Start to shape the tree, aiming for a wine-glass outline, removing branches less than 24 inches (60 cm) apart if this will not spoil the shape. Again, where there is a choice retain the one with the most or fattest buds.

4 If height is a problem, cut the central branch back to an outward-pointing side branch. If the tree is large you must remove big branches with care. A tree more than 15 feet (4.5 m) high should be tackled by a qualified tree surgeon.

5 Thin the fruit spurs as described for rejuvenating neglected apples (see page 142).

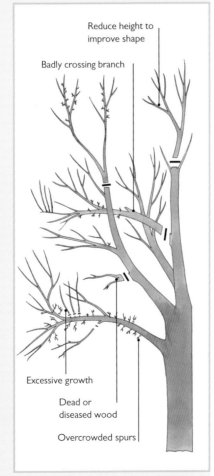

Reduce height to improve shape

Badly crossing branch

Excessive growth

Dead or diseased wood

Overcrowded spurs

(see page 142)

CALENDAR

EARLY SPRING
Plant your pear tree now. Use a stake and tree tie to keep it in place. You may need to plant more than one for good pollination. Make sure your trees are given an annual sprinkling of fertilizer and are well mulched with homemade compost.

MID-SPRING
If blossom comes early and frosts are forecast, be ready with a floating row cover to protect the flower buds. If you are growing it against a wall, ensure the system of wires is in place for training.

LATE SPRING
Make sure your young tree doesn't go short of water.

EARLY SUMMER
Thin out the numbers of fruit if the tree is heavily laden to one to two per cluster, as shown at right.

MIDSUMMER
Keep watering in the first couple of years.

LATE SUMMER
Trees grown in a restricted form, such as cordons and espaliers, need to be pruned back now.

EARLY FALL
Start to pick fruit as they ripen.

MID-FALL
Clear up fallen fruit and diseased leaves.

LATE FALL
Finish harvesting your fruit.

WINTER
Prune your pear tree. Remove crossing, diseased and damaged branches. Cut back long shoots but keep the short fruiting spurs that produce the flowering buds.

Plum, Gage and Damson

For a cooler climate, plums are one of the most reliable fruit, and their taste can rival even the sweetest peaches and cherries.

⬤⬤⬤⬤⬤ VALUE FOR MONEY
⬤⬤⬤⬤⬤ MAINTENANCE
⬤⬤⬤⬤⬤ FREEZE/STORE
CROPPING SEASON: MIDSUMMER–MID-FALL

If you want to eat tasty plums, gages and damsons, you have little choice but to grow your own. Grocery-store plums are usually restricted to tough-skinned varieties with an insipid watery flavor. But the juicy, sweet flavors of Victoria plums and greengages are something worth coveting. They're not the easiest tree fruit to grow, however. Late frosts can seriously affect their crop. Pests and diseases can be a problem too, and while they don't take very much pruning, it takes only a couple of years for a tree to get out of hand. Prune conservatively each year, mulch and feed well, and a tree should reward you with fruits through the midsummer and fall.

Zone 4 to 10, depending on varieties.

Where to grow As plums come into flower early, you'll need to make sure they're sited where they can be protected from late frosts. If your garden does suffer from late frosts, consider growing a plum tree against a west- or south-facing wall, so that you can throw a floating row cover over the tree to protect the flowers when frost is forecast.

They like good, rich soil that's well drained, but will do fine on heavier or lighter soils, which are worth improving with homemade compost each spring. At this time, also sprinkle a handful of general-purpose fertilizer around the base of the tree.

Planting and pruning Plums are best planted during the dormant season. You'll have a good choice from the plant store, but there's a better choice of varieties and sizes from a specialist nursery.

It's not possible to grow plums as cordons, but they can be trained against a wall as a fan (see page 141). Alternatively, site in a sunny open position in the garden for a larger tree.

Juicy fruit
Often untidy and unattractive trees for much of the year, plum trees are worthy of a space for their juicy fruit alone.

Once grown into the desired shape, the plum tree will need regular pruning (see pages 206–209).

Rootstocks

Plum trees, like other tree fruit, come grafted onto rootstocks to determine the size of tree.
Pixy The smallest rootstock, creating a tree up to 9 ft. 8 in. (3 m) in height. Starts cropping after three to four years.
St Julien A A slightly larger tree of up to 16 feet (5 m) will be produced with this rootstock. A good choice for poor soils, or for a large fan against a wall.

Types and varieties There are three main types of plum. European plums in general produce high-quality, uniform fruit, and will grow in mid-range climate zones. Oriental plums, which were brought to the United States from China via Japan, are juicier than European plums, although their flesh is not quite as sweet. American hybrids will produce tasty red or yellow fruits in a wider climate range than European or Oriental plums.

Gages are dessert plums, but their fruit are smaller and usually green or yellow. On the whole, gages are a slightly trickier tree to succeed with.

PLANTING A CONTAINER-GROWN PLUM TREE

1 Dig a planting hole that is larger than the rootball of the tree.

2 Plant the tree, and using a tree stake, tie in the tree to prevent it swaying in the wind. Mulch with homemade compost.

If your climate is inclement, think about choosing a damson. These fruits are perfect for making jam and are generally tougher than plums, surviving cold weather and resisting diseases.

Pests, diseases and other problems

Plums have a lot going for them taste-wise, but they do suffer from plenty of problems too.

Brown rot is a fungal disease that can attack plum trees. If your trees are hit, remove all affected fruit and twigs. Keep the area under the trees clean and tidy to limit the spread of the disease.

Trees can also be affected by plum curculio. If this insect attacks your fruit, spray with kaolin from just before bloom to six weeks after bloom.

One common problem with plums is a total lack of fruit. This is usually caused by late frosts damaging the flowers, causing them to drop off. If frosts are forecast when the tree is in flower, you'll need to try to cover as much of the tree as possible with a floating row cover to offer some protection.

Branches can sometimes become heavily laden with fruit, which causes them to snap. Try supporting heavy branches with a stake or other support. Alternatively, thin out the fruits to one every ¾ inch (2 cm).

Harvesting and storage

Plums, gages and damsons will crop, depending on the variety, any time between summer and fall.

Give the fruits a squeeze and when soft to the touch, they'll be ripe. Taste one or two before picking any more.

Some fruits, such as damsons, will crop later, and while they may still have an acidic flavor, they will be fine for making jams or chutneys.

In the kitchen Plums are the ideal late summer fruit. Picked straight off the tree, they're tasty and sweet. They can be used in desserts and pies too.

Damsons make excellent jam and are a great choice when making chutney. Here the rich, sweet flavors develop over time with the chutney tasting great after storing for at least six months.

VARIETY SELECTOR

Plum

- **'Stanley'**: exceptionally heavy cropping, purple-blue fruit.
- **'Shiro'**: yellow plum; excellent flavor.
- **'Burbank'**: red mottled-yellow skin, good flavor.

Gage

- **'Green Gage'**: best gage you can buy, small yellow-green fruit.

Damson

- **'Prune'**: good flavor, small fruit.

CALENDAR

EARLY SPRING

YEAR 1
Use a tree stake and tie in the tree to prevent it swaying in the wind. Mulch with homemade compost.

YEAR 2 ONWARD
Protect early blossom with a floating row cover if frost is forecast.

MID-SPRING

YEAR 1
Prune the tree in the first year in early spring. Cut back the leading shoot and all side shoots.

YEAR 2 ONWARD
Add a couple of handfuls of balanced fertilizer and a few bucket loads of homemade compost.

LATE SPRING

Carry out pruning of young trees now to create the desired shape.

Thin out the numbers of fruit if the tree is heavily laden.

MIDSUMMER

Ensure your tree doesn't go short of water. This is the time to prune older trees. Don't prune any later than this.

You may have to support the very heavily laden branches with a wooden stake to prevent them breaking off.

MID-FALL

Clear up fallen fruit and diseased leaves.

Juicy cherries
Sweet cherries can turn into huge trees, but if you're not careful birds will steal the lot.

Sweet cherry

If you love the taste of cherries, there is nothing better than being able to grow and pick your own.

✪✪✪✪✪	VALUE FOR MONEY
✪✪✪✪✪	MAINTENANCE
✪✪✪✪✪	FREEZE/STORE

CROPPING SEASON: MIDSUMMER–EARLY FALL

Sweet cherries deserve to be more widely grown. Their sensational flavor is second to none when picked fresh from the garden. However, they're renowned for being tricky to grow, and not without reason. They tend to grow into large, unwieldy trees and they're fussy about their growing conditions, requiring a warm spot and good weather conditions from early spring. However, there are now smaller-growing varieties that are available, and these allow you, where necessary, to protect the trees from late frosts as well as from birds, which have a habit of pinching all the best fruit.

Zone 5 to 9.

PRUNING AN ESTABLISHED SWEET CHERRY FAN

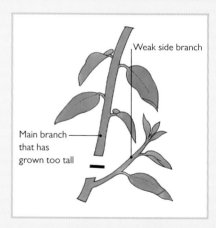

Weak side branch

Main branch that has grown too tall

1 Prune established fan-trained sweet cherries in summer to restrict the amount of leafy growth and encourage the formation of fruit buds for the next year. Remove the growing tips of new shoots when they have made five or six leaves (cut out completely any shoots growing directly toward the wall).

2 Shorten these same shoots to three buds in early fall. Remove any dead wood, and thin very congested spurs (remains of old shoots) at the same time.

3 Very tall shoots at the top of the fan can be cut back to a weaker side branch to reduce the size. Other strong upright shoots can be reduced in vigor by tying them down toward the horizontal.

Where to grow Sweet cherries require a sunny spot. They also need to be sheltered from strong winds and in a place where seasonal frost is least likely. Try growing against a sunny south- or south-west facing wall.

The most widely available cherries are grafted onto the 'Mahaleb' or 'Mazzard' rootstocks. This can produce a free-standing tree of over 16 feet (5 m) tall, too big for many gardens. There are now a couple of alternative rootstocks, such as 'Gisela', which produces trees around 6 ft. 5 in.–9 ft. 8 in. (2–3 m) high.

All cherries are best planted during the dormant season. Choose a fairly well-drained spot, and if necessary improve with some homemade compost or similar organic matter. Sweet cherries are prolific croppers, so each spring you should mulch the tree with a 2-inch (5-cm) layer of organic matter as well as a good handful of general-purpose fertilizer.

Types and varieties Unlike tart cherries, many sweet cherry varieties need pollinating by another cherry. To make things more complicated, some cherries are incompatible with others. For an easy life, it's safest to choose one of the few self-pollinating varieties. This way, you'll only need a single tree.

Pruning and training Trees can be pruned into a fan (see opposite and page 209) or allowed to grow into a tree. Sweet cherries fruit on old wood, so unlike tart cherries, it's a good idea to do as little pruning as possible once you've created the shape you want. Take off any crossing branches and any that look diseased or weak in the summer.

Pests and diseases The worst problem to affect cherries is birds eating them. This is frustrating, as you see the fruits ripening, only for them to disappear overnight! By keeping the tree small you will be able to drape a floating row cover over it during this time.

Fruit can also crack and sometimes fall off the tree before it is ripe. These problems are related to the weather, and there is little you can do. Some varieties are more affected than others. 'Lapins' is a good choice for cracking resistance.

Other diseases include brown rot (see page 147) and cherry leaf spot. Varieties resistant to cherry leaf spot are available, but if your trees suffer from either disease, clean up old leaves and fruit under the trees.

Harvesting and storage Sweet cherry trees can be more prolific than tart cherries, mainly because of their larger size. In a good year you can get as much as 100 lb (45 kg) from a tree. You can freeze cherries after being cleaned, but the best option is to eat them fresh.

In the kitchen Eating as a fresh fruit is the best way to appreciate this delicious crop.

CALENDAR

EARLY SPRING
Dig over the soil well and plant your tree. Use a tree stake and tie in the tree to prevent it swaying in the wind. Mulch with plenty of homemade compost. You may need to plant more than one tree, depending on the variety, to ensure good pollination. Mulch an established tree well and add a good few handfuls of general-purpose fertilizer.

MID-SPRING
If frost is still forecast, you may need to protect flowers from frost with a floating row cover. Now is a good time to prune your young tree.

LATE SPRING
Water the tree regularly in the first couple of years, and if the weather is dry thereafter.

EARLY SUMMER
Protect developing fruit from birds. Pick over the tree for ripe fruits when they're ready.

MIDSUMMER
Ensure your tree doesn't go short of water.

PRUNING A SWEET CHERRY BUSH

If bush cherries are not pruned they quickly become tall with few branches near the ground.

Once a bush form starts to fruit, reduce the number of main branches to seven or eight, to maintain an open tree that is easy to pick. Established trees may need only the top shoots thinned or cut back to reduce height, but prune back hard, old or neglected tree to stimulate new growth.

VARIETY SELECTOR
• **'Lapins' (Cherokee)**: large, dark red, almost black, fruits that crop in early summer.

• **'Compact Stella'**: makes a more compact tree with dark red fruits; self-pollinating.

• **'Stella'**: the most widely grown sweet cherry with dark red fruits; self-pollinating.

Sour succulence
Tart cherries are perfect for cooler climates, since they will tolerate lower temperatures than sweet cherries (see pages 148–149).

Tart cherry

Hardier cousins to the sweet, dessert cherries, tart cherries are great for desserts, pies and jams.

✪✪✪✪✪	VALUE FOR MONEY
✪✪✪✪✪	MAINTENANCE
✪✪✪✪✪	FREEZE/STORE
CROPPING SEASON: LATE SUMMER–EARLY FALL	

If your climate is chilly and unlikely to support sweet cherries, you may have more success with tart cherries. These cherries originate in south-west Asia and have been bred to produce varieties such as 'Morello' and 'Amarelle'. The fruits from these trees are more tart, or sour, in flavor than the sweet cherries (see pages 148–149) and are perfect for cooking with, or even for making drinks such as cherry brandy.

Zone 4 to 8.

Where to grow Tart cherries are actually a more suitable garden tree than sweet cherries. They grow to a diminutive 9 ft. 8-in. (3-m) tall tree. They can be trained as a fan, as well as being left to grow as a standard tree, and they also thrive on all aspects — even growing on a north-facing wall, where little other fruit does well. Nevertheless, they will still thrive in a warm, sheltered spot, and as they flower in mid to late spring, you may need to protect the blossom from frost if it threatens.

Types and varieties Unlike many sweet cherries, all tart cherries are self-fertile. This means they don't need another tree growing nearby to aid pollination.

As with other fruit trees, tart cherries are grafted onto a rootstock of another type. 'Mahaleb', 'Mazzard' and 'Gisele' are the most well-used rootstocks, and will produce a tree of around 9 ft. 8 in. (3 m), and is suitable for all forms, including fans grown against a wall. As far as varieties go, 'Montmorency', 'Northstar' and 'Balaton' are all good choices.

Pruning and training Tart cherries bear on new wood and older wood. Prune lightly each year, heading for a moderate amount of new growth (see pages 206–209).

Tart cherries make eye-catching fans (see below and page 209), which not only look decorative when in fruit, but also look very attractive when covered with blossom in spring, and they generally tolerate the shade cast by the wall or fence. 'Morello' is the variety usually grown, and this will do well even on a north-facing wall or fence, though the fruit will ripen a little later than if placed in a sunnier position.

For a compact tree that fruits early, choose a plant grafted onto 'Colt' rootstock.

Pests and diseases See Sweet cherry on pages 148–149.

Harvesting and storage A decent-sized tree can produce around 30–40 lb (13.5–18 kg) of fruit, and a fan tree somewhat less. Fruit should be picked when they've colored to a dark red and are fully ripe. Try to cut the fruit off with the stalk, rather than pulling it off the stalk. All the fruit won't necessarily be ripe at the same time, so you may need to pick over the tree a few times. Fruit can be frozen or used fresh.

In the kitchen Tart cherries are good only for cooking as they need a decent amount of sugar to sweeten them up. However, they do have an excellent flavor and are worthy additions to summer pies and desserts. For a real bumper crop, consider turning the excess into jam for eating in the winter months.

CALENDAR

EARLY SPRING

Dig over the soil well and plant your tree. Use a tree stake and tie in the tree to prevent it swaying in the wind. Mulch with plenty of homemade compost. Mulch an established tree well and add a good few handfuls of general-purpose fertilizer.

Now is a good time to prune your young tree.

EARLY SUMMER

Protect developing fruit from birds. Pick over your tree for ripe fruits when they're ready.

MIDSUMMER

Ensure your tree doesn't go short of water.

PRUNING AN ESTABLISHED TART CHERRY FAN

Surplus new shoot

New shoots that will replace it

Old shoot that has fruited

1 In late spring or early summer, thin the new shoots to 3–4 inches (7.5–10 cm) apart along the main branches, and tie them in to retain a good fan shape. Where possible, allow a shoot to develop at the base of each sideshoot that is bearing fruit.

2 When the crop has been gathered, cut the shoots that have fruited back to the replacement that was tied in during early summer pruning. If the fan starts to crop mainly around the edges, cut back some of the three- or four-year-old branches in early spring to stimulate new growth.

Correct cherry pruning
A good cut angles down away from the main stem of the tree.

Peach, Nectarine and Apricot

More suited to warmer climes, peaches, nectarines and apricots can also be grown in containers on a sunny patio.

⬤⬤⬤◯◯ VALUE FOR MONEY
⬤⬤⬤◯◯ MAINTENANCE
⬤⬤◯◯◯ FREEZE/STORE
CROPPING SEASON: LATE SUMMER–EARLY FALL

To enjoy peaches, nectarines and apricots at their best it's worth trying to grow your own. Heralding from China, they prefer a warm climate with a long growing season. However, they are fully hardy and actually need a cold period to encourage winter dormancy. But, because they flower very early — as early as late winter — the flowers may need to be protected from frost.

They are often grown as large specimens, trained as a fan against a sunny wall. However, there are now varieties available that are specially bred for growing in a pot. This means that they can be moved to somewhere frost-free very easily, and returned outside when the weather warms up.

Zone 5 to 9.

Where to grow If you have a sunny, south- or west-facing fence or wall, you could try growing a peach, nectarine or apricot tree against it. You'll need to improve the soil with some well-rotted compost. Plant the tree about 10 inches (25 cm) away from the wall, leaning toward it. Add a handful of general-purpose fertilizer in the spring, as well as a mulch of homemade compost.

Like sweet cherries, peaches, nectarines and apricots all flower very early in the season. If you're growing them outside, you may need to cover the emerging flowers with a floating row cover to protect them from frost. Take off the cover in the daytime to encourage pollination.

If growing them in a container, plant in multipurpose or soil-based container potting mix. Mix in a slow-release fertilizer and top this up each spring. Keep the plants well watered and give summer feeds with a tomato fertilizer.

Types and varieties The best choice outside is to grow trees as a fan, which will

Ripe apricots
Succulent apricots, peaches and nectarines are now a reality for most gardeners with many smaller forms suitable for growing in a container.

POLLINATING FLOWERS

1 If pollinating insects are few and far between in early spring, consider hand-pollinating your crop. Use a paintbrush to dab pollen onto the stigma of each flower.

2 When the fruit has set, thin the fruit in early summer to around one every 4–6 inches (10–15 cm).

help you protect them from the worst of the weather (in cold-winter areas) and the disease, peach leaf curl.

Growing in a container

If you want to have a go at growing them in a container, you'll need trees specially grown for this purpose. Make sure they're genetic dwarfs. The varieties recommended on this page should require very little pruning, except for removing dead, diseased or misplaced stems.

Pests and diseases

If you're growing in a greenhouse or sunroom, peaches, nectarines and apricots can suffer from spider mite. The biological control *Phytoseiulus* mite introduced onto the tree will help to control them.

Outside, there can be worse problems. Peach leaf curl is a fungal disease that affects both peaches and nectarines, and to some extent apricots. It causes blistering on the leaves, which become distorted and die. You can spray with a copper-based fungicide, but the best control is to try to keep the tree dry between mid-winter and mid-spring. Often, plastic sheeting is used to cover the tree, which prevents the disease from infecting it. It also helps to protect the tree from frost. But by far the easiest way to avoid this problem is to grow these fruit in a pot, keeping them undercover for this period of time.

Another fungal disease that can affect these plants is brown rot (see page 147).

There are also a number of pests that can affect peaches, nectarines and apricots. The peach tree borer is a moth, whose caterpillars bore into the base of the trunk, leaving small piles of sawdust on the ground. Mature trees withstand this damage better than younger trees. Attacks can be limited by spraying trees with horticultural oil in the fall.

Trees can also be affected by plum curculio (see page 147) and the Oriental fruit moth.

Pruning and training

The best time for pruning is in summer, which avoids problems of silver leaf, a debilitating disease. If the tree is growing up against a wall or fence, follow the advice on pages 206–209 on formative pruning to get the shape you want. Trees fruit on year-old wood. Each year, prune most of the side shoots out, but keep a couple and tie these in through the summer. In late summer, cut out the shoots that have fruited and the ones you tied in will replace them the following year. Late summer is a good time to cut out any dead or diseased wood too.

Harvesting and storage

Harvest peaches, nectarines and apricots when they're ripe, or almost ripe. If the flesh is soft and the fruit easily comes away from the tree, it's ready. Ripe fruit can be eaten straight away; unripe fruit can be laid out to ripen indoors.

In the kitchen

Best used as fresh fruit or can be made into jams or tarts if you have a glut of fruit.

VARIETY SELECTOR

Container

Peaches
• 'Bonanza', 'Empress', 'Garden Gold': all fruit in midsummer.

Nectarines
• 'Nectarina', 'Garden Beauty', 'Garden Delight': good choices for patio nectarines.

Apricot
• 'Floragold': the best.

VARIETY SELECTOR

Outdoors

Peaches
• 'Red Haven', 'Reliance', 'Harrow Beauty', 'Tropic Beauty'.

Nectarines
• 'Diamond Bright', 'Summer Fire', 'September Red'.

Apricots
• 'Perfection', 'Earlicot', 'Jerseycot', 'Goldcot', 'Hargrand'.

CALENDAR

EARLY SPRING

YEAR 1

Dig over the soil well and plant your tree. If you are growing against a wall, attach horizontal wires set at no less than 2-feet (60-cm) intervals. Cut back to start to train as a fan.

YEAR 2 ONWARD

Keep the protection against frost and peach leaf curl that you erected in late fall or winter in place. Mulch the tree well every year and add a good few handfuls of general-purpose fertilizer.

MID-SPRING

Hand-pollinate if necessary. Remove any polythene protection you had in place.

LATE SPRING

Start to tie in growth against the horizontal wires. Thin fruits when they reach the size of a walnut.

EARLY SUMMER

Water the tree in the first couple of years, and if the weather is dry thereafter.

MIDSUMMER

Start to pick fruits as they ripen.

LATE SUMMER

Keep picking fruits. If you need to prune in later years, now is a good time to do it. Trees fruit on stems produced the previous year, so old stems, including ones that have fruited, need to be slowly replaced with new ones to boost your harvest.

WINTER

Erect a rain- and frost-protection cover for your tree. This should be done in late fall in areas with heavy winter snowfall.

Fig

Keep a fig tree contained and it will reward you with sweet, sticky fruit in late summer.

✪✪✪✪✪	VALUE FOR MONEY
✪✪✪✪✪	MAINTENANCE
✪✪✪✪✪	FREEZE/STORE
CROPPING SEASON: LATE SUMMER–EARLY FALL	

The fruits of the fig tree are somehow rather exotic. Despite being grown in the UK since the 16th century, it wasn't until the 18th century that they became popular in walled gardens. Here, the warmth and shelter of the wall encouraged fruit ripening. They are widely grown with little attention all over the Mediterranean where the low rainfall, absence of frosts and long, hot summers encourage two crops of figs a year. In other areas, just one late summer crop is as good as you can hope for.

Plump figs
Figs can be more productive than you think, and kept under control, can make extremely handsome garden plants.

CREATING A PLANTING PIT

1 Dig out a pit and line it with four vertically placed paving slabs to create a square-shaped planting hole. Aim for a hole around 18 inches (45 cm) deep and 2 feet (60 cm) square. The tops of the slabs should stand above the soil surface so roots can't grow over. Fill the bottom 4–6 inches (10–15cm) with broken pots or rubble.

2 Fill the pit with soil and plant the tree in the center, but lean it toward the wall.

3 Cut back the main stem by a third and after attaching wires or canes to the wall, start to encourage the tree into a fan shape.

Zone 8 to 11.

Where to grow Fig trees are extremely vigorous, and will happily produce a plentiful supply of leaves, at the expense of fruit. For that reason, to be successful, it's best to try to contain the roots. Either grow in a container or line the planting pit with impermeable materials (see step by step).

Against a south- or west-facing wall is a good place to site a fig. The foundations of the wall will help to curtail its growth, and the drier conditions suits the plant well. However, during spring and summer the plant may require some additional watering if it is very dry. It's also a good idea to add a handful of general-purpose fertilizer to the base of the tree.

Figs are generally fairly unfussy about the soil they grow in, but they do need it to be well drained. If your soil is heavy, try adding some grit or well-rotted compost.

Types and varieties Unlike other fruit trees, figs haven't been grafted onto more well-behaved rootstocks — hence the need to curtail their growth. However, this makes choosing a variety to grow much easier.

Once you've chosen the variety, you'll need to decide on the shape of tree to buy. Trees are often sold as "bushes" in small pots. These are young trees that will take some time to settle in. Alternatively, you can buy larger forms, in the shape of a fan, for example — perfect for growing against a wall. If you're thinking of growing in a container, select either a young tree, or a larger, multi-stemmed bush.

Pruning and training To create a fan against a wall, you'll need to do most of your pruning in spring after the worst of the frosts are over. By summer, you'll need to start tying in the developing shoots, so the fruit can start to ripen. It's a good idea to pinch out the growing tips in summer too to encourage fruit ripening.

In a container, consider aiming for a multi-stemmed bush. This encourages more fruit to set. A couple of years after planting, prune the tree to ground level. This will encourage lots of shoots to emerge from underground. Removing around a third of them each year will keep encouraging more to be produced and keep the plant small.

Pests and diseases Figs are generally trouble-free. Birds will probably be your worst pest — they have a habit of picking the fruit just before they're ripe. Draping a floating row cover over the tree is your only option.

Harvesting and storage Figs develop on the axils of the leaves in young side shoots. They develop in fall and over winter as small pea-sized fruit. They grow on the following year and start to ripen toward mid to late summer. You'll need to pick figs when they're ripe. You can tell they're ripe as they look heavy, hang downward and often start to split. To appreciate their flavor, eat soon after picking.

In the kitchen Figs are often eaten as fresh fruit, straight from the garden. Alternatively, consider using in salads with mozzarella and Parma ham. If you really have too many, they can be dried — cut in half, sprinkle with a little sugar, and place in a warm oven direct on the rack for a few hours. The dried fruits can be eaten as a snack. You can also turn them into jam.

CALENDAR

LATE SPRING

YEAR 1
Usually bought in a container, fig trees are best bought in late spring when the worst of the winter weather is over. Restrict root growth by creating a planting pit to encourage heavier fruiting.

YEAR 2 ONWARD
Cut back as hard as you like, creating a shape that suits your garden. Cut out crossing, damaged or diseased branches too. Some figs may be set now, but if the season is short they will not ripen.

EARLY SUMMER
Water your tree, especially in the first few years. If you have restricted the roots, they may struggle to find enough water during dry spells, so water when necessary.

MID-LATE SUMMER
Check fruit regularly and pick when ripe. You may need to protect developing fruits from birds.

FALL
Where winters are cold, wrap for protection; bring potted plants to cool, not cold, locations indoors.

EARLY SPRING
YEAR 2 ONWARD
Apply a couple of handfuls of general-purpose fertilizer, plus a good layer of homemade compost.

VARIETY SELECTOR
- 'Brown Turkey': considered to be the most reliable variety. Produces a good crop of purple fruits with sweet, red flesh.
- 'Celeste': small, very sweet fruits.

SOFT FRUITS

Strawberries, raspberries and currants are the taste of summer. New varieties are now extremely high-yielding as well as bursting with flavor. While they're both healthy and nutritious, most soft fruits are also easy to grow and despite being expensive in the supermarket, at home this is one glut you won't mind having to deal with.

Strawberry

The sweet, succulent fruit of the strawberry is synonymous with summer.

✪✪✪✪✪	VALUE FOR MONEY
✪✪✪✪✪	MAINTENANCE
✪✪✪✪○	FREEZE/STORE
CROPPING SEASON: LATE SPRING–MID-FALL	

The strawberry has got to be one of the easiest fruits to grow. These small plants can be fitted into any garden — even window boxes will happily fit a few plants — and their fruits are bright, fragrant and sweetly flavored.

They're perfect for larger fruit gardens too. If you manage to keep the weeds off, a row of strawberry plants will provide pounds of fruit throughout the summer.

The large red strawberries we know today have been bred from the Chilean strawberry and the North American strawberry. A relatively new fruit compared to most, it wasn't until the early 20th century that breeding really took off. Today, however, they're a favorite in both gardens and supermarkets, and there are a wide range of varieties and types to choose from.

Succulent strawberries
A couple of years after planting, your strawberry plants will be rewarding you with pounds of fruit through the summer months.

Strawberry plants don't last that long, however; traditionally they're grown for just five years. At that point you dig out the old plants and start again. Buy certified disease-free plants from a nursery.

Zone 3 to 10.

Where to grow Strawberries are a bit fussy when it comes to soil. They don't like it too wet, or too alkaline, or too sandy. If you don't have perfect loam, the best solution is to add plenty of well-rotted organic matter.

The berries have a tendency to rot off if left on the soil surface too. Traditionally, growers would spread straw underneath the developing fruits to protect them. Nowadays strawberries

Delicate alpine strawberries
Smaller alpine strawberries are intensely flavored, and are also good for dry, shady areas of the garden.

are often grown through plastic sheeting that both keeps the soil warm and weed-free and protects the fruit.

If you don't have a large area to devote to strawberries, they can be added to your vegetable garden as a one- or two-year crop, or even grown in the ornamental garden. The leaves, flowers and small fruit of the alpine strawberry are extremely pretty in themselves and will thrive in a dry, shady spot.

Strawberries can also do well in containers, as long as they're well looked after. Using a large container will cut down on the amount of watering that's required, and in the summer they'll need feeding with a tomato feed to encourage flowering and fruiting. In a window box or hanging basket, go for the alpine strawberry.

Types and varieties Strawberries have been bred to fruit at different times. You'll often see varieties advertised as early, midseason or late varieties. In reality, this can mean picking your fruit from late spring to midsummer. To extend your harvest, ➡

Container strawberries
Strawberries make excellent container plants. Keep them well fed and watered and they'll reward you with an excellent harvest, free from slug and snail damage.

it's a good idea to choose a couple of varieties of different seasons. There are also varieties known as everbearing or day-neutral. These varieties typically fruit all season.

Buy strawberries in late winter or late summer. Often strawberries are sold in bunches of 10 bare-rooted plants — a couple of rows of 10 plants will be plenty for most families where a single plant can produce up to 1 lb (450 g) of fruit.

Pests and diseases Strawberries can suffer from a range of pests and diseases. To keep these at bay, encourage good, strong growth by ensuring the soil is weed-free, fertile and water-retentive.

Aphids can be a problem so you'll need to spray with an organic pesticide. Slugs can feed on the fruit. Use a sprinkling of organic slug pellets to keep them at bay. Vine weevil can eat the roots of plants, particularly those kept in containers or under plastic sheeting. You can use a nematode biological control

if they cause you a real problem. Gray mold can be a problem in wet areas. Thin out the leaves on plants to encourage some air movement and remove affected fruit. Remove runners as they develop, and once cropping is finished it's a good idea to cut down all the old foliage and destroy it. New, clean shoots will soon regrow.

Red stele disease can be a problem with strawberry plants. This fungal disease is most likely to develop in early spring or late fall when the soil is likely to be cold and wet. Resistant varieties are available for this and anthracnose disease, which tends to be limited to warmer climate zones (zone 8 and above).

Harvesting and storage
Strawberries can be picked ripe between spring and fall. Growing a crop in the greenhouse can also extend the harvest. Plants should be picked over at least twice a week. Strawberries can be frozen, but are not anywhere as good as when fresh.

PROPAGATING STRAWBERRIES

1 After a couple of years, your strawberry crop will start to decline. In the summer, plants will produce runners — long stems from the main plant. Select a runner and cut off in order to create the new plant.

2 Along each runner will be small plants developing with their own leaves and the start of some roots. Cut a single plant off and plant into small pots filled with multipurpose potting mix. Water well and leave in a sheltered spot.

3 By fall the plants can be planted out in the garden. Plant strawberry plants every 18 inches (45 cm). Although their crop will be small in the first year, it will increase dramatically by the second year.

'Eros'
A midseason cropper with attractive berries, which have a conical shape and a well-balanced flavor.

VARIETY SELECTOR

New varieties are being bred all the time and released each year. Look out for these new and more established varieties.

Early season

- 'Earliglo', 'Chandler'.

Midseason

- 'Honeoye', 'Red Chief'.

Late season

- 'Jewel', 'Allstar'.

Everbearing

'Tristar', 'Tribute'.

In the kitchen If you sicken of fresh strawberries, either on their own or with a dollop of cream, and you're tired of fruit puddings and pavlovas, excess strawberries can be made into jam, which will give you the taste of summer in the depths of winter.

Pest protection
Keep the birds off your crop with floating row covers, which can either be supported with a series of hoops (see below) or draped right over the plants.

CALENDAR

EARLY SPRING
Pull back the mulch you applied in winter when growth begins.

SPRING
Strawberries are sold through most of the year and can be successfully planted in spring, fall or even early summer. Prepare the soil by digging over well and removing any weeds. Add some well-rotted organic matter. You can lay a row of black plastic sheeting over the soil and bury the edges in the soil using a spade, ensuring the surface is kept tight to avoid puddles collecting. Cut slits in the plastic and plant every 18 inches (45 cm).

After bearing in spring, cut off all the leaves and compost them, thin out the plants to 10 inches (25 cm) apart, mulch with compost and water.

SUMMER
In dry weather, water directly through the planting hole under the plastic. Avoid watering onto the foliage directly as this can encourage diseases to spread. Consider giving a liquid feed to the strawberries, such as a tomato feed, which will encourage more fruit to set.

If you haven't used plastic sheeting, you can apply a mulch around the plants. This can be anything from straw to cardboard, or even "strawberry mats" that you can buy. This helps to keep the fruits dry and stops them rotting as they ripen. Cut off runners and pick fruits as they ripen. If birds are getting to the crop before you, drape over a floating row cover.

FALL
You may still get a few fruits from everbearers.

WINTER
Cover with organic mulch when the ground has frozen to a depth of 1 inch (2.5 cm).

Raspberry

Ripe, sweet raspberries just dropping off the plant are one of the joys of growing food. This plant is one not to be missed.

STAR PLANT
★TASTY CROP★
GREAT FOR JAM

○○○○○ VALUE FOR MONEY
○○○○○ MAINTENANCE
○○○○○ FREEZE/STORE
CROPPING SEASON: EARLY SUMMER–MID-FALL

Long-fruiting raspberry season
With careful selection of a couple of different raspberry varieties, it's possible to have fruit from early summer right into mid-autumn.

Raspberries are one of the most expensive berries to buy in the grocery store. This is because the fruits are a bit tricky to pick and don't transport well. Fortunately, growing your own couldn't be easier, and you'll only need to transport them from the garden to the kitchen.

They crop heavily too — each plant will produce well over 2 lbs (1 kg) of fruit, and as you need only a small amount of space and the plants require little care and attention, they are definitely worth a go.

Zone 3 to 7.

Where to grow Raspberries prefer a slightly acidic soil of between pH 6–6.5. If your soil is more alkaline than this, add sulfur. They don't do particularly well on sandy or clay soil either, but you can improve your soil structure easily with the addition of well-rotted organic matter, such as homemade compost or composted bark, which tends to be a bit on the acid side.

Raspberries prefer a sheltered spot and will crop most heavily in full sun, although they'll thrive in partial shade too.

While fall-fruiting types don't need any support, summer-fruiting types will need a series of stakes and horizontal wires to help keep their canes upright. As raspberries will remain in the same spot for many years, consider creating a special area for your raspberries: they'll need a bed around 3 ft. 2 in. (1 m) wide, but often a double row 6 ft. 5 in. (2 m) apart is better to aid netting and picking.

Unfortunately, raspberries don't do well in a pot, so they're worth growing only if you have some outdoor space.

Types and varieties Raspberries grow on canes, which grow from the base of the plant each year. One job each year will be to

Ripe raspberries
Fruit is ripe when the whole berry
slips off the plant, leaving the core
on the plant.

cut the old canes back, but how and when you do this will depend on the type of raspberry you are growing.

So, before you go any further with raspberries, you'll need to decide which type to grow. There are two main types and many people tend to grow both — this way you can extend the picking season right from early summer into fall.

The first type are known as floricane or summer-fruiting. They fruit on canes produced the previous year. They're a bit tricky to manage as while you're picking fruit off old canes, new canes will be growing, which you need to tie in.

The second type are much easier to look after. They are the primocane or fall-fruiting raspberries. They fruit later in the summer, but fruit on the canes produced earlier in the year.

How to grow The best time to buy raspberry canes is in spring or fall. They'll be sold as bare-rooted plants, usually in bundles of six, 10 or 12. Look for stout canes with tightly closed but healthy-looking buds. The roots should be dense and ➡

PRUNING SUMMER- AND FALL-FRUITING RASPBERRY BUSHES

SUMMER-FRUITING VARIETIES

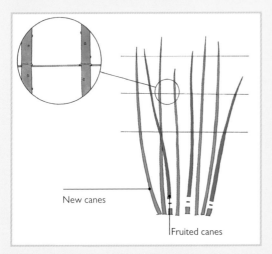

New canes

Fruited canes

Summer-fruiting raspberries carry their fruit on year-old stems. In the dormant season, cut out all those canes that have fruited, then tie in the new canes produced during the summer. If in time the clumps become congested, thin the canes to about 3 inches (7.5 cm) apart.

FALL-FRUITING VARIETIES

Fall-fruiting varieties carry their fruit on the current season's growth, so pruning is extremely simple. Just cut all the canes down to ground level during the dormant season.

'All Gold'
This pale yellow variety of raspberry, 'All Gold', is good but not as productive as 'Autumn Bliss'.

fibrous. Plants will need to be spaced at around 18 inches (45 cm) between canes, so your selected site will determine how many you buy.

Once you've chosen your site and bought your canes, you'll need to get them in the ground.

If you're growing summer-fruiting raspberries, you'll also need to create some support for the canes, and it's best to get this in place before planting (see step by step).

Dig over the soil and add plenty of organic matter. Raspberries don't like to be planted too deeply, and their roots spread just underground, so aim to plant just below the soil surface.

You won't get much of a crop in the first year, but if you prune appropriately and every spring, add a couple of handfuls of a general-purpose fertilizer and a good mulch of garden compost, the plants should last for many years.

SUPPORTING SUMMER-FRUITING RASPBERRIES

1 The easiest support consists of single posts and horizontal wires.

2 Using 7 ft. 8 in. (2.4-m) high posts, drive them into the ground by about 3 feet (60 cm), spaced 9 ft. 8 in. (3 m) apart.

3 Fix galvanized wire horizontally between the posts at 3 feet (90 cm) and 5 feet (1.5 m) high.

Pests, diseases and other problems

Although raspberries are among the easiest perennial fruit to prune, they do have a few enemies.

There are several fungal diseases that affect the canes of raspberries, such as cane spot and spur blight. The easiest way to manage raspberry diseases is to make sure that you cut out the old canes right down to the base each year and destroy them if they are diseased.

Birds can be a real pain too, stealing the fruit as it ripens. If birds are a problem, you can build a structure around your canes so you can drape a floating row cover over it during the fruiting season.

The main insect that targets raspberry canes is the cane borer. The adult beetle lays its eggs near the top of new canes, making them wilt. Remove and destroy any wilted canes as soon as you notice them.

Harvesting and storage

Raspberries can be harvested over a fairly long period, especially if you're growing both types. Fruit will be ready for picking when it's bright red and comes away easily from the plug. Picked berries will last longer if they're not squashed so choose a wide bowl or tray to keep them in — this also allows any bugs and small spiders to escape as you pick.

Once inside, raspberries can easily be frozen. Just bag them up in weighed amounts for jam making later, or lay them on a tray and freeze. If frozen on a tray, they keep their shape as you tip the frozen ones into a bag.

In the kitchen

Raspberries can be used fresh in summer desserts, sprinkled over ice cream or turned into purée. However, at some point during the season it's likely you'll have a glut. Raspberry jam is among the best-tasting of jams and will provide you with a taste of summer right through the winter.

4 Plant in between the posts. As the canes grow, tie them onto the wires. If they grow above the wire, curve them over and tie them in along the top of the wire.

'Glen Ample'
'Glen Ample' is bred in Scotland, can survive tougher weather conditions and crops well through the summer.

CALENDAR

EARLY SPRING
Buy your raspberry canes, improve the soil with organic matter, and plant shallowly.

SPRING/SUMMER
Mulch and add fertilizer each year in the spring. Water the plants in the first couple of years to get them established, especially during dry spells. They shouldn't need too much watering after that. You won't get much of a crop in your first year, but that will soon change. Follow advice for year 1 for the type of raspberry you have, then subsequent years thereafter.

SUMMER-FRUITING RASPBERRIES
YEAR 1
As new canes grow out from the base, tie in new growth to horizontal wires.

YEAR 2
Canes grown last year and tied in will start to fruit. New canes will start to grow, which need to be roughly tied in. At the end of year 2, cut down canes that have fruited to the ground. Spread out new canes along the horizontal wires and tie in.

YEAR 3 ONWARD
Repeat year 2.

FALL-FRUITING RASPBERRIES
SUMMER YEAR 1
Cut down all last year's canes to the base at the beginning of the year. New canes will emerge. There's no need to tie in.

SUMMER YEAR 2
Cut down all last year's canes to the base at the beginning of the year. New canes will emerge. There's no need to tie in. They should start to fruit by late summer.

YEAR 3 ONWARD
Repeat year 2.

Blackberry and hybrid berries

Juicy blackberries
Blackberries can be very productive, and if you don't have wild brambles growing nearby, it's worth having at least one plant in the garden.

You'll only need a single plant to produce enough dark, juicy clusters of fruit for the kitchen.

◕◕◔◔◔ VALUE FOR MONEY
◕◕◕◕◔ MAINTENANCE
◕◕◕◕◔ FREEZE/STORE
CROPPING SEASON: MIDSUMMER–MID-FALL

Blackberries and hybrid berries have the most delicious aroma and wild, juicy flavor, but their popularity in the garden is rather limited. It may be because the plants, on the whole, grow large, with some needing around 13 feet (4 m) of wall or fence space. It also may be because the spines of many are fierce, and pruning a blackberry becomes quite a tricky task. Or it may be because wild blackberries are often to be found growing nearby, giving the gardener free access to a large, wild crop. If, however, you don't have a wild clump of brambles near your home, fortunately there are now smaller, better-behaved varieties of blackberries and hybrid berries that have been bred without spines, perfect for growing up a wall, or even a single post.

Zone 5 to 8.

Where to grow All blackberries and hybrid berries need some support for their

CARING FOR BLACKBERRIES AND HYBRID BERRIES

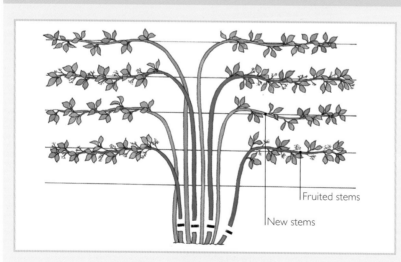

Fruited stems

New stems

1 As new stems emerge, tie them onto the horizontal wire frame using soft string.

2 Only last years stem's will fruit — pick the fruits as they become ready.

3 At the end of fruiting, cut back fruited stems to the ground (see above). Next year's fruit will come from this year's stems.

VARIETY SELECTOR
Best of the blackberries

- 'Chester': a cold-hardy, thornless blackberry.
- 'Black Butte': huge berries are produced by this variety, but you'll need to keep tying it to its supports.
- 'Triple Crown': a large-fruiting, thornless variety with excellent flavor.

VARIETY SELECTOR

Best of the hybrid berries

- **'Buckingham Tayberry'**: a spine-free version of the tayberry with large, red fruit from midsummer onward.

- **'Boysenberry'**: the berries are much darker, producing large black berries. Needs plenty of space.

- **'Loganberry Thornless'**: another spine-free version of an old favorite, producing large, red fruit in the summer.

wild stems. A wall or fence is fine with horizontal wires attached. Alternatively, you can set up a series of posts and wires in open ground as with summer-fruiting raspberries. Another alternative is to allow plants to scramble over a pergola or arch. Whichever you go for, you'll have to be prepared for pruning throughout the year.

Blackberries do best in sun, but will also thrive with some shade too. They're not the most attractive of plants, so pick a spot that's out of the way and used for little else.

In the ground Wherever you decide to plant you'll need to get the soil prepared beforehand. On the whole, blackberries are fairly unfussy about the soil, however, plants do prefer it slightly acidic. They don't like waterlogged soils and prefer good, deep, rich soil. It's a good idea to add a few bucketloads of homemade compost before you plant.

Plants flower later than other fruits so are unlikely to be affected by the frost. They're tough too, so a good choice for cold gardens.

Types and varieties Wild blackberries have always grown along the edges of woodlands and on scrubby ground, particularly where the soil is good. Prior to 100 or so years ago very little breeding was carried out as these wild plants were bountiful enough on their own. More recently, however, breeding has attempted to increase the size of fruits, reduce the size of plants and remove the thorns. There are now a fairly large number

of blackberry varieties that are available to gardeners.

Hybrid berries are the result of the ability of the blackberry to cross with the raspberry. They grow in much the same way as blackberries and require the same amount of space and pruning regime, but their fruits are often larger and redder colored. The first hybrid berry to be discovered was the loganberry in 1883 in Santa Cruz, USA. Since then, breeders have purposely crossed blackberries and raspberries to create plants that produce these blackberry-like fruits that are ready to harvest earlier in the season.

Pests and diseases Generally trouble-free, but birds can be a problem. Floating row covers will be your only solution to prevent birds from stealing your harvest.

Harvesting and storage Blackberries will start to ripen in midsummer, but may go on into fall. The fruits will be ready for picking when they turn from red to a shiny black color. It's harder to tell with hybrid berries, and depending on the variety they may still be bright red when ripe. Try picking a couple of berries to try before you start picking a whole plant. Some varieties can crop very heavily — you may get up to 22 lbs (10 kg) of fruit from a single plant.

Lay the fruit out on a tray outside once picked. Any spiders or other bugs should escape before you take them into the kitchen.

Fresh fruit doesn't last long so should be eaten immediately. Alternatively, they can be laid on a tray and frozen. Once frozen, tip them into a freezer bag. This way their shape is kept intact.

In the kitchen The fantastic flavor and aroma of blackberries can be kept all year in a jar. Making jam with a large crop of blackberries is ideal. For smaller harvests, try adding to summer puddings, or for a later harvest, combine with apples to make crumbles and pies.

Loganberries
Hybrid berries are a cross between blackberries and raspberries. They generally produce larger fruit than blackberries but retain some of the aroma of wild brambles.

CALENDAR

SPRING
YEAR I
Plant shallowly in the soil, spreading the roots to encourage the production of new shoots. Ensure you have wires in place to attach the new growth.

SUBSEQUENT YEARS
Add a good layer of mulch, such as homemade compost, and a handful of general-purpose fertilizer.

SUMMER
YEAR I
As the new shoots emerge, tie them into the support system.

SUBSEQUENT YEARS
New shoots will need to be tied in, but keep these separate from last year's stems. Start to pick fruit from last year's stems.

FALL
YEAR I
There'll be no fruit in the first year, but don't prune back the plants.

SUBSEQUENT YEARS
Keep picking fruit.

WINTER
YEAR I
Nothing to do.

SUBSEQUENT YEARS
Once fruiting has finished, cut out all fruiting canes at the base. Re-tie this year's growth, spreading it out along all the wires. Shorten the lateral shoots to 2 inches (5 cm).

Black currant

STAR PLANT
SUPER FOOD
HIGH YIELD

Bunches of glossy black currants are the jewels of the fruit garden. They're easy to grow and productive too.

●●●●○ VALUE FOR MONEY
●●●●● MAINTENANCE
●●●●● FREEZE/STORE
CROPPING SEASON: EARLY SUMMER–EARLY FALL

If you've never eaten black currants, it's probably because you've never grown them. They're expensive at the supermarket, and as they're not the sweetest of berries they're often left on the shelf. Grow your own, however, and you'll be rewarded with lots of delicious and beautifully scented fruits packed with vitamin C that, with the addition of a little sugar, have a fantastic flavor.

Currants are easy to grow too. Black currants are the most simple — just a single, simple annual prune is all they need.

Zone 3 to 7.

Where to grow Black currants are tough plants that do well in most situations. They will fruit best in full sun or part shade. They don't like waterlogged soils or either extremely acidic or alkaline soils, but if you add

Black currant harvest
Black currants are heavy croppers — you can expect up to 11 pounds (5 kg) of fruit from a single plant.

plenty of organic matter and feed the plants, they should thrive in most soils.

Some varieties can grow fairly large, up to around 5 ft. (1.5 m) in height and spread. There are now newer varieties that are much smaller but fruit just as well, so are a better choice for most gardens. If you're growing lots of berries, it's a good idea to place them all together, as you can protect the whole lot from birds come summertime. A single black currant bush will last for around 15 years, so make sure you select a good spot where you can easily access the plants for pruning and harvesting. With up

to 11 lbs (5 kg) of fruit per bush, there's probably not much need for more than one or two in your garden.

Pests and diseases Generally trouble-free, but sometimes mildew can be a problem. New varieties claim to be resistant to it. Reversion disease, or big bud (where buds become round and swollen), is caused by mites. There's nothing you can do and plants will eventually die. If you do suffer from it, you'll need to dig up the plant and start again.

PLANTING A BLACK CURRANT BUSH

1 Dig out a planting hole in a well-prepared patch of soil. Make sure the soil surrounding the hole is loose and uncompacted.

2 If you've bought bare-root specimens, soak them in a bucket of water for an hour or so. Otherwise, take the plant out of the pot.

3 Plant to the same level as previously grown or so the bare roots are well covered, fill in with soil and compact with the heel of your boot.

Harvesting and storage By midsummer bushes should be thick with fruit. Berries will hang on the bush for a few days, but it's a good idea to pick them as soon as they're ripe. Most fruit will ripen simultaneously, so you can't help but get a glut. You can avoid this somewhat by choosing different varieties to grow that will be ready for picking at different times. It is easiest to cut whole sprigs of berries, then clean up in the kitchen later. They're fairly thin-skinned fruit so can easily damage — take your time and lay them out as thinly as possible as you harvest.

Once in the kitchen, pick off the stems as well as the remains of the flower, if it's evident. Fruit can be frozen too.

In the kitchen Black currant cordial is simple to make and an ideal way to use up a glut of fruit. Alternatively, put black currants through your juicer to keep the high levels of vitamin C. Black currant jellies and jams are also easy to prepare. Ice creams, fruit puddings, pies and tarts are also worth trying with black currants because of their bright color and subtle flavor.

VARIETY SELECTOR

- **'Ben Lomond'**: a disease and cold-resistant variety that bears large fruit.

- **'Ben Sarek'**: heavy-yielding but with a really compact habit. Good for a small spot.

ANNUAL PRUNING OF BLACK CURRANTS

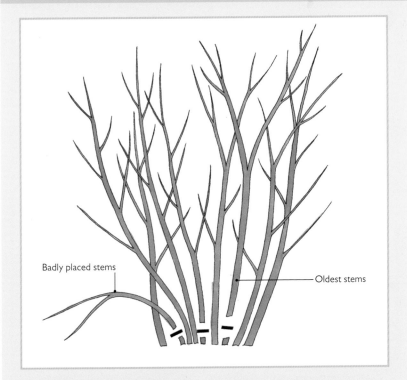

Badly placed stems

Oldest stems

1 Prune plants in the winter, since young stems produce the most fruit, and stems older than three years produce very little.

2 Take out the very oldest of stems at the base of the plant. Take out those that are badly placed too. Aim to remove about a third of the stems each year.

CALENDAR

WINTER
YEAR 1

Plant bushes at least 5 feet (1.5 m) apart. Plant around 1 inch (2.5 cm) deeper than the original planting depth to encourage shooting. Cut back each stem to one bud above soil level.

SPRING

Add a handful of general-purpose fertilizer and a mulch of homemade compost.

SUMMER
Nothing to do.

FALL
Nothing to do.

WINTER
YEAR 2 ONWARD
Nothing to do.

SPRING

Add a handful of general-purpose fertilizer and a mulch of homemade compost.

SUMMER

Around six to eight stems should start to fruit. Protect from birds and pick the fruit as it is ready.

Red and White currants

Although not as useful as black currants (see pages 166–167), white and red versions can look stunning in the fruit garden, and produce just as heavy a harvest.

⬢⬢⬢⬢◯ VALUE FOR MONEY
⬢⬢⬢⬢◯ MAINTENANCE
⬢⬢⬢⬢⬢ FREEZE/STORE
CROPPING SEASON: MIDSUMMER

Red and white currants are closely related to gooseberries, but their growth and fruiting are different so they need slightly different growth requirements.

Zone 3 to 7.

Where to grow Red and white currants will do well against a fence or wall. They'll do well in sun, but are quite productive in the shade too. You can grow them as a bush in open ground, or against a wall as a fan or cordon where they can take up less space. You'll need to look out for plants trained in this way at the plant store or otherwise train your own from very young plants. However, most plants on sale will be as two-year-old bushes and are more appropriate for growing in the open.

These currants do fine on a wide range of soils, but an annual feed and mulch will certainly help. Again, these currants can produce well in excess of 11 lbs (5 kg) of fruit per plant, so don't plant too many.

Pests and diseases Gooseberry sawfly can be a pest to red and white currants. This pest can rapidly strip the leaves bare with its larvae's voracious feeding habits in mid-spring. Keep an eye out on the backs of leaves for the pest occurring and quickly reach for a spray of insecticide, otherwise the plant will struggle to produce any currants at all.

Aphids cause wrinkled leaves but can be ignored.

Other problems include birds (where floating row covers are required), and various

PICKING AND FREEZING CURRANTS

1 When fruit are ready, cut whole fruiting stems with scissors and carefully lay them on a tray.

2 Take the fruit indoors and carefully remove each fruit by running a fork along the stem. The fruits are extremely delicate and are easily crushed, so be gentle.

3 For freezing, lay them on a tray and freeze. Once frozen, tip into a bag and return them to the freezer.

Ruby jewels
The glassy look of red currants makes them look almost like jewels.

Opaque gems
White currants are not so useful in the kitchen, but can look great as a garnish on a plate.

CALENDAR

WINTER
YEAR 1

Plant bushes about 5 feet (1.5 m) apart. Cordons can be planted as close as 16 inches (40 cm) apart. Plant to the same level as in the pot. Cut back all the main branches by half and create a small stem free from side branches at the base.

SPRING
Add a handful of general-purpose fertilizer and a mulch of compost.

SUMMER
Nothing to do.

FALL
Nothing to do.

WINTER
YEAR 2 ONWARD

Cut back new shoots that emerged in the summer by half, aiming to create a goblet shape.

SPRING
Add a handful of general-purpose fertilizer and a mulch of compost.

SUMMER
Protect fruit from birds and pick when ready. Remove any crossing side branches and cut the rest back to two buds, which will go on to produce fruiting buds.

FALL
Nothing to do.

fungal diseases. If stems start to look infected, it's a good idea to cut them back.

Harvesting and storage Red currants and white currants will happily remain on the bush even when very ripe. But if they're not protected from birds, they may disappear rather rapidly. For jams and jellies, you can pick them as soon as they color up, but for eating fresh or freezing it's best to leave them as long as possible as the sweetness intensifies. Cut whole strings of currants and clean them up in the kitchen later, being careful not to crush them.

In the kitchen White currants look very elegant, used as a garnish, but they're no different in flavor to the red variety. Red currants are often made into jelly or used as with black currants in pies and desserts, or fresh in fruit salads or with ice cream.

VARIETY SELECTOR

- 'Redstart': a high-yielding red currant that is ready for harvest later in the season. It has a compact habit too.

- 'Jonkheer van Tets': a much earlier fruiting variety of red currant, with large brightly colored currants.

- 'White Versaille': one of the few white currant varieties available. A decent variety with pearly-white translucent fruit ready for harvest in midsummer.

Sweet treats
These jewels of the fruit garden can be used in desserts or turned into jellies.

Blueberry

Get the conditions right, and blueberries can be a productive and easy plant to grow.

○○○○○ VALUE FOR MONEY
○○○○○ MAINTENANCE
○○○○○ FREEZE/STORE
CROPPING SEASON: MIDSUMMER–EARLY FALL

Blueberries are from the ericaceous family of plants. They need acid soil conditions to thrive and dislike being overfed. If you understand the growing requirements of these plants and get it right, these American plants, which don't reach over 6 ft. 5 in. (2 m) in height, can be well-behaved and extremely productive. They also look great, with their pretty white or pink bell-shaped flowers in spring and their attractive fall color. They are known as one of the superfoods, with high levels of antioxidants. While they're often cooked in muffins and pancakes, the steady stream of ripe, juicy berries from the garden in summer may not make it past the fresh-fruit stage.

Zone 3 to 9.

Where to grow For some gardeners, the soil conditions may allow you to plant blueberries directly in the ground. However, for most, where the pH is above 6, you'll either need to change your soil conditions or grow blueberries in a pot.

Anything below pH 6 is perfect for these acid-loving plants. They can be grown in some shade, but will fruit best in full sun. You'll need to space them around 5 feet (1.5 m) apart and are best planted with any other fruit, since they're very attractive to birds. As a result, you'll need to drape a floating row cover over the plants as the fruits start to ripen. You should grow at least two different varieties to aid pollination.

If you have soil above pH 6, the easiest method of cultivation is in a container or acidify the soil with sulfur. You'll need to use acidic potting mix, and use an acid fertilizer — these help to keep the pH down and the plant thriving. You'll also need to water with rainwater. Most tap water will be too alkaline, so a water barrel in the garden to collect water

The super blueberry
Blueberries have many health benefits, and with their long period of harvest, will provide you with fruit for several weeks during the summer months.

from your eavestroughs is essential. Use a slow-release acid fertilizer each year, and top up as necessary in the fruiting period with a liquid acidic fertilizer to boost your crop.

The other alternative is to create a planting pit or a raised bed in the garden. The best way to do this is to dig out to a depth of 8 inches (20 cm), line it with permeable weed-control fabric and re-fill with acidic potting mix. To help keep the soil acidic, you can add sulfur chips (quantity depending on the initial soil acidity), available from the plant store, each spring.

Types and varieties Wild blueberries were an important part of the diet of native Americans, and the collection of wild berries is still carried out today. They're processed into muffin fillings, juices, and jams. *Vaccinium corymbosum*, the highbush blueberry, has more recently been used in breeding programs to produce more productive, larger and more vigorous plants, which can reach up to 6 ft. 5 in. (2 m) high. These northern highbush blueberries are generally tolerant of cold winters too, which makes them ideal for cold gardens. They may not do so well in warmer climes, however, but the southern highbush varieties can cope with both heat and drought. As well as *V. corymbosum*, there's also *V. angustifolium* — or the lowbush blueberry. Breeders now are crossing these two species to come up with hybrids. They reach only around 30 inches (75 cm) high, with slightly smaller berries, but these are intensely flavored, more like the wild blueberries of old.

Pests and diseases

Generally trouble-free, but birds stealing ripe fruit will be a problem for most gardeners. Floating row covers are the only solution. If plants do start to struggle, the soil conditions may be to blame. Plants hate to dry out and like organic rich, moisture-retentive soil. It's worth checking the pH of the soil every so often too, and if it's above pH 6, take action to reduce, either with sulfur chips or an ericaceous feed. If you run out of rainwater, plants will tolerate being watered with tap water, but try to avoid this for long spells. Plants sometimes can flower when frosts are still likely, which can damage their potential to fruit in that year. Where plants have started flowering but frosts are still likely, cover overnight with a floating row cover.

Harvesting and storage

A single plant can produce up to 8 lbs 8 oz (4 kg) of fruit, but 4 lbs 4 oz (2 kg) is more likely.

Fruit will ripen through the summer. Some varieties, such as 'Duke' and 'Patriot', will start to be ready in early summer. Others, such as 'Bluecrop' and 'Sunshine Blue', are ready later, in midsummer onward. Fruit will be ready when it turns blue and there is no green or red color to the fruit. Individual fruits will be ready at different times, so you'll need to pick over your bushes every few days for between four to six weeks. Ripe berries will store for a few days in the fridge or they can be frozen immediately.

In the kitchen

Add fresh blueberries to pies, muffins, pancakes, and puddings, or eat fresh, sprinkled into fruit salads or over breakfast cereals and oatmeal.

CALENDAR

SPRING

YEAR I

Container-grown plants are best planted in the spring. Check the pH of the soil and if suitable, plant out in the garden. Alternatively, create a planting pit (see step-by-step) or grow in a container.

YEAR 2 ONWARD

Mulch with organic matter, such as leaf mold, old pine needles or bark.

SUMMER

YEAR I

Make sure plants are kept well watered, preferably with rainwater.

YEAR 2 ONWARD

Give the plants a feed especially made for acid-loving plants. Start to pick the fruit.

FALL

Nothing to do.

WINTER

YEARS I & 2

There's no need to prune in the first six years.

YEAR 6 ONWARD

Start to prune plants from the base. Remove about a fifth of the older shoots, selecting those with fewer fruiting buds — these are much bigger than the leaf buds.

CREATING A PLANTING PIT

1 Dig out an area at least 8 inches (20 cm) deep and around 5 feet (1.5 m) wide.

2 Lay a sheet of permeable weed-control fabric in the bottom, reaching up the sides, and refill with peat and sand.

3 Plant a couple of blueberry plants within the pit.

VARIETY SELECTOR

- 'Patriot', 'Bluecrop', 'Brigitta': Northern highbush varieties (ideal for gardens that have cold winters with periods of frost).
- 'Sunshine Blue', 'Misty': Southern highbush varieties (better for warmer gardens, where winter frosts are less likely).
- 'Polaris', 'Northblue', 'Chippewa': hybrids/half highs (very hardy, but much smaller than the northern highbush varieties, and more likely to succeed in a container).

Cranberry

Similar to blueberries, cranberries can do well in acidic soils, and particularly where the soil is permanently wet or waterlogged.

✿✿✿✿✿ VALUE FOR MONEY
✿✿✿✿✿ MAINTENANCE
✿✿✿✿✿ FREEZE/STORE
CROPPING SEASON: EARLY FALL–EARLY WINTER

Cranberries need acid soil and plenty of moisture to do well. For most people this will mean growing them in a container. However, you could consider creating a planting pit and filling with ericaceous potting mix (see page 171). While the fruits of cranberries are sharp and acidic and are useful only for jellies, these plants are extremely attractive, their dark red, large fruit covering the small, shaggy bushes in late summer. For an eye-catching display, grow cranberries in a plastic-lined hanging basket, but you will need to make sure they are watered regularly.

Zone 3 to 7.

Where to grow If you have a wet, soggy, acid area of the garden, cranberries are the plants to grow. If you still fancy growing them but your conditions aren't right, you'll need to create an acidic bog garden.

Types and varieties There are few varieties available to gardeners. 'Early Black' produces large, dark fruits, while 'McFarline' has redder fruits.

Harvesting and storage Cranberries are ready for harvesting in fall, but you can wait until much of the fruit is ripe and pick in one go. Cranberries stored in an airtight container can be kept for up to three months in the fridge, or can be frozen for even longer.

In the kitchen It's unlikely you'll ever grow enough cranberries for juicing, but you may grow enough for making some sauce to go with your turkey.

CALENDAR

SPRING

YEAR 1
Plant in a container, hanging basket, sunken cranberry bed (see step-by step on page 171) or directly in the garden if your conditions suit.

YEAR 2 ONWARD
Cut out some of the stems to avoid overcrowding. You can do this with hedge shears, but it's better to cut out at ground level.

SUMMER

Nothing to do except keep your plants well watered.

FALL

If there are any fruit, wait until they're ripe and pick.

WINTER

YEAR 1
Nothing to do.

YEAR 2 ONWARD
Trim plants to avoid them getting straggly. Add some acidic organic matter, such as leaf mold, old pine needles, or shredded bark, or a layer of lime-free sand to encourage new shoots to root.

Fall fruits
The dark-red cranberry fruit will smother your plants in late summer and create a pretty fall display.

Grapes

Establish these plants for a couple of years and they'll start to reward you with bunches of sweet, juicy fruit.

✪✪✪✪◇ VALUE FOR MONEY
✪✪✪◇◇ MAINTENANCE
✪✪✪◇◇ FREEZE/STORE
CROPPING SEASON: LATE SUMMER–EARLY FALL

Grapes have a reputation for being tricky to grow. It's true they take a couple of years to establish, and in this time you'll be little rewarded for your efforts, but once established, a grape vine will produce vast quantities of grapes with very little effort.

Grape vines are large, vigorous plants, and left to their own devices quickly become unruly, but there are some simple training and pruning methods that, applied every year, will keep your plant in check and fruiting well.

While most people will be familiar with vineyards, where rows of outdoor grapes are used for making wine, in the garden the dessert grapes are most useful and rewarding, producing a plentiful supply of grapes for the table through late summer and fall.

Zone 7 to 10 (European wine grape), 3 to 7 (labrusca American grapes), 7 to 9 (muscadine grapes), 5 to 10 American–European hybrids.

Where to grow While all vines are frost-hardy, they need a long growing season with plenty of sunshine for the fruits to grow and ripen. Varieties vary in their requirements, but generally the dessert grapes need a longer season than wine-making grapes. If in doubt, ask at your local nursery or plant store. Vines are best grown up against a wall or fence as their weak stems need support. Alternatively, you can grow them up against a pergola or arch, so long as they receive plenty of sunshine. Vines are also very pretty plants and can easily be squeezed into the ornamental areas of the garden.

Grapes are vigorous plants. Your soil should be on the acid side of neutral (around pH 6.5), and be free-draining. To improve the soil structure, it's worth adding a good mulch of organic matter each spring, alongside a handful of general-purpose fertilizer. ➡

Juicy grapes
With recent breeding, growing juicy, sweet dessert grapes is a reality for most gardeners.

PRUNING AND TRAINING GRAPES — THE GUYOT METHOD

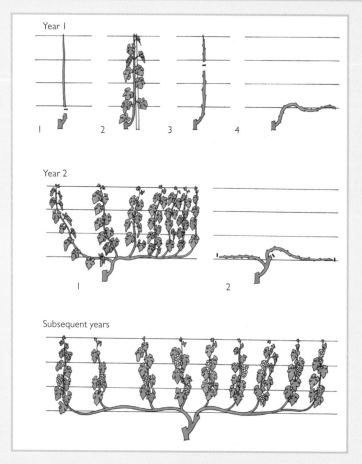

Year 1

1   2   3   4

Year 2

1   2

Subsequent years

There are many methods of pruning and training grapes, but for the garden the Guyot method is one of the best. The stems are supported by horizontal wires spaced about 12 inches (30 cm) apart fixed securely to stout posts. Leave a gap of 6–12 inches (15–30 cm) behind the wires if growing against a fence or wall.

Year 1

1 After planting in the dormant season, cut the previous season's growth back hard to one or two buds.

2 During the first summer, train a single vigorous shoot vertically, tying it to the wires or a cane. Remove any other shoots.

3 In fall or early winter, when growth is complete, cut back to about 30 inches (75 cm) of the current season's growth.

4 Loosen the ties, then bend the shoot over horizontally and tie to the bottom wire.

Year 2

1 During the second summer, numerous new shoots will be produced. Train these up the wires, spreading them out as shown. When the main shoots reach the top of the wires, remove the growing tips. Shorten any side shoots to five leaves.

2 At the end of the growing season, cut out all the shoots except two that have grown from near the top of the upright part of the main stem. Shorten these two selected shoots to about 30 inches (75 cm), then tie them down to the bottom wire.

Subsequent years

Train the new summer growth to the wires. At the end of each season, select two new shoots to shorten and tie in, then cut out the remainder.

Types and varieties In some areas, you can buy vines that have been grown on their own rootstocks, and can easily be propagated by taking hardwood cuttings in winter. In other areas, there may be soil pests that feed on and kill vines. To prevent pests, the plants need to be grafted onto a different rootstock. Your local nursery should be able to advise whether this is the case for you and should stock vines grafted onto appropriate rootstocks.

Most vines are sold as rooted cuttings, probably just a year old. They'll look like just a thin, single shoot and will need some time to establish in your garden. Vines may also be available as larger, more established plants, and these may be suitable if you want to grow in a container and don't want to wait a couple of years for your first crop.

The only decision you'll really need to make is which variety to grow. This will depend on whether you want wine or dessert grapes, as well as seeded or seedless, and of course, flavor.

Pests and diseases Vines suffer from relatively few pests and diseases.

Pests such as grape berry moth and Japanese beetles can be a problem. The larvae of the grape berry moth feed on tender stems, blossom buds and fruit. Larvae can also overwinter in fallen leaves so it is important to clean up the leaves in the fall. If your vines are affected, spray with BT spray. The adult Japanese beetles feed on leaves and fruit and can be quite destructive; however, biological controls are available.

Diseases such as mildew and botrytis can also affect the leaves and fruit. While these diseases are difficult to control once the plant is under attack, making sure the plant is well watered and fed should help the plant to defend itself. With mildew, spray the vines with potassium carbonate or sulfur.

The fungal disease black rot can also attack vines and fruit. Black rot discolors the stems and leaves and causes the grapes to shrivel and turn black. When this occurs, the grapes are called "mummies." If your vines are affected, clean up all mummies and spray with copper sulfate. Resistant varieties are available.

Harvesting and storage Grapes should be picked when ripe and eaten fresh. There will be a window of a few weeks to pick the fruit, which are best left on the plant until you need them. Cut whole bunches using scissors or secateurs, being careful not to handle the fruit too much as the grapes can be easily damaged. For wine-making, fruit can be picked all in one go.

In the kitchen Best served on their own or with cheese and biscuits. They can also be juiced and combined with other fruit to make a delicious drink. Alternatively, turn the bunches into wine and impress your friends.

VARIETY SELECTOR

Dessert grapes

- 'Vanessa': seedless, crisp texture.
- 'Jupiter': seedless blue berries on medium-sized cluster.
- 'Swenson Red': seedless table grape.
- 'Early Muscat' (*Vitis vinifera*): grape-y tasting grape; may be tricky to ripen.

Wine grapes

- 'Marechcal Foch' hybrid: red-wine grape variety.

CALENDAR

WINTER

YEAR 1

Provide a suitable support system, and plant vine with a thick mulch of organic matter. Cut back to around 2 feet (60 cm) from the base.

YEAR 2 ONWARD

Cut back side shoots to two buds. Cut back the main stem to the highest healthy bud or below if it has grown too big for your support.

SPRING

YEAR 1

Train the vertical shoot as it grows.

YEAR 2 ONWARD

Train vertical and side shoots as they grow. Add a handful of general-purpose fertilizer and a deep layer of homemade compost.

SUMMER

Cut off side shoots to five leaves. If necessary, thin out fruit early in the summer, especially with young plants to encourage them to establish well. On older plants, fruit will start to ripen in midsummer.

FALL

Keep picking fruit if any are ripe. Along a wall or fence, set up horizontal wires fixed using vine eyes 12 inches (30 cm) apart. Over an arch or pergola, plants will need to be encouraged through the trellis and tied in where necessary. On a single post, plants will need to be pruned to be kept in check and tied in to the post.

Gnarled vines
Old grape vines can make attractive ornamental plants as well as productive ones.

Gooseberry

Gooseberries are well-behaved fruit, suitable for containers or small gardens

✪✪✪✪✪	VALUE FOR MONEY
✪✪✪✪✪	MAINTENANCE
✪✪✪✪✪	FREEZE/STORE
CROPPING SEASON: LATE SPRING–MIDSUMMER	

A traditional fruit, gooseberries have been popular since the 1700s. They're unlikely to be available in most supermarkets, but are easy to grow in the garden. They form small bushes in the open, or they can be trained as a cordon or even a fan against a wall or fence. They can even be grown in pots. Their fruits develop in the summer and can be picked early for making jams and desserts or left to ripen fully on the bush where their sweetness intensifies, and they can be eaten fresh.

Zone 3 to 7.

Where to grow
They prefer a slightly acidic soil, so it's a good idea to dig in, or mulch, with plenty of organic matter before planting. Fruit production can be affected by frosts, so select a sheltered spot in your garden, avoiding any frost pockets. However, they still do well on a shaded wall or fence. Place with other soft fruit if you can, such as currants and raspberries, and protect with a single fruit cage, since plants will last for many years. You'll get around 11 lbs (5 kg) of fruit from a single plant, so bear this in mind when deciding how many to buy. Cordons will produce much less per plant, perhaps just 2 lbs (1 kg), but you'll be able to squeeze many more plants into the same space.

Types and varieties
While there were once hundreds of varieties available, most plant stores will stock just two or three. The biggest variety is in the color of the fruit, coming in green, white, yellow and red. Another choice you'll have is the form or shape of the plant you want, and this will determine the characteristics of the plant you select. For more on pruning and training the plant forms below, see pages 206–209.

Juicy gooseberries
Gooseberries are not as popular as other fruit superfoods, such as blueberries; however, these pretty bushes are easy to grow and productive, too.

Bush Most plants in the plant store will be sold as two- or three-year-old bushes. This is fine if you want a free-standing, small bush.
Fan If you want to grow it against a fence or wall, a fan is a good use of space. Plants will need to be trained into a two-dimensional form, so select a plant that you think you can train easily.
Cordon A cordon is basically a vertical main stem with short fruiting spurs coming off it. This allows you to fit more plants into a small space, but they will need careful pruning to make them productive. You'll need to select a plant with a good, strong central stem.
Standard This is basically a bush on a leg. The standard form makes picking easier as the fruits are higher up. You can either buy a standard already grown or train your own by slowly pruning all the side branches from the base.

Pests and diseases
Gooseberry sawfly can be a real pest, stripping the plant bare from spring onward. You'll need to keep an eye out for these caterpillar-like pests on the underside of leaves and spray with an appropriate pesticide. Gooseberry mildew can coat the leaves in a white powder, severely weakening the plant. Make sure your plants don't go short of water, that they're pruned appropriately, and ensure you mulch well in the spring with homemade compost. Some varieties, such as 'Invicta' and 'Pax' have some resistance to the disease, otherwise you'll have to opt for a fungicide approved for use on gooseberries.

Harvesting and storage
A good way to harvest gooseberries is in two stages. The first is when the berries are just beginning to ripen, around early summer. This crop is especially good for making jams and preserves, or using in pies or crumbles. They're still a bit sour, but have large amounts of pectin in the fruit. The rest of the fruit should be picked in midsummer. These fruits should be fully ripened and can be eaten fresh as the

PRUNING GOOSEBERRIES

Gooseberries fruit on shoots that are a year or more old, so they continue to fruit well even if pruning is neglected. However, harvesting becomes a prickly and difficult task and with age, the lowest branches may be so close to the ground that the fruit becomes splashed with soil.

After harvest, remove any badly placed branches (those crossing, too low to the ground, or crowding the center, see above). Cut low branches to an upward-facing bud.

In winter, reduce the length of the summer growth from the tips of the main branches by half, and reduce the sideshoots, which produce the fruit, to two buds from the old wood (see above).

Also, cut out any shoots showing signs of mildew (dark spots or patches), and every few years cut out one or two old shoots that are tending to die, leaving suitable replacement shoots to take over.

sweetness should have intensified, or can be made into chutney. Fruit can be frozen. Top and tail the fruit before freezing in plastic food bags. Alternatively you can stew then freeze after sieving.

In the kitchen While some people like the sweet flavor of ripe gooseberries, they're more often used cooked. They're a great fruit for preserves and chutneys, and are often used as an accompaniment to meat and poultry dishes. They can also be used in sweet pies and puddings.

VARIETY SELECTOR

Green berries
- 'Invicta': high yielding.
- 'Jumbo': big berries.

Yellow berries
- 'Hinnonmaki Yellow': heavy cropping.

Red berries
- 'Red Jacket': nearly thornless.
- 'Hinnonmaki Red Captivator': abundant, exceptional quality.

CALENDAR

SPRING
YEAR 1
Prepare the soil and plant gooseberries, giving around 5 feet (1.5 m) per plant. Mulch with organic matter. Cordons can be spaced every 12 inches (30 cm). Remove any stems below 8 inches (20 cm) of the main stem and cut back main branches by half.

YEAR 2 ONWARD
Add a handful of general-purpose fertilizer and a mulch of compost.

SUMMER
YEAR 1
Water during dry spells.

YEAR 2 ONWARD
Start to pick fruit. Remove any crossing side branches. Water during dry spells.

FALL
YEAR 1 ONWARD
Nothing to do.

WINTER
YEAR 1
Cut back new shoots that have grown this year by half.

YEAR 2 ONWARD
Prune back growth, try to create a goblet-shaped bush with an open center and around eight main branches. If growing a cordon, aim for a plant up to 5 feet (1.5 m) high.

Rhubarb

This hardy perennial is easy to grow and provides the earliest kitchen garden crop for making desserts and pies.

✪✪✪✪✪ VALUE FOR MONEY
✪✪✪✪✪ MAINTENANCE
✪✪✪○○ FREEZE/STORE
CROPPING SEASON: LATE SPRING–LATE SUMMER

Rhubarb is not strictly a fruit, as it's the stems that you harvest and eat. However, it is mainly used as a fruit in the kitchen for turning into desserts and puddings. It's one of the earliest crops for harvesting from the garden, as stems will have started to grow in early spring and it is these early stems that are the most tender. However, once your plant is established you'll be able to keep picking stems until early summer. For an even more tender and earlier crop you can blanch or force rhubarb from mid-winter for stalks in late winter or very early spring.

Zone 4 to 8.

Where to grow This perennial plant will last more than 10 years in your garden, so you'll need to consider where to place it. Rhubarb grows fairly large, and with its huge broad leaves and bright stalks, it is attractive too. Each plant will need a space of around 3 feet (90 cm), and two or three plants are easily enough for most households. Plants prefer a sunny spot and enjoy ground that is moisture-retentive. However, they are not too choosy: so as long as you improve the soil with homemade compost, they should be happy in most soils.

Plants need a period of cold to grow well each year. When leaves die back in the fall, make sure you remove the leaves to the compost heap and expose the crown to the worst of the winter weather.

Types and varieties Varieties are separated into seasons, as some will come into growth earlier than others. Select a more compact variety, as some older varieties turn

FORCING RHUBARB

1 Cover the crown in straw from mid-winter.

2 Cover with a terracotta forcing pot. If you haven't got one, use an upturned large plastic pot or trash can.

3 Lift the lid of the pot after a few weeks to check if the stems are ready for picking.

Tender stems
The tenderest stems of rhubarb are those produced at the start of the season.

(see step-by-step). Stalks are etiolated, in that they stretch out in the dark conditions in search of light. Their color is paler than stems grown in the light and as they've grown quickly are more tender.

Pests and diseases Rhubarb is generally trouble-free, and a great plant to grow if you don't want to worry about pests and diseases. Viruses may weaken plants over time, so after 10 years or so, or if the plant starts to grow more weakly, it's best to replace. If soil is very heavy, the crowns of the plants can rot. Keep adding a good layer of homemade compost every year to maintain good soil structure.

Harvesting and storage You shouldn't harvest any stems the first year after planting and only a few early on in the season in the second year. In year three, if the plants have established well, you can start to pull stems from early spring to early summer. Reach down to the center of the plant and push the leaf stalk downward to break off as near to the crown as possible. Take as much as you need at each harvest.

Stalks will last a week or so in the fridge, but they can also be chopped and frozen.

In the kitchen Rhubarb stems are sour on their own so need sweetening with sugar and are ideal for turning into jams and chutneys. Rhubarb is also good in crumbles, pies, and puddings, either on its own or combined with other fruit from the garden. It's often also served as a sauce alongside meat such as duck or pork.

into giants in the garden. You can grow rhubarb from seed, but it's much easier to buy at the plant store or mail order as young one- to two-year-old crowns in fall or spring.

In the garden You can force rhubarb to produce an earlier and more tender crop

4 When the stems have reached the top of the pot, lift off the forcer and cut the stems at the base.

CALENDAR

FALL
YEAR 1
Fall is the best time to plant (although spring is also possible). Dig in plenty of organic matter and plant so the top bud is just 1 inch (2.5 cm) below the surface of the soil.

YEAR 2 ONWARD
Do nothing.

WINTER
YEAR 1
Do nothing.

YEAR 2 ONWARD
Remove old leaves and compost.

YEAR 3 ONWARD
Force plants as required. If you're digging up plants don't repeat this process for a couple of years to give the plants time to recover.

SPRING
YEAR 1
Don't pick any of the young stems.

YEAR 2
Pick just a few of the young stems, but leave some on to help the plant to establish.

YEAR 3 ONWARD
Harvest the stems regularly.

SUMMER
YEARS 1 & 2
Water plant as necessary to help it to establish and add a general-purpose fertilizer.

YEAR 3 ONWARD
Keep harvesting stems until midsummer.

TENDER FRUIT

If you just can't help but try to grow something tricky, go for one of the tender fruits. You'll need hot, sunny conditions for long periods, but if you get good weather you may well be able to show off an exotic fruit salad to your dinner guests.

Kiwi

If you have a warm garden, a kiwi can produce an exotic touch to your edible garden, but beware: they need plenty of space.

○○○○○ VALUE FOR MONEY
○○○○○ MAINTENANCE
○○○○○ FREEZE/STORE
CROPPING SEASON: LATE FALL

Kiwis are also often known as Chinese gooseberries — referring to where they grow in the wild. This large, rampant plant produces broad, downy leaves, fragrant white flowers and brown-skinned furry fruits with a sweet green pulp. Since they are exotic plants, they need a warm site and temperatures in between 41 and 77°F (5 and 25°C) to fruit. They will grow in colder areas, but the production of fruit may be limited. Kiwis grow into huge plants, so they need plenty of space and plenty of pruning.

Zone 3 to 7 (*Actinidia kolomikta*), 4 to 9 (*A. arguta*), 7 to 9 (*A. delicosia*), 8 to 10 (*A. chinensis*).

Where to grow Kiwis twine and clamber as they grow and need appropriate supports to keep them from flopping. This is usually achieved by a series of posts and wires or even trellises attached away from the wall. The wall should be west- or south-facing, and away from any harsh winds, which kiwis hate. If you have plenty of space in a polytunnel, however, it may be worth devoting some space.

Kiwis prefer a pH of 6–7 and good soil, rich in organic matter.

Types and varieties In the past, you had to grow a male plant to pollinate a female plant. However, recent breeding means you can now buy self-fertile varieties that do away with the need for a male plant. Unfortunately, this has also resulted in the fruit on these varieties being somewhat smaller than those produced by the older types.

Pests and diseases Kiwis are generally trouble-free.

Harvesting and storage It will take three to eight years before vines start producing fruit. Kiwis should be ready for picking by the fall, and a slight squeeze of the fruit will tell you if they've softened and are ripe. They keep for weeks if picked slightly underripe.

In the kitchen This fruit is best eaten fresh, added to fruit salads, cheesecakes or even turned into juice.

Tender vines
The kiwi needs warm temperatures to produce a good crop.

CALENDAR

WINTER
Plant kiwis at least 20 inches (50 cm) away from a south- or west-facing wall, or against a series of horizontal wires fixed between sturdy posts. They'll need around 16 ft. 4 in. (5 m) of wall space.

SPRING
Mulch plants well with organic matter and sprinkle a handful of general-purpose fertilizer every year.

SUMMER
Train shoots onto the wires, tying in as you go. Kiwis fruit on shoots growing off one-year-old wood so it's best to create a framework of shoots that can be cut back each year.

FALL
After a few years, your plant should be producing fruit that should ripen in early fall.

WINTER
Cut back stems that have fruited back almost to your established framework along the wires. Make sure those stems produced this year (which should fruit next summer) have been tied in.

TIP

To boost your harvest, in early summer cut shoots which are bearing fruit to five leaves above where the fruit are developing. This encourages the fruits to swell and ripen.

VARIETY SELECTOR

A. delicosia
- **'Hayward'**: most popular; sweet/tart.
- **'Tewi'**: tried and tested.

A. chinensis
- **'Jintao'**: relatively fast to start bearing fruit.

A. arguta
- **'Anna'**: can be winter hardy.

Passion fruit

Passion fruits need a hot climate to succeed, but because they can be grown in containers, it's possible to grow them almost anywhere.

○○○○○ VALUE FOR MONEY
○○○○○ MAINTENANCE
○○○○○ FREEZE/STORE
CROPPING SEASON: LATE SUMMER–EARLY FALL

Passion fruits are climbing plants, producing incredibly beautiful flowers. In fact, many people grow passion fruits for their flowers alone. If you do manage to grow some fruit, you'll be rewarded with a sweet and fragrant pulp attached to hard black seeds.

Zone 9 to 11.

Where to grow Passion fruits can struggle to survive in temperatures below 50°F (10°C). If your area dips below this in winter, you'll need to winter passion fruits in a sunny window. Because passion fruits bear fruit on the current year's growth, they can be kept fairly compact, and because of this are suitable for growing in large containers.

Outside, they're best up against a wall with either trellis or a series of horizontal wires attached. As they grow upward, they attach themselves using tendrils and produce large plants.

Types and varieties While there are many species and varieties grown for their ornamental value, there are two species that

> **TIP**
> If the plant fails to fruit after flowering, try pollinating by hand using a paintbrush. Gently brush over the flowers, passing pollen from one flower to another.

are grown for fruit. The first is *P. edulis f. flavicarpa*, which produces yellow fruit that can lack sweetness, and *P. edulis*, which produces purple-skinned fruit often found in supermarkets — they are highly regarded and much more sweet and flavorsome. There are several varieties of each but it is likely you will find just the species for sale.

Pests and diseases In a greenhouse you may find aphids, scale insects and red spider mite to be a problem. Use an appropriate organic insecticide or biological control.

Harvesting and storage Fruits are ripe once they start to shrivel or drop. You can pick them earlier and ripen in the fruit bowl if you prefer. Once picked, they'll last a couple of weeks kept in a cool place.

In the kitchen The purple-skinned fruits are much sweeter and tastier than the yellow-skinned fruit, and the sweet pulp is ideal for adding to ice cream or sorbet or over other fruit. The yellow fruit can be turned into jams or chutneys.

VARIETY SELECTOR

- **'Common Purple'**: naturalized in Hawaii, thick skin.
- **'Noel's Special'**: yellow fruit with richly flavored orange pulp.
- **'Purple-Gold'**: hybrid of yellow and purple forms.

Unripe passion fruit
The incredible flavor of the passion fruit can be achieved only in warmer climes.

CALENDAR

SPRING
Plant out and mulch with plenty of homemade compost. Add a handful of general-purpose fertilizer each spring.

SUMMER
Encourage the plant to attach itself to your support structure — either wires or trellises. Select two main stems along the support. The side shoots of these can be allowed to grow each year and fruit.

FALL
Pick fruits when they're ripe.

WINTER
Once they have fruited, cut the side shoots back to the main stems.

Cape gooseberry

A distant relative to the tomato, these plants are best grown from seed and should start to bear fruit by midsummer.

⬤⬤⬤○○ VALUE FOR MONEY
⬤⬤⬤○○ MAINTENANCE
⬤⬤○○○ FREEZE/STORE
CROPPING SEASON: LATE SUMMER–EARLY FALL

Cape gooseberries produce small orange fruits that develop in pretty paper-thin lantern-shaped cases. They're often used as a garnish in restaurants, but their pineapple-flavored fruit can be incredibly sweet and juicy. They're an easy-to-grow annual, just like tomatoes.

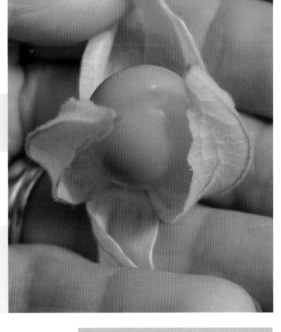

Hidden treasure
Peel back the papery case to reveal the sweet orange fruits of the cape gooseberry.

Where to grow Seed should be started off in early spring in the greenhouse and young plants kept somewhere warm until all threat of frost has passed. They can be planted into the greenhouse border, but can do well outside too. Plant out in a sunny spot and if they grow too large, be prepared to give them a bit of support such as tying them onto a cane. They can be grown in large containers on the patio too.

Types and varieties There are several varieties available. Some are now more compact and are ideal for growing in containers.

Pests and diseases Cape gooseberries are trouble-free.

Harvesting and storage Leave the fruits hanging on the plant until required, then pick the fruits when they're orange and fully ripe. The paper-thin casings will start to fall from the fruit when they're ripe.

In the kitchen You can turn cape gooseberries into a jam or jelly. If you don't get that many, eat them raw.

CALENDAR

SPRING
Sow seed in a small pot, keeping the temperature between 64 and 70°F (18 and 21°C). Once the seedlings have grown, prick out individually into larger pots. Plant outside once all threat of frost has passed, and cover with a cloche on cool nights.

SUMMER
Provide supports in the form of canes if the plants start to get too big. Water regularly and feed with a tomato fertilizer once the fruits start to form. Fruits should start to ripen in midsummer.

FALL
Keep picking fruits as they ripen. Pull out the plant at the end of the season and compost.

VARIETY SELECTOR
- 'Golden Berry Little Lanterns' and 'Golden Berry Pineapple': these two varieties produce compact plants and plenty of fruit.

Delicate buds
With their papery lanterns, cape gooseberries can make attractive, if a little straggly, plants.

Melon

For a taste of the sublime, try growing melons: simple to grow in the garden and on the patio.

- ✪✪✪✪○ VALUE FOR MONEY
- ✪✪✪✪○ MAINTENANCE
- ✪✪○○○ FREEZE/STORE
- CROPPING SEASON: LATE SUMMER–EARLY FALL

Melon on the vine
Melons need long, hot summers to ensure they ripen.

A relative of the cucumber, melons are tender, sprawling plants that need plenty of warmth and plenty of space to grow. However, intense breeding means that there are now varieties that will do well everywhere.

Where to grow Melons need a warm and sheltered spot to do well. Strong winds can damage their foliage and affect the growth of the plant, particularly in the spring, and in cold areas the melons just won't ripen by the end of the summer. Sweet melons grow best at temperatures around 77°F (25°C), whereas watermelons prefer it even warmer — up to 86°F (30°C). If your garden never reaches these heights you could try growing melons in a cold frame, which provides some shelter and additional warmth. Where this fails, a greenhouse will be your only option. However, as they turn into large plants, you may not feel devoting your greenhouse to just a couple of melons is really worth it. Melons are annuals and can fit into your vegetable and fruit garden

Maturing cantaloupe
Growing melons in the garden, like this cantaloupe, can make attractive plants, especially when trained (see right).

easily, but as large, sprawling plants, they need plenty of space — around 6 ft. 5 in. square (2 m sq). If you are growing outside, consider covering the soil with black polythene; this will help keep the weeds down, the soil warm, and also provide a dry surface for the fruits to develop. Melons like plenty of moisture too, and the black plastic will help to keep the moisture in. However, it may be necessary to water through the drier summer months and provide an additional liquid feed of tomato fertilizer once the plants start to flower.

Types and varieties There are hundreds of varieties of sweet melon, most can be classed as fitting into a few different types. Cantaloupes have grooved or rough skins and are often green with orange-colored flesh. Musk types are often smaller with

VARIETY SELECTOR

Cantaloupes

- 'Sweet Granite': early-ripening variety.
- 'Ambrosia Hybrid': extra juicy and productive.

Honeydew

- 'Super Dew Hybrid': fragrant white flesh, very productive.
- 'Venus Hybrid': bright green flesh.

smoother skin and tend to have orange or green-colored flesh. Finally, there are the honeydews with their yellow skin and creamy white flesh. Cantaloupes are renowned for succeeding in cooler climates where the others fail. However, recent breeding in developing varieties that can succeed in more temperate climates are beginning to be available to the amateur gardener.

Watermelons have darker, more ferny leaves and need a very warm climate to succeed. However, new smaller-fruiting varieties are more likely to succeed in home gardens as the growing season required for the fruits to ripen is shorter.

Pests, diseases and other problems Fruit can split if water becomes sparse. Make sure the plants don't go thirsty. This will also help to reduce powdery mildew, which can also be a problem (see page 85). Sometimes the base of the stem can rot away too. To avoid this, build up the soil to a point and plant into it, which encourages water to drain away from the plant. When planting out, plant proud of the soil by an inch (2.5 cm) or so. In the greenhouse, spider mite can be a problem. If you get a mosaic pattern on the leaves and stunted growth, your plant may be suffering from cucumber mosaic virus. Destroy the plants immediately, taking care not to infect other nearby plants.

Melons can also be targeted by the cucumber beetle (see page 85) and the squash bug (see page 85).

Harvesting and storage Look out for the stalk cracking. Once this happens, the fruit should be ripe. Sweet melons should also start to give off a very sweet smell. With watermelons, if the underside starts to yellow where it is sitting on the ground, this generally means the melon is ripe. Cut off the fruit with a pair of secateurs and take inside. Fruits should last a couple of weeks in the kitchen. If the fruits haven't ripened by the onset of fall, consider covering them with a glass cloche or similar. This greenhouse effect will help the fruits to ripen more quickly.

In the kitchen Melons are most often used either as a dessert or as part of a starter. Melon goes well with Parma ham and cheese, for example, but equally well just sliced up and eaten fresh.

VARIETY SELECTOR
Watermelons
- **'Bush Sugar Baby'**: compact vines, small, sweet melons.
- **'Crimson Sweet'**: round with dark red, sweet flesh.

GROWING MELONS IN CONTAINERS

1 Grow just one or two melon plants from seed from mid-spring.

2 Transplant each plant into a large 12-inch (30-cm) diameter pot filled with multipurpose potting mix and a slow-release fertilizer. Either allow the plants to trail or create a structure using canes.

3 Tie in the plant with soft string as it grows up the supports.

4 Additional support may be required for the large fruits — use nets tied to the supports to stop the fruits pulling the rest of the plant down.

CALENDAR

MID-SPRING
Start melons off in a warm place three weeks before the last frost date. Sow seeds individually in small pots, maintaining a minimum temperature of 61°F (16°C).

LATE SPRING
Seedlings are large and grow quickly. Keep plants well watered and pot into larger containers if necessary.

EARLY SUMMER
Plant out in the garden one week after the last frost date. Don't plant too deep, making sure the stem is completely proud of the soil surface. Leave around 3 ft. 2 in. (1 m) between plants.

MIDSUMMER
Stop the main shoot by pinching out the tip, then pinch out the side shoots once they've grown. This repeated pinching out encourages branching and fruit development. Make sure the plants are fed and watered regularly.

LATE SUMMER
Protect from wet soil any fruits that develop. Check fruits and harvest when ripe.

Citrus fruit

If you have a large greenhouse, why not bring a bit of the Mediterranean indoors?

○○○○○ VALUE FOR MONEY
○○○○○ MAINTENANCE
○○○○○ FREEZE/STORE
CROPPING SEASON: MID-FALL–MID-WINTER

With shiny, bright evergreen leaves and heavily scented flowers, citrus plants are pretty enough for any garden. Any fruit is usually brightly colored too — lemons, limes and oranges can give your garden a really exotic feel. However, unless you live in a frost-free zone don't even think about trying to keep a citrus plant outdoors all year round. Despite some varieties surviving sub-freezing temperatures, their fruit will drop and flowers fall. What's really needed is a sunny windowsill where they can be enjoyed

Zesty container plants
Citrus plants are best grown in containers — so you can easily move them in and out of the garden throughout the season.

through the winter months, then returned to the patio in the summer, when the temperatures rise.

Zone 8 to 10.

Where to grow Citrus trees can reach around 33 feet (10 m) tall and almost as wide. In warm climates, where the temperature stays well above freezing all year round, citrus trees flower and fruit throughout the year.

TRAINING A CITRUS STANDARD

1 When planting your standard, tie in the leading stem to a stake with a figure-eight knot. Remove one third of the length of each side shoot as shown.

2 Between late winter and early spring the following year, prune the leading stem back to a healthy bud at around the required final height of the trunk. Remove any sideshoots that were shortened the previous year, but leave any new sideshoots in place — these will help to thicken the trunk.

3 When the tree has developed three to four shoots above the trunk, prune them back by three to five leaves. Remove all shoots below these on the trunk to create the standard shape. Repeat every year to create a bushy, spherical shape.

In more temperate climes, where the thermometer often dips below freezing in the winter, you can still encourage repeated fruiting and flowering, but you'll need to grow the plant in a container and move it around your garden.

For a container-grown specimen you'll need to buy a plant that is either naturally small, such as a calamondin, or grow a variety that has been grafted onto a dwarfing rootstock, which keeps it naturally compact.

The roots of citrus tend to grow more vertical than horizontal, so choose a long, deep container and fill with potting mix. It's worth mixing in a slow-release fertilizer at planting time too. Plants will need repotting every three or four years, but will need plenty of feeding and watering in between.

If you're growing in a container, you'll want to keep the plant naturally compact. The best time to prune is in winter after the fruits have been picked. Trees fruit on both old and new wood, so it's about keeping the plant to a shape you want and ensuring any dead, diseased or dying branches are removed. It's also worth making sure no suckers grow from the base as these will be from the rootstock.

Types and varieties
There are plenty of different types of citrus. Lemons and limes are reputed to be some of the easiest to grow and, as you're not likely to get lots of fruit, will be perfect for slicing into drinks. Oranges are available in a number of varieties, such as large navals and blood oranges, as well as the smaller mandarins, such as satsuma and clementine. Then there are the bitter oranges, such as the Seville, for making marmalade, and calamondin oranges, which are mainly grown as a small ornamental plant. Finally, the other common citrus grown in gardens is the grapefruit, with both the traditional yellow and the Florida pink available to gardeners.

Pests and diseases Like all plants that are protected from frosts and kept indoors for the winter, they're liable to suffer from typical indoor pests such as aphids, whitefly, scale insect and spider mite. You'll need to bring out all your defences — either organic sprays or biological controls to keep these pests in check and prevent them from damaging your plant.

Harvesting and storage Citrus mainly flower in winter and spring and fruit in late fall or early winter. Keep an eye on your plant as individual fruits will ripen separately. They will often sit on the plant for some time once ripe so it's not crucial to pick them immediately. Cut them off the plant using a pair of secateurs. Fruit can be stored in a cool place for several weeks.

In the kitchen You'll be lucky if you harvest a dozen fruits from your container-grown tree. And as they ripen separately you'll only be getting one or two at a time. The peel can be candied and the fruit can be juiced, but in the limited quantities you get, you should definitely savor their taste fresh as the flavor of home-grown citrus can't be beaten.

CALENDAR

SPRING
Once your plant is suitably potted up, keep it somewhere well lit, but out of direct, harsh sunlight. Stand the pot on a tray of gravel or similar material and keep this topped up with water to just below the base of the pot. This helps to raise the humidity, especially when they're kept indoors. As the soil starts to dry, give the plant a thorough soak. Start to liquid feed with a fertilizer high in nitrogen.

SUMMER
In early summer, once all threat of frost has passed, move out to the patio. Carry on feeding every couple of weeks with a balanced fertilizer. Mist plants regularly with water to keep the humidity high and keep an eye out for pests.

FALL
Start to feed with a more balanced fertilizer and one that contains trace elements. Keep an eye out for the weather and when it starts to drop below 45°F (7°C), consider taking your plant indoors to a sunny window for the remainder of the year. Reduce the amount of watering.

WINTER
Fruit should be starting to ripen, so pick when they're ready. At the end of fruiting, you can prune your plant as necessary. Shorten straggly stems and anything that's diseased or damaged. Repot if the plant is getting too large.

VARIETY SELECTOR
Oranges

- **'Washington Naval'**: ripens early and is claimed to have a superior taste to other navals.

- **'Sanguinelli'**: this blood orange produces dark-colored flesh and a very sweet blood-orange flavor.

- **'Calamondin'**: produces small, acidic fruits on small bushes suitable for a windowsill.

VARIETY SELECTOR
Lemons

- **'Four Seasons Lemon'**: as its name suggests, it flowers and fruits throughout the year.

- **'Variegata'**: produces stripy green and yellow fruit, again throughout the year.

Limes

- **'Tahiti'**: with yellow fruit and a fairly sweet flavor, this lime produces a good crop.

NUTS

There are not many nuts that are worth growing in the garden, but if you have the space, hazelnuts and filberts, almonds and walnuts are worth trying. They need little care or attention, but you may need to wait a few years before you see any nuts.

Hazelnut and Filbert

While the common filbert will yield some small nuts, it's only the choicest varieties of hazelnut and filbert that produce the largest.

STAR PLANT
SMALL TREE HIGH YIELD

○○○○○ VALUE FOR MONEY
○○○○○ MAINTENANCE
○○○○○ FREEZE/STORE
CROPPING SEASON: EARLY FALL–MID-FALL

Furry cases
The frilly cases enclose large succulent nuts — but beware of squirrels stealing your crop.

Hazelnuts and filberts are one of the most expensive nuts to buy. They are eaten fresh and don't store well, so they are only in the supermarket for a short season, usually in early to mid-fall. This is true for the garden too. If you manage to beat the squirrels to the crop, you'll get beautiful nuts shrouded in a pretty, frilly green or purple husk. Plant a tree now — you may have to wait as much as three to four years for your first nuts.

Zone 5 to 8.

Where to grow The native hazel, *Corylus americana*, tends to grow on a number of shoots. Hazels are commonly found in the wild, on woodland edges, and in hedgerows. They can crop well in the wild too, allowing you to harvest some of their bounty. In the garden they will do best when provided with an area of their own. Hazelnuts and filberts are fairly unfussy when it comes to soil, but they're renowned for being shy to produce nuts on very fertile ground. They'll produce their biggest crop when grown in full sun, with a semi-fertile, moist soil. When planting, it's best to grow at least two of each species, and plant them 10–13 feet (3–4 m) apart.

You'll often buy very young plants, that are perhaps just a couple of years old. You'll need to train these into the most sensible shape for your garden. Hazelnuts and filberts can be grown on a single trunk, usually to a height of around 18 inches (45 cm). At this height they should be trained into an open bush shape through pruning or grown as a multi-stemmed shrub.

Types and varieties While the wild hazel tends to be small, it is the varieties bred from it that produce the larger hazelnuts.

Hazelnuts and filberts produce both female and male flowers on the same plant, and so in theory you should not need more than one in a garden. However, as a general rule, they do set fruit more successfully if there is more than one variety grown locally. If you have the space, grow two or three in a small group.

Pests and diseases The dreaded squirrel is the worst pest by far, stealing your harvest before you've had a chance to collect any nuts. There is little you can do to prevent them from doing this.

Harvesting and storage While the squirrels tend to harvest hazelnuts (also known as cobs) and filberts before they're fully ripe, it's best to leave them on the tree if you can until the frilly husks start to turn yellow, usually in early fall. You should be able to pick most of the crop together, then store in a cool, dry place such as in slatted trays or nets.

In the kitchen The frilly cases enclosing the largest cobs and filberts can look fantastic. The sweet, succulent nuts are best eaten fresh.

CALENDAR

WINTER
Buy bare-root plants and plant in the garden, at least 10 feet (3 m) apart. Mulch the soil well with a hefty load of homemade compost.

SPRING
If rabbits or deer are likely to be a problem, consider using a tree guard around the trunk. Cut back the main shoot by around half. This should induce branching. Keep around six of these to form an open bush shape. Mulch your plants in early spring from year 2 onward.

SUMMER
Water well in the first couple of years.

FALL
This is the season for harvesting, but you'll have to wait a few years before nuts are produced.

WINTER
Start an annual pruning regime in late winter. Cut back new growth by about half until the tree reaches around 6 ft. 5 in. (2 m). Then each year after this cut back to this height. Any higher and you won't be able to reach the nuts. Remove any crossing, diseased or damaged stems in winter too.

VARIETY SELECTOR
Blight-resistant varieties
- 'Santiam': high-yielding hazelnut.
- 'Lewis': hazelnut admired for its smaller nut size.
- 'Clark': recommended hazelnut.
- 'Jefferson': filbert.

Hazel catkins
In early spring, the male catkins provide pollen to insects as well as the small, inconspicuous female flowers.

Almond

Closely related to the peach, almonds need a warm, hot summer to produce a crop of these nuts.

⦿⦿⦿⦿○ VALUE FOR MONEY
⦿⦿⦿⦿○ MAINTENANCE
⦿⦿⦿⦿○ FREEZE/STORE
CROPPING SEASON: EARLY FALL–LATE FALL

Originating in the Mediterranean, the almond is grown for its slightly bitter nuts. Almonds need a good spring where the blossom can bloom, unaffected by frosts, and warm conditions throughout the summer. If you can provide these conditions, they're definitely worth a go. The trees can be trained to stay fairly compact, and can be grown up against a sunny fence or wall. If you're lucky, you'll be picking your first almonds after just a few years. A well-established tree will produce bucketloads of nuts each year.

Zone 7 to 9.

Where to grow Almonds can be grown as standard trees. Choose a sunny spot, on a decent, well-drained soil. Alternatively, choose a sunny fence or wall and grow as a fan against it, using horizontal wires to help train the branches.

Almonds, like peaches, can be grown on rootstocks to keep them more compact. This is a good idea for most gardens and especially if you intend to grow them against a wall. Nevertheless, they'll still need around 19 ft. 6 in. (6 m) of wall space to thrive.

Types and varieties There are a few different types of almond but it's the sweet

Tender trees
Almonds produce beautiful trees as well as a good crop, where it's warm enough.

almond, *Prunus dulcis*, that's the best. This one contains less of the bitter chemical associated with almonds and has the most palatable flavor.

Pests and diseases Peach leaf curl, which produces distorted leaves with patches of red blistering, can be a real problem to gardeners. The best solution is to copper spray the tree. Almonds are affected by other peach pests and diseases (see page 153).

Harvesting and storage It's best to wait until the nuts fall off the tree, usually in mid to late fall. Gather up the shrivelled fruits and take out the nuts, wiping them clean as you go. Leave them somewhere inside to dry off. Once dry they will store well.

In the kitchen Tricky to crack open, almonds are a favorite eaten fresh. Alternatively, you can roast them and cover them in chocolate or grind to a flour and use in cakes and pastries.

> **TIP**
> Pollination may be patchy in early spring, and some varieties prefer to be cross-pollinated with another tree. If your tree is flowering but not producing any nuts, try brushing the pollen from the flowers onto the stigmas to encourage fruit to set.

CALENDAR

WINTER
The best time to plant an almond. Stake and mulch well. Prune back the main shoots by a third, and keep just one leading shoot.

SPRING
After the first year, mulch the plants with some homemade compost and a top dressing of general purpose fertilizer.

SUMMER
A good time to prune after the first year as summer pruning will prevent diseases from entering the tree. Almonds fruit best on young wood from the previous year, so aim to cut out some of the old wood to encourage new stems to grow.

FALL
After a few years, start to harvest the nuts as they begin to fall from the tree.

VARIETY SELECTOR
• **'Nonpareil'** and **'Livingston'**: both have light pink blossom in early spring, and nuts by fall.

Walnut

Walnuts turn into huge trees, but if you've got the space and time, they have huge crops too.

○○○○○ VALUE FOR MONEY
○○○○○ MAINTENANCE
○○○○○ FREEZE/STORE
CROPPING SEASON: MID-FALL–LATE FALL

If you're lucky, walnuts can start to produce nuts after just eight years, but you may have to wait much longer. Trees can reach up to 65 feet (20 m) tall when mature, but will take up to 20 years to get to half that size. By that time, you should be collecting bucketfuls of nuts.

The Persian walnut, *Juglans regia*, grown for its nuts, is perfectly hardy, despite originating in Iran and China. Walnuts are also renowned for secreting a chemical into the soil that stops some other plants from growing around them so it's best not to plant walnuts next to a shrub or in an ornamental border, for example, but are best left to field situations.

Zone 4–8 (*J. regia*), 6–8 (*J. nigra*).

Types and varieties Within each species there are a few cultivated varieties that you may be able to track down.

Bumper harvest
Walnuts need plenty of space, but if that's what you've got they'll reward you with a bountiful harvest for years and years.

In the garden Best planted in an area of the garden which has little other use. Avoid frost pockets, as early growth can be hit by late spring frosts. Nut production will be limited in colder areas. Tress will eventually reach 65 feet (20 m) high and 65 feet (20 m) wide.

Pests and diseases Trouble-free.

Harvesting and storage Gather the nuts when their outer husks begin to crack and start to fall from the tree. This should be in fall. Clean off the husks and wipe clean. Dry in the sun if you can or indoors if it's wet. Store in a wooden box in a cool but airy place.

In the kitchen Walnuts are popular eaten fresh. Large harvests can be used in baking, especially in cakes and desserts, or you could try pickling them!

CALENDAR

WINTER
Plant a two- to four-year-old tree in winter. Look for one that has a good, straight trunk. Use a stake to keep the tree in place, and add a 3 ft. 2-in. (1-m) diameter area of mulch to the soil after planting to retain moisture and provide nutrients. Make sure you plant the tree away from other plants.

SPRING
Water well in the first year.

SUMMER
Keep watering in the first few years.

LATE WINTER
This is the best time to do any pruning as outside of this season there is a risk the tree will "bleed." Take off lower branches in the first few years to encourage the central leading shoot to grow. Remove any competing leading shoots.

After a few years, look out for walnuts developing on the tree and harvest when ripe. Re-mulch every year for the first few years.

VARIETY SELECTOR
Persian walnut

- 'Chandler': medium-sized, upright tree, which bears young.
- 'Franquette': late-ripening, pest-resistant variety.
- 'Allegheny': hardier variety.
- 'Kentucky Giant': hardier variety.

PART 3: HOW TO GROW

Once you've selected the varieties you want to grow, you'll need to equip yourself and your garden to make sure you're prepared for any eventuality. From the gear you need to finding out more about your soil and how to improve it, it's worth learning more about the tools and techniques that make for a successful food garden.

Tools and equipment

There are some essential tools that will be used almost every day. While others aren't essential, they'll save you time and effort in the long run.

There are a number of tools and equipment that are essential for good gardening and food growing. If you've never gardened before, it's worth spending some time getting the right tools, as well as ones that are both comfortable and effective in use.

If you've already got a few pieces of equipment, it's worth adding some more to your essential kit, as well as reviewing what you already have. For instance, if your spade or rake is uncomfortable to use, it's probably the wrong size. For these and other tools, it's worth buying ones that fit your body size perfectly, as while gardening with a well-suited tool can be a pleasure, using one that's ill-fitting is a real pain.

One of the first things you need to think about is protecting yourself by wearing appropriate clothing, gloves and footwear, which will allow you to do the jobs required unimpeded. Then there are the essential tools for digging, planting and weeding.

There are a few hand tools here that no gardener should be without — a spade, fork, rake and hoe, for example.

Then there's cutting. Cutting back plants and pruning are a regular job, especially where fruit are concerned, so a decent pair of pruning shears, as well as other cutting equipment, can be a good buy. Along with pruning, tools for harvesting, such as knives or snippers, are a good choice too. Finally you'll often have to move things around the garden. Pots, potting mix and plants need to be transferred from one area to another and here, a sensible piece of equipment for moving these things, based on your requirements, is also worth investing in.

Clothing, gloves and footwear

Whatever clothing you decide to wear, it will probably slowly get ruined. Don't think about gardening in your best clothes, but wear comfortable, loose-fitting clothes. A garment with plenty of pockets is a good choice, so you can keep your string and pocket knife handy.

Footwear is another area worth considering. You're likely to get muddy, so consider investing in a decent pair of waterproof boots. Stout walking boots or even steel toe-capped boots are a better choice if you're thinking of using powered machinery such as a rototiller.

Gloves are an essential item of clothing for the kitchen gardener. While some gardeners prefer to garden without any, they can be useful in some situations. When you're working in the greenhouse, or sowing seed, consider using disposable latex gloves or thin rubber gloves. This will allow you to do delicate work such as pricking out or sowing seeds, but will keep your hands clean. For rougher work, such as digging and pruning, select thicker leather gloves. Going for ones that have a gauntlet up the wrist will ensure you stay protected when pruning the spikiest blackberry. Don't skimp on gloves for quality as the best, softest leather allows you to work easily. Rough, badly stitched cheaper versions make glove-wearing awkward.

Maximum gardening efficiency
A good range of tools and equipment will make your gardening life a lot easier. Always buy the best-quality equipment you can afford and look after it: bladed tools like these heavy-duty scissors should be wiped dry and sharpened regularly.

Tools for digging, planting and weeding

Spades and forks A spade and fork are tools most people keep in their shed, but if you're buying them new, consider first whether they're lightweight and comfortable to hold. It's always worth visiting your plant store to try them out first. They should:

- **Have stainless steel blades or tines:** These are not much more expensive than other types, and stay clean and sharp for years.

- **Have a strong shaft:** Spades and forks often come under a great amount of physical force as you use them for various jobs around the garden. Make sure the shaft is either smooth wood or metal.

- **Have a comfortable handle:** While T-shaped handles are still common, a D or Y shape will be more comfortable. Avoid any with finger spacings as everyone holds their tools differently. Make sure the handle is secure and doesn't wobble.

- **Be a size to suit you:** While standard forks and spades actually have fairly large heads, border forks and spades,

with their slightly smaller heads, are often a much better bet. If these are too big, look out for good-quality children's versions, which are often just smaller versions of adult tools and can be more comfortable for some.

Rake A good border rake is essential for drawing out furrows or creating seedbeds. Choose one where the handle reaches your nose when held vertically — this means it will be comfortable in use. Other than this, go for one with stainless steel blades and a comfortable, lightweight handle.

Hoe Hoes are essential weeding tools and if you plant your vegetable plot in rows, they are fantastic at quickly clearing away unwanted weeds from your plot. You'll use a hoe from earliest spring right into winter, so it's worth choosing one that's comfortable and effective.

There are lots of different types of hoes on the market — some cut the weeds at the base, and others are designed to uproot them just below the surface.

While some hoes need to have their blades sharpened so that they can cut weeds cleanly, others, made from stainless steel, don't need to be resharpened. Try out the hoe before you buy it and make sure you can use it comfortably without stooping.

ESSENTIAL TOOLS AND EQUIPMENT

Loppers
Good for pruning old fruit trees, and helping you to clear your patch when you start out. Good for cutting thicker stems.

Penknife
Kept in the pocket at all times, a knife is useful for harvesting and cutting string.

Gloves
A decent pair of thick gloves is useful when tidying up fruit, especially prickly gooseberries, blackberries and raspberries.

Hoe
On large plots where you've planted in rows, a hoe is a quick way of getting rid of weeds.

Soil rake
An indispensable tool for creating seedbeds and drills.

Spade
Good for digging over your plot in the spring or fall and essential when planting trees and soft fruit.

Draw hoe
A draw hoe makes earthing up potatoes a quick and easy task.

Hand trowel and fork
Essential when working close to the soil. A trowel is good for planting and a fork is good for weeding.

Pruning shears
A sharp pair of secateurs is essential for all light pruning tasks.

Garden fork
A good tool for lifting root vegetables like carrots and potatoes, as well as helping move compost and other mulching materials around.

ROTOTILLER

Another piece of equipment that is very useful, especially on largers plots or allotments, is a rototiller. The gasoline version is very expensive, and as you'll only be using it a couple of times a year when the beds are empty, this may not be cost-effective. You can rent rototillers from rental shops, but again, cost can be prohibitive. If you are part of a gardening club or have gardening-friendly neighbors, consider chipping in together to get one to share. Aim for one that is easy to start and easy to maintain.

There's also another type of hoe, often used on the vegetable plot but more commonly used for drawing up soil and creating drills. Onion hoes or draw hoes can be useful for earthing up potatoes, say, or when you want to create long lengths of drills.

Trowel and hand fork Although a trowel is an essential piece of kit for planting, a hand fork is more useful for weeding on your hands and knees. They often come as a pair, and it's worth having them both in your armory. Make sure the handles are comfortable. A wooden handle is usually the best, along with a stainless steel blade or tines. Trowels and hand forks are renowned for bending under pressure, so look at the shaft and make sure there are no weak joints.

Use a marker line
A marker line is useful when planting out to ensure you plant your seedlings in straight rows.

Tools for cutting

Cutting back berries and pruning fruit trees requires a good pair of pruning shears. Go for the bypass type. While anvils are more useful for cutting dead wood, bypass shears can cut both live and dead wood effectively. Select a pair that is comfortable to hold — they are sold in different sizes so try before you buy. And make sure the catch is easy to reach, whichever hand you use. Blades should be sharp and easily sharpened when necessary. The best shears will allow you to have blades replaced once worn out. Finally, go for a pair with bright handles as you'll often lose them in a pile of prunings.

Loppers, which are basically long-handled shears, are good for thicker stems and awkward-to-reach places. Again, a bypass pair is best. Pruning saws are a good choice too if you have a lot of fruit trees. They can give a cleaner cut than loppers and are sometimes easier to use in tricky-to-reach places. Blades often fold inside the handle for easy carrying.

Moving things around the garden

A plastic, flexible carry trug is one of the most useful recent introductions to the gardener. They are excellent for harvesting crops or collecting weeds or prunings. One of these is essential for a garden of any size, and as they come in such a wide range of colors, there'll be one to fit your style.

On top of this, a wheelbarrow is always a good investment — useful for carrying heavier or more awkward materials around the garden, such as potting mix and young plants. Go for one with a pneumatic tire and a plastic pan. Make sure the handles are comfortable and that it has a good balance — you don't want it to tip over when it's full of your prize plants.

There is a range of other trolleys and pot movers available to the gardener, but most things can be carried in either a trug or barrow.

Measuring and planting equipment

A marker line, basically made of two pieces of wood with a string attached to each piece, is always useful when it comes to planting straight rows. Alternatively, use a wide plank, marked at spacing intervals. This can be kneeled on over the bed while you plant. Or use a narrower rod or feet/meter rule that can be used for spacing. Once you get your eye trained, you'll probably end up leaving this one in the shed, but it can be useful when you first start out.

Tools for harvesting

A sharp folding knife is really useful for the gardener. As well as using it to harvest crops such as zucchini, cucumbers and grapes, it's also useful for cutting string when you want to quickly tie something in. Choose a small one, with a comfy handle and a sharp blade that easily folds in and out. Other tools, such as a good pair of scissors or snippers, can also be useful for harvesting crops.

Hoe your plot
Spring and fall are the key times for hoeing, but weeds can soon appear at any time following rain. It's best to keep your plot fairly weed free at all times to stop it getting out of hand.

MAINTAINING YOUR TOOLS

- Keep your tools somewhere dry. A shed or a garage is perfect.

- Try to keep them as clean as you can, which helps prevent them from rusting.

- For tools like secateurs, use an oily rag to keep them in good shape.

- Some tools will need to be sharpened — usually on an annual basis. There are a range of sharpeners available to the gardener — go for one that will allow you to sharpen all your tools.

Growing from seed

Whether you're sowing direct in the ground or raising plants in pots, here are some tried and trusted techniques that will ensure your plants grow well.

The satisfaction you get from growing your own food is definitely increased when you've raised the plants yourself from seed. Growing from seed can be more cost effective than buying plants, especially for most vegetables and herbs, and you'll get a crop in the same year you started raising the plants. Sowing indoors is essential for crops that are tender and need a head start, or for tricky-to-germinate seeds that just never seem to do well when sown in the ground. However, for many, starting the seeds off in the soil is the most sensible option.

Sowing in the ground

Some vegetables, salads and herbs can be sown direct into the ground. It makes sense when you want a large number of a specific plant as it saves you time and effort raising lots of plants in small pots. Some plants fare better when sown where they are to grow. This is true of most root crops such as carrots and parsnips, whose roots don't like the disturbance of being transferred.

If you do decide to sow direct, you'll need to keep a careful eye on your plot. The soil temperature and moisture need to be right, and there are usually hidden dangers, such as pests like slugs and snails that will devour your tiny seedlings as soon as they emerge.

SAVING SEED

While buying seed ensures good germination and the right variety, saving seed each year can be an economical and fun way to grow plants. It's easier to save seed from some plants than others. Peas and beans, for example, can be left on the plant at the end of the season, and whole pods removed and dried in the greenhouse. Tomatoes, too, can be squished in a sieve and fermented in water for a couple of days, then their seeds saved. Remember to store seeds in a dry and cool environment to ensure they remain viable until the following year. However, if you've grown more than one variety, you may find they've cross-pollinated and you get a whole new plant!

Timing

While some crops such as garlic and onion sets can be sown in fall, others prefer the spring, when the soil starts to warm up. This is true of crops such as carrots and beets. You can use a soil thermometer to check the temperature of your soil to make sure it's warm enough — for most crops, the soil temperature should be over 41°F (5°C). However, for tender crops such as green beans and corn, the soil should be around 54°F (12°C) for the seed to germinate. In these cases you'll need to wait until later in the spring to sow direct.

Preparing the soil

For all seeds, a good seedbed is essential to help them grow. The soil should be raked to a fine tilth to ensure the seeds sit comfortably on the soil and don't slip down large cracks or sit on stones where they will dry out. To do this, draw out a drill using the edge of the soil rake. Alternatively, use a plank of wood across the bed that you can kneel on and use a hand trowel to draw out the soil.

If the soil is dry, watering the base of the drill will help get your seeds off to a good start.

Next, you'll need to make sure you follow the advice on seed sowing depth, then cover with the fine soil from the drill. It's also worthwhile to always mark your drill with a plant label noting the plant, variety and date sown. If nothing appears in a few weeks you'll know something has gone wrong and you can try again. Alternatively, if just a few seedlings come up, you can always resow the same variety into the gaps.

Although seed drills are best for most crops, where you sow a single line of seed, others can be planted in bands, three to four seeds deep in a single row. This is a good idea for crops such as cut-and-come-again salads, spring onions, radish and peas.

Other crops, such as fava beans and corn, should be planted in blocks rather than rows. In the case of fava beans, this helps when you're trying to keep the plants upright, whereas with corn, planting in a block aids pollination.

Thinning

Thinning is a process of removing excess seedlings. It's common to oversow, resulting in too many seedlings for the space allowed. You can pick over the seedlings and remove the weaker ones. These can be used to fill gaps in the rows further along. Alternatively, for some crops such as leeks and carrots, you can leave thicker sowings intact, but start pulling the crops when they're baby-sized, leaving others to grow on to maturity.

Direct sowing
Growing from seed is the cheapest method of raising plants. If soil and climate allow, planting directly in the soil saves both time and effort.

Sowing in pots

Sowing in small pots in a greenhouse or windowsill is a failsafe way of raising plants. You control the soil conditions, moisture, warmth and light and it's easier to keep out slugs and other pests.

Where to grow

A propagator (an enclosed unit with a clear top) provides a good environment for seeds to germinate. It helps to keep the humidity high and warmth in. For certain crops that need a high or constant temperature, heated propagators are available. These can either be used on a windowsill or in a greenhouse.

If you don't want a bulky propagator on your windowsill, you can still raise plants from seed. Use a clear plastic bag tied around the small pot that you sow into.

WAYS TO SOW

Pots A good choice for plants with big seeds that grow quickly and will soon fill the space in a pot. Examples include marrows, zucchini, cucumbers and eggplants.

Modules Where you want plenty of plants, these can be sown into modular trays, then planted out directly into the ground. Examples include cabbages, beet, leek and onion seed.

Root trainers Deeper modular pots are good for plants that develop large root systems quickly. Examples include corn and pole beans.

Seed trays A good choice if you don't mind pricking out plants once they've germinated. Ideal for lettuce, herbs and other salads.

Eavestrough A good idea is to sow your peas straight into a length of eavestrough. Sow in bands, and once germinated in the safety of a greenhouse, these can be slid straight into a prepared drill in the vegetable garden.

Propagator seedlings
Raising seed in propagators is useful when you want to get a head start, say, with greenhouse crops such as tomatoes and peppers.

SOWING SEED

Whatever container you're sowing seed in, you'll need to follow the germination advice provided here.

● First, select either a sowing or multipurpose potting mix. Most vegetable seeds aren't too fussy, and you could use a good-quality peat-free version.

● When sowing seed on the surface of the potting mix, aim to sprinkle the seed evenly. When planting individual seeds, place in the middle of the pot, and for zucchini, cucumbers and other flat-seeded vegetables, it's best to place them on their side.

● In a module, you may want to plant two seeds, then if both come up, just pinch out the weaker one — this will ensure you don't have any gaps later.

● A fine sprinkling of potting mix can be used to cover the seed, helping to retain moisture, or alternatively you can use a dusting of vermiculite, which is useful for those seeds that require light to germinate, such as celery.

● Water with tap water and use a fine rose to ensure the seeds don't get washed down through the potting mix.

Prick out your seedlings
If you have sown your seeds in a seed tray, you will need to prick out young plants into individual pots.

Pots, trays and modules

Traditionally, seeds are sown in large seed trays, and once germinated, they can be pricked out into individual small pots. To save time, seed can either be sown directly into pots or into module trays. Module trays are trays that have been divided into separate growing units. They're usually square so you can fit plenty of plants into a single tray. For most people who want to raise a lot of plants but don't have lots of time and space, module trays are the best choice. These can also be fitted into propagators, or plastic wrap can be placed over the surface of the tray until seedlings start to appear.

Pricking out

If you've sown individually in pots or modules, you won't need to prick out seedlings, but for those you sowed in open trays, once the seedlings have germinated they need to be transferred to individual pots. Fill small pots with multipurpose potting mix and use a pencil to create a small hole in the center. Then, using the pencil, plant label or similar, gently tease out the seedlings from the soil of the tray. Only pick up the seedling by the tip of the leaf, never the stem, which can be easily damaged. Then lower into the prepared hole and carefully firm up. These transplanted seedlings will need a bit of care and attention for the next few days until they settle into their new home.

Aftercare

Once plants have grown on in their pots and modules, they will be ready for planting out. Plants that you are keeping in a container can be planted out into larger containers as soon as they're ready. Other plants that are to be planted out in the soil, such as peas and fava beans, are fairly unfussy when they get planted out. Other tender vegetables, such as corn and runner beans, will need to be kept under cover until the conditions are right.

If you are keeping your plants in small containers for a long time, bear in mind that the fertilizer in the potting mix will last for only around five weeks. After this, it's a good idea to apply a liquid fertilizer or pot on into a larger container. Also, don't sow too early as plants dislike being left in small pots for a long time, and sometimes struggle to recover once planted out.

Using covers

Covers can be used to cover the soil and raise the temperature to help seeds get a head start.

Floating row covers

The most economical cover, floating row covers can be used on the surface of the soil after you've sown your crop. It will help

Flourishing seedlings
In mid-spring your greenhouse should be packed with young plants and seedlings. Having a removable bench will allow you to squeeze more into the space you have available.

MAKING SOWING EASIER

Most seed comes in its natural state; however, some is treated to make sowing easier and more successful.

Seed mats These are mats that have been impregnated with seed. They're usually sold to fit into a small or large container for container growing, and are ideal for some herbs such as basil. It also means you don't need to handle small tricky seeds.

Seed tapes For vegetables usually grown in rows, you can buy tape impregnated with seed every few inches/ centimeters. Typically, these are available for vegetables such as lettuce, carrot and parsnip, and again are ideal if you struggle to handle small seed. However, your choice of varieties may be limited.

Treated and pelleted seed Most seed available for amateur gardeners is not treated, but some may be treated with a fungicide. It will say on the packet if this is the case. Others may be pelleted (surrounded in a clay-like casing to make seeds bigger and therefore easier to handle).

lift the temperature underneath it by a few degrees and encourage germination. You'll need to anchor the edges with bricks or pieces of wood.

Plastic tunnels
Long tunnels or cloches are available that can be lifted over a row of newly sown seeds. Again this warms the air within the tunnel and encourages germination, especially early in the season. They're easy to lift off and move to another part of the garden

Individual cloches
Bell cloches or lantern cloches are more expensive but can be good to protect individual larger plants, for example zucchini, cucumbers and melons.

Storing seed
If you've got seed left over or are storing your own, it's a good idea to store it properly so it can be used the following year.
- Use a plastic container with a sealed lid.
- Make sure your seed packets are labeled with the plant and variety name.
- Add a sachet of silica gel to help keep the moisture levels down.
- Keep in the fridge or somewhere cool and dark.

Buying plants

Whether you're buying seeds or plants, it's worth shopping around for the best-quality and best-performing varieties.

CHOOSING PLANTS AT THE PLANT STORE

- Check the stems of plants — make sure they're unblemished and have no cracks or fissures.
- Look out for pests and diseases on the stems or leaves, and avoid any that show signs of yellowing.
- When buying a tree, look for a straight, strong leading shoot from the base.
- If you're buying a pot-grown plant, tip the plant out of the pot and check the roots. Make sure they look healthy, have reached the edge of the pot, but are not cramped for space or starting to wind around the inside of the pot.
- When buying young plants, look for bushy plants that have been cared for well with healthy green foliage.
- Ask for advice — good plant stores should be packed with staff who know their stuff. Also ask about their returns policy and what happens if your plant dies.

Starting off your food garden will need some capital investment. You can keep the cost down by growing many of the plants from seed. However, for places where you'll only need one or two plants, the expense of a packet of F1 seeds may not be worthwhile. When it comes to fruit, even more will be invested, but buy at the right time of year and the right stage of growth and your plants will settle in well and reward you for years to come.

Seed

Seed is obviously the cheapest method of growing, but in many cases you'll need a heated propagator, as well as pots and potting mix. For many crops, however, particularly those that can be sown direct or don't need special cosseting, seed is best. Certainly for crops that are sown in long rows such as lettuce, peas and beans, it makes sense to buy a packet with plenty of seed. Also, in general, root crops do better when grown undisturbed, so sowing carrot, beets and parsnip for example, direct in the ground, will be better than buying young plants. When out buying seed, you'll need to compare between the different varieties. Although many long-standing older varieties are still available, many do not perform as well as the newly bred varieties. In general, opt for an F1 variety where you can (although these may be slightly more expensive) and go for varieties recommended throughout this book.

Seed is a valuable commodity, and if you don't use all your seed up, think about storing it for later in the year, or even next year (see page 203). The best time to buy seed is in the winter — this is when the fresh stocks are released by the seed suppliers, and also a good time for you to plan your gardening year (see page 20).

Young plants

Buying young vegetable plants can seem expensive but is sometimes more economical than buying seed and it will certainly save you time. For some crops you'll really only want a handful of plants, if that. For some, such as Brussels sprouts, eggplants and sweet peppers, just a couple might do. Buying plants means that it saves you having to raise these plants from seed, some of which are fairly tricky to grow. It also means that you can try several different varieties of the same plant, but not waste any seed.

In general, some brassicas and tender crops such as tomatoes, sweet and chili peppers, and eggplants are the most popular, but if you've forgotten to sow other crops, a quick trip to the plant store may mean you can still grow them this year.

While plant stores start to stock young vegetable plants from early spring, your choice will be limited. More and more mail order suppliers are now offering young vegetable plants by mail order, and you'll need to get your orders in by late winter to have the pick of the varieties on offer.

Perennial vegetables

Although some perennial vegetables such as globe artichokes and asparagus can be raised from seed, most people buy plants. These are often sold in early spring and planted directly in the soil. It is best to buy these plants from a mail order supplier to give you the best choice of varieties.

Other ways of growing

Some crops aren't raised from seed or as young plants, but as tubers, sets or bulbs. Seed potatoes are basically single tubers that are usually sold in small bags. These are available for mail order or in plant stores in late winter and early spring. Onions and garlic are best planted either in spring or fall, and the bulbs and sets are widely available at these times.

Herbs

It's definitely worth growing herbs that you use a lot from seed, such as parsley and cilantro. For other perennial herbs, such as tarragon and thyme, plants are your best option.

Berries

Berries such as raspberries and strawberries can be bought in late winter, early spring and sometimes in fall. The best choice

will be from mail order suppliers, and as they lift them from their nursery they'll be sent directly to you, which means they're kept very fresh and their roots won't have dried out.

It's a good idea to get them into the ground as quickly as you can. Where there is a choice, don't go for plants that are too big or old, as young, small plants always settle in much quicker.

Trees

Plant stores can have a great choice of fruit trees, and if you're spending a lot of money on a fairly mature specimen you'd want to see it first to make sure it's a good shape. Find a good nursery or plant store near to you. If you want anything unusual, or are after just one-year-old trees, a mail order nursery will almost certainly be cheaper and have a wider choice. The best time to order is in winter or late summer for a spring or fall delivery.

Plant-store herbs
When stocking up your herb garden, it is best to buy perennial herbs as plants. Choose robust, healthy-looking specimens.

Pruning and training fruit trees

Gardeners often dread pruning fruit trees, but if you prune correctly in the first few years, trees will only need a regular tidy-up.

Pruning a fruit tree is like pruning any other plant. It's a way of getting rid of unwanted branches — perhaps because they're diseased or growing in the wrong place — to create a shape that suits the space allotted to the tree and to maximize fruit production. Get all these right and you'll have an attractive and productive plant that will last for years.

The pruning you do in the first few years — called formative pruning — is essential to creating the shape that you want. Once in that shape, the tree should be pruned back into the desired space each year.

Pruning

Once you've bought your young tree and planted it according to the specific guidelines in the relevant entry in the fruit directory, you'll need to start pruning it into shape. On the following pages is some general advice on how to create the most popular shapes.

When to prune

Apples and pears are most often pruned in winter. Plums, apricots, cherries and nectarines should be pruned in spring and summer.

GROWING A FRUIT TREE AGAINST A WALL

- If you're growing a tree against a wall, then you'll need to attach horizontal wires to allow you to train the tree easily.
- For fan trees aim for a horizontal wire every 12 inches (30 cm). For cordons and espaliers 18 inches (45 cm) should be sufficient. Measure and mark accordingly.
- Use eye bolts or vine eyes secured into the wall or fence. These should be kept off the surface of the wall to allow air to circulate behind the tree.
- Attach wires horizontally. If required use a straining bolt at one end to help keep the wire taut.

Persevere with your pruning
Creating a beautifully shaped tree will take a few years, but once grown and trained properly, subsequent care will be so much easier.

Spur or tip-bearer?

Most apples and pears are spur-bearing — they produce fruit buds on new shoots that develop from short woody shoots known as spurs. Some varieties are tip-bearing — they tend to produce flower buds on unpruned two-year-old shoots. If you were to prune these back to produce short spurs you would remove most of the flower buds, and, therefore, the fruit. If you have an old tree and do not know the variety, observe how your tree fruits. If most of the fruit is borne toward the tips of the shoots, it is a tip-bearer; spur varieties will have lots of fruit on short spurs close to the main stems.

There are two types of buds that you should be able to recognize on a fruit tree in winter. In general, when you're pruning, it's best to prune to a leaf bud.

SPUR BEARER

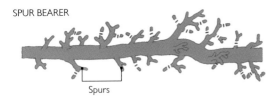

Spurs

Fruit buds

These are the buds that produce flowers, and subsequently fruit. They're generally larger than the leaf buds. These are the buds you really want to promote to encourage decent fruiting.

Leaf buds

Leaf buds are smaller than fruit buds and although your tree needs these to produce leaves to photosynthesize, they do not increase fruiting.

TIP BEARER

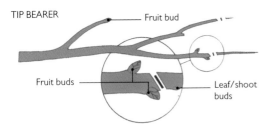

Fruit bud

Fruit buds

Leaf/shoot buds

Tree fruits dealt with on these pages include apples, pears, plums, cherries, peaches and figs. Also included are intensively pruned forms such as cordons and espaliers, as well as bush-trained versions on dwarfing rootstocks that produce trees more shrub-like in size and shape than the tree shapes seen in traditional orchards. Specific information on each fruit can be found in the individual entries in the fruit directory.

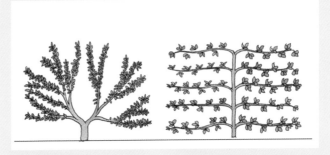

Fan

Branches fan out on either side, starting from a very low stem. Good for peaches, nectarines, figs and cherries that need a warm spot against a fence or wall.

Espalier

A central stem with horizontal branches usually trained against a fence or wall. Takes a long time to train but can look very attractive, and is good for apples and pears.

Cordon

These are usually trained up a single stem, sometimes at an angle of 45 degrees. Perfect for fitting lots of trees in a small area, but needs a wall or fence to train against.

Bush

A freestanding tree with a clear trunk and open center.

PRUNING TECHNIQUES

KEY apple pear plum cherry peach fig

Espalier

An espalier has a vertical trunk from which horizontal branches are trained in pairs around every 20 inches (50 cm).

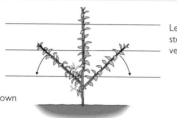

Leave the leading stem to grow vertically.

Tie branches down horizontally.

Nip out the leading shoot to encourage more branching.

Prune the horizontal stems back to a healthy bud.

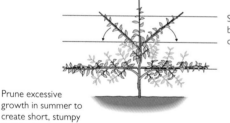

Select two more branches and tie down horizontally.

Prune excessive growth in summer to create short, stumpy fruit buds.

Cordon

Cordons can be squeezed into the smallest spaces against a wall or fence, and allow you to try out several varieties close together.

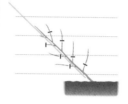

Cut back branches to three buds.

Cut back side branches in summer.

Cut the main stem, and remove excess branching.

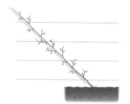

This leaves a collection of short, stumpy fruit buds.

YEAR 1: Choose three strong stems. Tie two horizontally and leave the middle one to grow vertically. Remove any other stems.

YEAR 2: In the winter, nip out the leading shoot to encourage branching below. This should be near to where you want the next set of horizontal branches to be formed.

In the summer, tie in a further two stems to the next tier of horizontal wires. Keep repeating this process until you have the desired number of horizontal branches.

Horizontal branches should be pruned in summer, as with cordons, to develop short, stumpy fruiting buds.

STEP-OVERS

The pruning information also applies to step-overs, which are essentially single-armed espaliers.

YEAR 1: Once you've planted, tie in the tree to a cane positioned to the angle required. Leave the leading shoot but cut back any branches to just three buds from the trunk.

In the summer, cut back any of these side branches that have grown back to just beyond where you pruned them in the winter.

YEAR 2: Cut the main stem at the point you want the tree to reach. If it isn't there yet, leave it until year 3. Prune the side branches in the summer back to near where you pruned them previously. This will help to build up a collection of short and stumpy fruiting buds.

Bush

The bush is the most common fruit tree shape. The height of the tree will depend on where you cut the leading shoot.

Prune the main stem.

The following year, cut back 3–5 side shoots and the leading shoot.

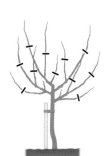

Shorten branches by a third in year 3.

Continue in subsequent years.

Fan

With no central stem, a fan is made up entirely of a network of branches leading to further branches.

Prune the central stem back to four healthy buds.

If the tree arrives with branches, remove all but two.

Trim back the two selected branches and remove all other shoots.

Prune back subsequent branches from the two main branches, leaving four main stems on each side.

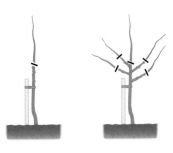

YEAR 1: Once planted, prune the main stem down to around the point you want the main trunk to start. Make sure there are some decent buds below this point. If there are any side branches cut these back by around two-thirds.

YEAR 2: Select three to five strong side shoots. Aim for those that will help develop a goblet shape. Cut these back by about two-thirds. Cut the remaining side shoots at the main stem.

YEAR 3: No more heavy pruning should be necessary. Shorten the main branches by about a third to a leaf bud. Tidy up the tree to keep it in a shape you want.

YEAR 1: Prune to around 18 inches (45 cm), making sure there are some decent buds below this point. Fix canes on the horizontal wires at around 45 degrees. If you have any side branches, select two now; otherwise, wait for others to be produced in the summer, then cut off all others. Train these two stems onto the canes. These will be your two main branches.

YEAR 2: Prune back the two main side shoots by about two-thirds. Remove any other side shoots. Onto either side branch, attach two canes above and one below. Select the summer side branches to be tied into these canes and remove all others.

YEAR 3: Prune the eight side branches you have developed by about one-third. If space allows, you can create more side branches from these. Side stems produced from these main branches will need pruning back in the summer.

Growing in containers

Whatever size space you have, you'll be able to grow some fruit and vegetables, but pick what you grow wisely.

While many people have large plots at their disposal, there are even more with just a small patio, terrace, balcony or window box. Even if you do have a large garden, bringing it closer to your kitchen makes sense. Who wants to traipse down to the end of the garden to pick herbs, when a well-positioned container next to the back door can provide you with a decent supply? One of the problems of growing food on the patio is that, unlike flowering plants that can carry on flowering for months, for much of the time the pots and baskets containing edible crops don't look particularly good. However, choose your crops wisely and be a little creative, and your containers of fruit and vegetables will look attractive and appetizing for much of the year.

How to grow

You can use multipurpose potting mix for your containers, preferably peat-free. Growing bags often work out a little cheaper, and these are easy to carry. They're formulated for growing crops so do well for container vegetables. There shouldn't be any need for specialist potting mix for your crops, except perhaps with blueberries or cranberries. Here, it's best to go with an acidic potting mix. For any permanent, larger plants (such as trees), it's well worth using a soil-based potting mix as it will be heavier and prevent tall plants from toppling over.

If you want to save some money, homemade potting mix performs very well too (see pages 222–223). Make sure it's well

Fresh herbs
Growing herbs in containers on the patio can make attractive features as well as a useful supply for your kitchen.

Peppers on the patio
Sweet peppers make attractive patio plants, despite
not being the most productive of crops.

WHERE TO GROW

Vegetables, salads, herbs and fruit can all be grown in
containers, but you'll need to select wisely.

Large planters Growing your own food is becoming
so popular that companies have started designing large
planters for patios. These are often raised off the ground
so no bending is required. They're a great idea if you
lack space in the ground but want to grow some larger
vegetables such as spinach, beets, shallots, as well as rows
of herbs and salads. If you do invest in a large planter,
think about where you'll site it, as once filled with potting
mix it will be difficult to move. A sunny spot is best.

Pots For most crops, opt for pots at least 12 inches
(30 cm) in diameter. While quick crops such as salads will
do fine in shallow containers, plants that produce edible
roots, such as carrots, do better in a fairly deep container.
In general, the deeper the pot the better, as plants are less
likely to run out of water and you can water less often.
You can also use containers on the patio for fruit that you
can't grow in the ground, such as blueberries, or those
that need to be moved to a sheltered area in the winter,
such as citrus.

Baskets Baskets can be a good choice for vegetables
and salads. Although not many vegetables trail, cucumbers
and melons can prove successful in a basket, as can
tomatoes. Other crops can be successful too, but it's
best to go for short plants as anything too tall becomes
unwieldy. Try spherical carrots, bush beans and herbs such
as parsley and basil.

Window boxes Plants in window boxes are often the
most tricky-to-grow food. Their position usually means
they struggle for good light, and their width and depth
make them unsuitable for any but the smallest crops.
However, if you choose plants with pretty foliage, then
they can look good and be productive too. There are now
varieties of tomatoes to fit in window boxes; chili peppers
can look good; and a regular supply of radish and salads
such as rocket and mizuna will soon help them fill out.

On the windowsill There's nothing wrong with
growing food on your windowsill. Small pots of herbs
can be kept for weeks on a windowsill; however, if you're
buying them from a supermarket it's best to pot up into
slightly larger containers and add some slow-release
fertilizer. The windowsill is a good place for sprouting
seeds too.

Ornamental yet functional
Chili peppers do well in greenhouses, on the patio or even on the windowsill.

rotted and that any large, undecomposed chunks have been removed. Putting it through a sieve is a good idea. If you want, homemade potting mix can be supplemented with decent garden soil too, but it's worth removing any large stones first and checking for obvious problems with the soil.

Whatever you use, it's worth adding a slow-release fertilizer to your pots when you fill them up.

Many crops can be sown direct in containers, sprinkling the seed over the surface, then covering with a light dusting of potting mix. For mixed containers, however, it may be worth raising plants in small pots, then transferring to larger containers later. For tender crops such as basil, it may be worth starting the containers on a windowsill, then moving the containers out once all threat of frost has passed. Similarly for early containers of carrots and salad, try starting them off on a windowsill in early spring, then moving them outside toward the end of spring.

Crops that do well in containers

Large, slow-growing crops generally don't do well in pots. They can look fairly unattractive for most of the year and need plenty of care and attention. For this reason it's worth avoiding some of the slow-growing brassicas such as Brussels sprouts and winter cabbages. Similarly, steer clear of parsnips and other winter crops that will take up space on your patio all summer as they grow and develop.

The best crops for containers are those that grow quickly. They'll need less care as you'll be harvesting them, and also leave you space to grow others. Salads are perfect. Lettuce, arugula and mizuna, for example, are all good choices, as are quick-growing radishes, turnips, carrots, chard, beets and spring onions. Onions do surprisingly well in containers but don't look particularly nice, as do garlic and baby leeks. Peas, fava beans, bush and pole beans all do well, but the amount of watering you'll need to do with these will vary, and if you miss a single watering, the peas and pole beans may not recover.

Crops such as zucchini, squash and potatoes need only one plant in each container, but can produce a really good crop.

Plenty of varieties of tomatoes, cucumbers, sweet peppers, chilies and eggplants perform well in a container on the patio.

Many of the herbs are worth growing in a pot or basket and are useful if positioned close to the house. Cilantro, basil and parsley are the most often used, but large pots containing bay, rosemary, thyme and oregano also work well.

Salad leaves for the kitchen
Cut-and-come-again salad leaves are perfect for growing in containers and are very convenient to harvest if positioned on the patio.

Mix and match
Containers don't have to contain just one plant, a mixture of edible plants and herbs can be grown together, as with these baskets of tomatoes and herbs. You could also add some edible flowers for interest.

TRICKS TO SUCCESSFUL CONTAINER GROWING

- Choose varieties that are small and have been specially bred for containers. Flick through the most recent seed catalogs as more and more are appearing each year.
- Once you've harvested some of your container vegetables you'll be left with gaps. Think about having some young lettuce plants that can be used to fill in gaps as they appear.
- Some vegetables will do better on their own, such as potatoes. Other crops such as bush beans and salads can be squeezed in with other crops.
- Mix and match several containers together. A blueberry bush can look great in late summer and fall, but its structure can also be appreciated earlier in the year when positioned next to containers of young vegetables.
- Move your containers around. You can easily move containers from sun to shade or reposition the better-looking pots toward the front of the patio.
- Consider installing an irrigation system and water timer. The worst thing about growing food in containers is the watering, and an irrigation system will both save you time and can be more water-efficient than watering by hand.
- Avoid crops that need extra care when you're likely to be on holiday, or make friends with a neighbor and ask them to water your plants while you're away.

Making your containers look good

Think about the containers to use. Larger containers are a good choice as plants are less likely to run short of water and wilt. Choose glazed (or plastic pots) in preference to terracotta, which can dry out quickly and crack in cold weather. And don't grow just traditional vegetables — try some more unusual or interesting crops, as well as growing flowers.

Another way to make your edible containers look good on the patio is to have somewhere they can be put when they're not looking great. Wheel them out once they've grown a little and enjoy them when they look their best.

Some crops, such as carrots, will take several weeks before the seeds germinate and plants grow to a decent size. Whole pots of feathery carrot foliage and orange tops peeking out of the soil can look great once grown on, but not when first sown.

Another way to make your containers look good is to grow a mixture of plants. Having some edible flowers as well as herbs mixed in with your vegetables can make them look more attractive. Or try using more unusual varieties — purple bush beans or yellow snow peas, for example.

Watering in the garden

Some crops really do benefit from watering at certain times in their growth cycle, whereas others don't benefit from any additional watering. With containers, watering is essential, and sometimes necessary up to twice a day. There are techniques that make watering both quicker and easier, as well as more effective.

Rainwater or tap water?

For most people the water they get out of their taps is the easiest water to use in the garden. It's clean, cheap and easy to use with a hose. However, if you water a lot and your supply is on a water meter, it could end up being more expensive than you think. Water from the water mains supply is often fairly alkaline too, so is not always ideal for certain crops such as blueberries.

To keep the cost (both environmental and economic) of watering down, consider investing in one or two water barrels. These can be attached to the down spouts of your eavestrough using a rain diverter, and water from your roof is then diverted into the water barrel. Place the water barrel on bricks or a stand, so you can put a watering can underneath to fill up.

If you really value the water that falls on your house, you can even invest in larger, underground storage tanks. Electric pumps can also be fitted to remove the need to use a watering can and allow you to use a hose from your barrel or tank.

Soak in new plants
Watering shouldn't be a burden, but it's a good idea to give crops a good watering as they are first planted out.

Ways to water

Whichever source of water you use, you'll need to decide the way you'll water. There are pros and cons to each.

Watering can

This is the slowest way of watering, but also the most efficient as you water only where required. This is a good choice if you are using a water barrel, but also good on a community garden plot or place where you don't have tap water available. A small can with a fine rose is useful for watering seedlings.

Hose

If you want to water quickly, a hose is the best bet. You'll still need to stand there to water so you can direct the hose to where the water is really needed, but it's much quicker than using a can. There are a range of nozzles available that allow

WAYS TO REDUCE WATERING

If you're finding yourself out every evening watering, here are a few tips to help keep watering to a minimum:

Mulches and membranes Use either thick layers of organic material or permeable or non-permeable weed-control fabrics. These help to keep the moisture in the soil and reduce evaporation.

Timing of crops If your crops need a lot of watering in midsummer, consider changing the timing of your growing. Start plants off earlier so they're ready for harvest before the very hot period.

Keep weeds down Weeds also use up water, so where necessary keep weeding regularly.

HOW TO WATER

Whichever way you decide to water, there are a few other golden rules.

● Use only tap water for watering seedlings as this limits the spread of disease.

● When watering, try to do so either mid-morning or late in the evening.

● Try to direct the water to the roots of the plant. If the water is just running off, consider inserting an upside-down cut-off plastic drinks bottle next to the crop and water into that — this is particularly effective for large single plants such as zucchini or tomatoes.

● Try to avoid watering onto the plants themselves and water just at the base of the plant. This helps to discourage diseases from entering the plant.

These crops should be watered a few weeks before they're ready for harvesting or as the crop just starts to form to help swell the crop: broccoli, fava beans, green beans, peas, potatoes and corn.

These crops do benefit from regular watering right through their growing season: eggplant, celery, zucchini, cucumber, fennel, leek, lettuces, oriental salads, pepper, radish, runner beans, spinach and tomatoes.

In general, fruit and nut trees shouldn't need to be watered. However, to aid good establishment they should certainly be watered for the first couple of years, especially in dry spells or in dry regions. After that, just applying a thick layer of mulch in early spring, as well as keeping any other plants and weeds away from the base of the tree, should be sufficient. Berries, however, can benefit from additional watering, especially as the crop begins to form. Black currants and raspberries, for example, will produce a larger crop if watered as they ripen. However, most plants, once established, should be able to fend for themselves, and again keeping weeds down and adding a layer of mulch or weed-control fabric should be sufficient in most areas to give you a decent crop.

you to change the spray pattern, which can be useful when you're watering containers and in the greenhouse to stop the plants from being blasted.

Sprinkler

A sprinkler is attached to your hose and left on for an hour or so. It's fairly difficult to direct to exactly where you want it, and it can waste a lot of water. However, it does mean you can get on with other things in the meantime.

Irrigation systems and water timers

Irrigation systems are worth thinking about when designing your garden. Attached to the water mains pipe with a water timer, they can be programmed to switch on for a period each day or even twice a day. They are efficient in using water as they need to stay on only for a limited period and can save a lot of time and effort.

There are a couple of different types available. The first is a leaky hose system where the whole length of the hosepipe leaks water and is good for along a bed. The second uses specific drippers, which are good for growing bags and containers. Whichever you use, it will mean having black pipes around your garden, so worth thinking about whether they'll end up being more trouble than they're worth.

What needs watering when?

These vegetable crops shouldn't need any additional watering, once established: artichoke, asparagus, beet, Brussels sprouts, cabbage, carrots, cauliflower, garlic, kale, onions, parsnip, pumpkin, rhubarb, shallots and rutabaga.

Hosepipe help
Young plants should be able to survive without too much additional watering, but in dry years, a good soak with a hose may be essential.

Organic gardening

Strict organic guidelines may not be for all, but every gardener can change their gardening habits to reduce their impact on the natural environment.

When people think about buying organic food in the supermarket, most will be thinking about the health benefits first. While it's true that pesticide residues have been shown to be lower in supermarket organic produce than conventionally grown food, there is still no agreement that organic food is better for you. Some studies have shown antioxidant levels and vitamins to be higher in organic produce, but others show the converse.

In the garden, other considerations may be more important. With the limited number of pesticides available to amateur gardeners, it's extremely unlikely that residues will be present on your vegetables — so long as you use them according to the instructions. Similarly, the health benefits in terms of nutrition are also likely to be negligible. However, where it is agreed that organic gardening can make a difference is in its impact on the wildlife in your garden as well as the wider environment.

At its essence, gardening should be about working with nature. Understanding not just how the plants in your garden thrive, but also the wildlife that shares the space with you.

Working with nature
Mixing flowers with vegetables and fruit is an ideal way to try to reduce the impact of pests and diseases on your crops, without turning to sprays.

Slug pellets, pest-control sprays and fungicides can all have an impact on the wildlife in your garden, and the use of peat and fertilizers can have a much wider influence on the natural environment. There are three key areas in the garden where the choices you make of the products and techniques you use can have a dramatic effect on the environment.

Raising plants

When you decide to start raising plants, there are basically two things you need: seed and potting mix. Organically grown seed has been available for many years, and the quality of it has been shown to be just as good as conventionally grown seed. While it's unlikely that non-organic seed will affect the wildlife in your garden, the production of the seed itself can require high inputs of both fertilizers and pesticides. Although it's not always possible to buy organic seed, particularly of the varieties you want, where possible it is a good idea to do so.

When raising the seeds, you'll need a supply of growing medium in which to do it. If you want to be both organic and environmentally friendly, the best compost to use is your own (see pages 222–223). Homemade compost and leaf mold can make excellent growing media and are ideal for use in large containers. However, most people still visit their local plant store for bags of multipurpose potting mix, which often contain peat. Peat bogs have been shown to act as a carbon sink, and the wildlife they contain is considered worthy of conservation. Unfortunately, harvesting peat for multipurpose potting mix can both release carbon and destroy the natural habitat. Peat replacements are now not only widely available, but in some cases perform just as well, or even better, than peat-based potting mixes. There is certainly no need to use peat as a soil improver as homemade potting mix, manure or mushroom compost perform the job even better.

For containers, too, peat-free potting mixes can be just as good as peat. For most seeds, a good peat-free potting mix works well. It's only with extremely fussy and difficult-to-germinate seeds that some gardeners still feel the need to use peat.

Feeding plants

Feeding plants to many means adding chemical fertilizers to your garden. It's true that standard fertilizers can be extremely useful in the food garden and ensure that your plants are as productive as possible. If you don't want to use a chemical fertilizer, there are plenty of good organic versions instead, including chicken manure pellets that can provide a real boost to your plants.

Wildlife havens
Ponds, trees and lots of flowers provide a haven for all
sorts of wildlife, from frogs to hoverflies, which will all help
to keep problem pests at bay.

Whichever fertilizer you go for, you should also be
supplementing your soil with organic matter. Homemade
compost (see pages 222–223) is greenest and best, but
mushroom compost, manure or even composted municipal
green waste are also very good. These materials, added as a
mulch of around 2 inches (5 cm) depth, provide a slow release
of nutrients, help to improve soil structure and texture, and
support a healthy community of soil microorganisms that
help both to keep your soil fertile and to protect plants from
root diseases.

Controlling pests and diseases

When it comes to controlling pests and diseases, it's easy
for gardeners to reach for the sprays. When gardeners see a
pest eating your crop, many will do anything to get rid of it.
However, with planning, many pests and diseases can be
resisted through the use of organic methods.

Crop rotation (see page 23) is one of the best ways of
preventing your plants from falling foul. Moving crops around
your garden helps to prevent a build-up of disease in a certain
area. Also, if your plants do suffer from certain diseases,
unfortunately the best advice may be to stop growing them
for a few years.

For those crops you want to grow every year, floating row
covers can be the most useful weapon in an organic gardener's
armory. This material will keep all sorts of pests at bay. You can
also use jets of water from a hose to blast off aphids, or pick off
caterpillars and squash the eggs of butterflies with your fingers.
If you do reach for a spray, try an organic one. In reality they
may not be quite as good as their chemical counterparts, but if
you apply them regularly they can help to control the problem.

Another way of controlling pests organically is to use
biological controls — these are natural enemies of the pests that
you release into the garden in huge (but microscopic) quantities.
They can work well for whitefly and red spider mite in the
greenhouse, as well as vine weevil and slugs outside. However,
you have to order these by mail. Get your timing right as they
are fairly expensive.

There are now organic slug pellets available that have been
shown not to harm wildlife. Other methods, such as copper
tape and physical barriers, can provide protection for your
plants, especially when they're young and vulnerable.

WILDLIFE GARDENING

While all of these methods of organic gardening will help
minimize your impact on the wildlife both in your garden
and in the wider countryside, there are other things you
can do to actively promote wildlife in your garden.

Don't cut all your lawn Leave a patch to grow and
flower that will provide both food and shelter to insects
and small mammals.

Dig a pond Ponds are a haven for wildlife and also
encourage garden-friendly frogs to take up residence,
which will help control your slug population.

Plant a tree or a mixed native hedgerow Planting
some native trees or shrubs will provide both food and
shelter to many animals.

Don't be too quick to tidy up Leave some plants
over winter before you cut them back, or leave an area
of fallen fall leaves into spring to provide a wildlife habitat.

Create a compost heap It's a great way of recycling
materials from your own garden and it can provide
shelter and warmth to a range of wildlife.

All about soil

The soil you have and the weather you experience in your garden can affect what you grow. While you can't do very much about the weather, there is much you can do to improve or alter the soil to make your crops healthier and your yields bigger.

Drainage

If you have a clay soil, you may need to improve drainage. Essentially, free-draining soil ensures the plants don't sit in waterlogged conditions and that there is plenty of air in the soil to allow the roots to breathe. To improve drainage, you can dig coarse sand into your soil, but probably the easiest option is to apply a 2-inch (5-cm) layer of organic matter each year until it is suitably improved. Organic matter will be pulled underground by the soil microorganisms and helps to create air spaces, improving the ability of water to move down the soil profile.

Fertility

All soils need to be fertile to support plant growth. There are a range of micronutrients that plants need, as well as a plentiful supply of nitrogen, phosphorus, potassium, calcium, magnesium and sulfur. While most ornamental gardens have plenty of nutrients, in the vegetable and fruit garden where you are constantly taking out plants and harvesting crops, you will be removing nutrients from the soil. These need to be replenished. Organic matter again has plenty of these nutrients that are released slowly over time, ideal for growing plants. However, it may also be necessary to supplement with additional fertilizers.

Types of fertilizers
General-purpose fertilizers

These generally contain nitrogen, potassium and phosphorus. They should contain quantities of these fertilizers in the ratio of something like 7:7:7 (the ratio should be listed on the packs).

TYPES OF SOIL

It's worth thinking about the type of soil you have in your garden before you decide how you need to treat it.

Whether you have a stony, sandy, clay or even loamy soil, you'll need to constantly improve it. As plants grow they use nutrients, which need to be replaced. You'll also need to replace the organic matter in the soil that slowly disappears due to the actions of the soil microorganisms.

Stony Soils that are stony are usually free-draining, so dry out quickly. They may also lack nutrients. You may find digging it over tricky too because of all the stones you hit. Root crops such as carrots and parsnips may find growing in stony soil a challenge as it will be difficult for their roots to grow straight.

Sandy Sandy soils are also free-draining and dry out quickly, but are much better for growing root crops as the roots can grow unimpeded. Sandy soils may also be easy to dig over. However, the fertility of sandy soils may be limited and will need improving.

Clay You know you have clay soil if you dig when the ground is wet and all the soil sticks to your spade. Essentially, clay soil is made up of very fine particles that easily stick together. It usually holds nutrients well, but can be difficult to drain. It can be slow to warm in the spring too.

Loamy Loamy soils are essentially the ideal soil for gardening. They contain some clay to hold nutrients, but some sand to help with drainage.

Know your soil type
The soil you have can affect what you grow, but adding plenty of well-rotted organic matter can help to improve even the worst of soils.

Chicken pellets, made from chicken manure, are a good example, though they tend to have slightly more nitrogen than potassium and phosphorus. However, they are good all-round fertilizers that can be used across your plot.

Straight fertilizers

These contain generally just one nutrient, such as nitrogen, in sulfate of ammonia. These can be useful if you know your garden is deficient in one nutrient. For instance, epsom salts is a fertilizer that supplies magnesium and can be useful for crops such as tomatoes and raspberries if they show yellowing between the veins of leaves.

Seaweed extracts

These claim to provide plenty of micronutrients. They generally won't sustain the soil on their own, so should be supplemented with other fertilizers if used at all.

Soil pH

The pH of your soil describes how acid or alkaline it is. While some crops such as blueberries and raspberries prefer acid conditions, others are less fussy. You should be aiming for around pH 6.5–7. For brassicas, it's better if the soil is around pH 7.5.

To test the pH of your soil, you can buy a cheap pH testing kit from your plant store. If your soil is too acid and you want to raise the pH, you can do something called liming. Adding ground limestone to your soil will help to raise the pH. You'll need to know the current pH of your soil first and what general type of soil you have (whether loamy, clay or sandy) to work out how much lime to add.

For soils with a high pH, reducing it is more difficult. Use sulfur chips to acidify the soil supplemented with some organic matter, such as composted bark, to slowly reduce the pH over time.

Supplementing soil with organic matter

Adding bulky organic matter to your soil will benefit your garden in many ways:

- It provides nutrients to your plants immediately as it will contain some nutrients in an available form.
- It helps with drainage and makes working your soil, such as digging it over, much easier.

Composted bark
Composted bark and other organic materials provide a long-term supply of slow-release nutrients as well as improving the soil structure for the roots of the plants.

- It also provides a slow-release fertilizer to your plants — microorganisms slowly break down complex organic molecules and release nutrients for plants to take up.
- It helps to make the soil lighter and airy. This aids plant growth by providing plenty of air spaces in the soil around the roots.
- It encourages friendly microorganisms to grow around the roots; they help to defend the plants from plant diseases.
- It holds on to water and so reduces how often you have to irrigate.

Bulky organic matter can be added as a mulch to your soil, often in the spring. But there are lots of different types out there, so how do you decide which to go for?

Homemade compost

Compost you make yourself is a good place to start, but you may not always have enough. It's free, hasn't traveled very far and is an extremely good soil improver. However, you may have weeds germinating from the compost.

Leaf mold
Compost should be well rotted before it's used in the garden.

Recycle your waste
Homemade compost (see pages 222–223) is a great way of recycling garden waste locally.

Leaf mold

Made just of leaves in your own garden, leaf mold shouldn't have any weed seeds in it. While it can be a good soil improver, it doesn't tend to hold much in the way of nutrients.

Horse or cow manure

Horse or cow manure is a rich organic matter with plenty of nutrients and ideal to really improve your soil if it is very deficient in nutrients. However, you must make sure that it has matured for a few months before you add it to your soil.

Spent mushroom compost

This material contains straw, chicken manure and calcium. It's nutritionally very rich and is an excellent soil improver, but because it contains calcium, it should be used only where you don't mind if the pH of your soil goes up.

Composted bark

This is a waste product of the forest industry and tends to have a slightly lower pH, so is good for soils where the pH is too high.

Mulching or digging in
Compost can either be added as a layer on top of your soil (mulch) or dug into the ground.

Municipal green waste compost

More and more local authorities are collecting green waste from householders and composting this material. Some towns then sell it back. This material can make an excellent soil improver as it tends to be like homemade compost. Contact your local town to see whether they supply it in bulk.

PREPARING THE SOIL FOR PLANTING

No digging Some people think that gardening is all about digging, but many now believe that digging isn't necessary. If you have created narrow beds for your crops, it's unlikely you'll ever have to walk on the bed. This way you won't compact the soil.

Adding a mulch of organic matter in early spring of at least 2 inches (5 cm) deep will help to reduce weed growth and provide a medium into which you can directly plant. Once the crops are established, you'll need to make sure the weeds are kept down by hoeing, so this way digging could be a thing of the past.

Single digging For those more traditionally minded, digging over your plot in early spring is part of the gardening calendar. Digging over can help to break up the large clods of soil, particularly when you have clay soil, as well as allowing you to remove stones. It's also a way of removing the weedy growth established through the less productive months.

Double digging This is a method of really getting to grips with your soil and improving it quickly. This is hard work, but if you're keen to improve the soil conditions rapidly, it can be worth it.

You need to dig out a single trench to a spade's depth, around 12 inches (30 cm) wide and put the soil into a wheelbarrow. Then spread a layer of organic matter in the bottom of the trench. Dig another 12-inch (30-cm) trench along the bed and put the soil from this trench on top of the organic matter. Repeat this along the bed, and in the last trench empty out your barrow of compost.

Making compost

A great way of recycling waste from your kitchen and garden—no garden should be without a compost heap.

Making your own compost is fun and rewarding, beneficial to the garden, as well as being extremely environmentally friendly. Garden compost has all sorts of uses — from improving the soil in your fruit and vegetable beds, to raising plants from seed and growing in containers. Recent studies have shown garden compost to be an excellent alternative to bought growing media — for growing vegetables like potatoes — in pots. Not only does it save you a trip to the plant store, but also it saves money in the process.

If you work hard you can have garden compost ready for use in as little as three months. For those wishing to take it at a more leisurely pace — and without much added work — compost made one season will be ready for use the next.

What type of bin?

There are a range of compost bins available, but they can be split into two main groups.

The first is the plastic cone or cylinder shape with a tight-fitting plastic lid — essential if you suffer with pests such as rats. These are a great choice if you have only a small garden and don't expect too much waste to be generated.

There are also large "bay" type bins, often made from wood. These are a great idea if you intend to produce a lot of compost, and if you invest in more than one bay it means you can add, mix and remove the compost very easily. For a homemade bin, this style is perfect — try using old pallets or doors.

Where to site the bin

The best site for a compost bin is in a warm, sunny spot. This helps the compost to heat up and start to decompose. However, in most gardens you'll want to use the sunniest parts

of your garden for either relaxing or growing plants. Composting will work on a shady site but will take more time. Also, make sure you site your bin on bare soil — not on a concrete surface.

What to add

You can compost almost all plant and vegetable matter — as long as it isn't cooked. Materials that you add to your compost are usually either rich in nitrogen — such as grass clippings and vegetable peelings; or rich in carbon — leaves, plant stems and even cardboard and newspaper. The best combination is a 50:50 mix of these two groups of ingredients. Other materials you can add include tea bags and eggshells. You shouldn't add fish, meat, bones or any cooked food as this will attract vermin. Also avoid perennial weeds as the composting process may not kill them and you may accidentally introduce them to your garden.

To mix or not to mix

Ideally you should be adding a mix of materials whenever you fill up the bin. Add it bit by bit, or fill it up in one go. Composting will really speed up in summer; you should make sure the bin is kept moist and doesn't dry out.

Mixing is also recommended: use a garden fork to turn and aerate the compost. Mixing the heap will also help to bring uncomposted material at the edge of the heap into the middle, and the composting process will begin again. If you turn once a month in the summer, your compost will be ready in as little as three months. If you choose not to mix, you'll still get great compost — it will just take longer.

Uses

If the compost heap gets really hot, it can kill any seeds — flowers, vegetables or weeds. However it's unlikely it will kill all seed, so be prepared for some unwanted visitors. You can use compost to fill trenches for beans, where the compost is buried, or use it as a mulch in the vegetable garden — but be prepared to do some weeding, or cover the top with a weed-control fabric.

Compost can be used in pots and containers too. Sieving it will help remove large uncomposted pieces, and mixing it with good-quality garden soil in a 50:50 mix produces an excellent container-compost in which to grow all sorts of vegetables. Think about applying a mulch of coarse sand or bark to prevent weeds from germinating.

Gathering fall leaves
It can take over a year to make good leaf mold. Use for acid-loving plants.

Bin it
Wooden bay-type bins needn't be an eyesore if they are painted to blend in with other outbuildings.

DO COMPOST

- Shredded paper (although not shiny magazine-type paper), cotton and woolen fabrics
- Uncooked vegetable trimmings, peelings and tea bags
- Annual weeds
- Tops of perennial weeds
- Old bedding plants
- Soft hedge clippings
- Dead leaves
- Lawn mowings

DON'T COMPOST

- Woody material like prunings and Brussels sprout stems—these need to be put through a shredder first
- Synthetic fabrics
- Food scrap
- Meat or bones
- Diseased plant material
- Soil pests
- Any weeds with seed heads
- Perennial roots

OTHER TYPES OF COMPOSTING

There are a few other types of composting systems that can help you recycle all your kitchen and garden waste.

WORMERY

If you don't generate much garden waste, but plenty in the kitchen, including cooked food such as pasta and rice, a wormery may be for you. Add kitchen scraps to this type of compost heap filled with worms and you can produce extremely fertile compost. The easiest way to set up a worm bin is to buy a kit with worms included. Keep in a sheltered spot — and somewhere frost-free in winter — and the worms will reward you with rich compost all year round.

BOKASHI BIN

Kept in the kitchen, you can add all sorts of kitchen waste to a bokashi bin, including fish, meat and cooked food. Add a special type of bran and the compost can be transferred into the garden — either onto the compost heap or buried in your garden. Bokashi bins and the special bran are available by mail order and are a good way to recycle all manner of kitchen waste.

LEAF MOLD

A name given to compost produced entirely from leaves. Fall leaves decompose more slowly than other materials and if you have a lot they can be composted on their own. Leaf mold is slightly acidic so can be used for acid-loving plants such as blueberries and bilberries. It contains few nutrients so is also good for seed sowing. To make a leaf bin, use four wooden posts, with wire mesh. Alternatively you can fill black garbage bags, tie up tight, and leave to one side.

Dealing with weeds

Every gardener has to deal with weeds, and it's best to face them head on. If you neglect a patch of your garden, for even just a couple of months, it's likely it will get swamped by weeds. Weeds not only look unsightly, they compete with your plants for moisture, food and light. They can also harbor diseases. So for the vegetable and fruit gardener, it's best to create a plot that's weed-free.

There are a range of methods to help you create a weed-free plot. Choose the one that suits you based on the amount of time you have available and the effort you are prepared to put in. Once you've managed that, there are a range of techniques to keep your plot weed-free for years to come — although some require more effort than others.

Types of weeds

There are two main types of weeds that are a bane to gardeners: annual and perennial weeds. Annuals grow from seed very rapidly, they usually flower quickly too and spread their seed widely. They can quickly colonize a freshly dug plot, as sometimes their seed can last for years in the soil, and once uncovered will quickly germinate. Because they're quick to grow, their rooting system doesn't become particularly developed and so if you manage to uproot or slice the plant in two, it's unlikely to regrow. Perennial weeds are trickier to get rid of. They can last for years in the same spot, and if removed, they can often regrow from the smallest piece of root in the soil. In the garden it's often the perennial weeds that cause the biggest problem when you're clearing a site that has not been used for years, but the annual weeds start to be more of a problem once the site has been cleared and bare soil is a common sight.

Clearing a site

Some people are lucky enough to take over a perfectly clear site, without any perennial weeds, but for most there will be some initial work to be done.

Covering

If you have time on your side, you can cover the ground with a material that prevents weeds from growing and ones already growing slowly die. Cardboard (a cheap option), plastic weed control fabric or a thick layer of homemade compost all work. Carpet used to be a common sight, but this is now not recommended. You'll need to leave the cover over the soil for at least six months to get rid of most weeds. Some will linger on after this time and digging or spraying will be inevitable.

Spraying

If you're short on time and don't mind using chemicals, a weedkiller is a good option. A product that contains glyphosate is recommended as it quickly breaks down in the soil. If it hits a plant, it travels through it to the roots and kills it off. This product is best used when the weeds are growing vigorously in spring, but care should be taken to ensure it isn't sprayed on plants you want to keep.

Digging

Digging can be a good option once you've either covered your plot for some time or used a weedkiller. If you have a big area to deal with, consider investing in a gasoline-powered rototiller – either hiring one for the weekend or buying one. This will quickly plow through large areas, and is useful each year when you empty your beds.

If your plot is smaller or awkward in shape, a spade will be your only weapon. You'll need to keep bending down to remove every shred of root you can find as each piece will quickly regrow.

Maintaining weed-free soil

Once you have a weed-free plot, it's best to keep it that way and especially avoid any more perennial weeds getting a foothold.

Mulches

Using a deep layer of organic matter each year can help to keep your plot weed-free as it smothers the annual weed seeds that fell on the plot the year before. If you don't have access to organic matter in those quantities, consider using a plastic (permeable is best) weed-control fabric. You can cut slits in this to plant through, and it's best used on permanent plots such as fruit gardens. It can also be used with annual crops such as potatoes, but it can work out to be very expensive.

Weed haven
Bare soil is a magnet for weed seeds. Try using mulches or covering with a material that prevents weeds from growing.

OTHER TECHNIQUES TO KEEP WEEDING DOWN

Green manures Try using a green manure in the winter. This covers your plots with a short-term crop, preventing weeds from growing as well as protecting the soil from erosion. When the land is needed in the spring, the green manure can be dug into the ground to provide more nutrients to the soil. Examples of green manure include buckwheat, rye grain and oats. However, you must ensure that the crops are dug in before they set seed.

Raised beds Perennial, spreading weeds often encroach from the edge of your beds and can be tricky to keep under control. One way to keep this problem contained is by creating raised beds. The fixed edges of wood or other materials raised off the soil level will ensure weeds can't grow onto your plot.

Tools for the job A good hoe is essential for weeding (see page 197). For working close to the soil, a hand fork or trowel is useful. When using a weed killer, a watering can with a fine rose is essential. Even better would be a dedicated sprayer that produces a fine mist that covers the plants well. Whatever you use for your weed killer, ensure that you either use it only for that job alone or you rinse it out thoroughly.

Hoeing and hand weeding

Another simple method to keep weeds down is to dig over your plot in early spring, leave it until the annual weed seeds exposed on the surface have germinated, then hoe off or spray using a chemical. You will get more weeds growing after this, but not as many.

When you plant out your crops, consider the spacing you are using between crops and between rows. Wide spacing can allow you to walk down a row and hoe as you go. Narrow spacing may mean you can't get a hoe down the row, but the density of the crop will smother any germinating seeds. Any weeds that do grow may need to be pulled out by hand. Try using just your fingertips around the crops, but using a hand fork can be useful too. Play around with the spacing of your crop and work out what's best for you.

Regular hoeing
Hoeing is a task you'll need to do throughout the growing season to keep on top of the weeds.

Pests and diseases

Throughout the gardening year it's likely that unexpected things will happen that will affect your crop. If your plants aren't looking as healthy as they should, the problem is likely to be caused by the soil, weather, or a pest or disease.

If you've planted out at the appropriate time and protected your plants where necessary with floating row covers, and you've been watering and feeding as required, a pest or disease is likely to be to blame for any problems. Pests and diseases are something that all gardeners have to live with, but there is plenty you can do to help limit the problem occurring in the first place.

General advice

Rotation, interplanting and companion planting

Rotating different crops around your garden on a four-year cycle has been shown to help reduce the build-up of diseases. It's unlikely rotation will have any effect on pests such as aphids and caterpillars, as they can move around the garden easily, but any diseases that remain in the soil are best avoided by moving the crop families around (see page 22).

Companion planting
Planting marigolds around tomatoes is a well-known example of companion planting. The marigolds not only protect the tomatoes from white fly, but look attractive too.

Interplanting is a method of mixing crops up together and making more of the space you have as well as protecting your crops. Some pests, such as carrot root fly, can be tricked into thinking there are no carrots around by surrounding them with onions, for example.

Companion planting is an extension of this, where you use a plant that provides some sort of protection to a specific crop. Perhaps the most well-known is planting French or African marigolds around tomato plants to protect them from white fly. There are other examples too, but there is little hard scientific data to prove them.

Soil fertility

One way to keep your plants healthy is to provide sufficient food and water. If a plant is growing without any stresses, it's more likely to be able to withstand attack.

Hygiene

Keeping the garden tidy and clean can help to reduce problems building up. This is especially true for the greenhouse, which should be emptied and washed out with a disinfectant once a year to help get rid of any pests over-wintering in crevices. While it's not always necessary to cut down all your plants as soon as winter arrives, you should be removing any plants that are showing signs of diseases, including the leaves and stems of fruiting trees and shrubs. It's best not to compost this material in case the disease survives and you return it to the garden.

Harvesting and storing

When harvesting crops, make sure you're picking them carefully and not damaging them in the process. Look over the harvest and discard or use immediately any that look blemished or damaged. When the produce is stored, it's a good idea to keep checking over your harvest every week or so. Any diseased crops should be removed quickly before they spread into the rest of the harvest.

Variety selection

Many breeders are selecting varieties not just on the basis of yield and flavor but also disease resistance. Tomatoes and potatoes that are resistant to blight are now becoming more available, and if you suffer from blight this is the best way to avoid it. Other crops too will boast disease resistance. While it's likely these crops may resist the disease for longer, it will still be necessary to keep an eye on them as it's likely that at some point the disease will break down the resistance and you'll need to treat with some other method of protection.

Gardening with wildlife in mind

While many birds, mammals, insects, fungi and bacteria can be a pest, others provide you with your very own army, protecting your plants throughout the year. Frogs and birds help to keep larger pests, such as slugs and snails, off your garden and therefore should be encouraged. Insects such as ladybugs, lace wings and hoverflies actually eat many of the pests you find in your garden and these should be welcomed by providing pollen- and nectar-rich flowering plants. Below ground, having a healthy population of soil microorganisms helps the roots of plants to protect themselves from root diseases. There are plenty of things you can do to help encourage friendly wildlife into your garden (see page 217).

Garden pests
Flying insects

Flying pests are best avoided by using barriers where possible. A floating row cover can protect against all sorts of pests, such as aphids and carrot root fly.

If you opt for a pesticide, you'll need to decide whether to use a systemic treatment or a contact treatment. Systemic means that the chemical is taken up by the plant, and as soon as the pest attacks, it will be killed as it eats both the plant and the chemical — this means you don't have to spray all of the pests but just the plant. Direct treatments work only where they are sprayed, so you'll need to direct these onto the pests themselves. They're considered to be more friendly to wildlife as, provided you spray in the evening, they won't affect bees or other pollinating insects. Organic sprays also usually work in this way.

Aphids

Aphids can multiply at an incredible rate and can quickly weaken your plants, and can even cause their death. You'll need to keep an eye out for these pests as they can be easily blasted off with a hose pipe. You can use insecticide sprays too to clear them off, but even better is an army of ladybugs — encourage them into your garden and they can help keep your plants pest-free.

Slugs and snails

These are often the most feared problem to the gardener, especially early on in the season when they can easily decimate a whole row of seedlings overnight. Think about how you'll protect your plants before you even open a packet of seed.

Slug pellets are both effective and cheap, and there are now organic versions too. Barriers work by creating a physical barrier that the slugs and snails don't like to cross. Crushed egg or shellfish shells are common, but if the barrier is breached, slugs will quickly move in. Slugs can also move underground so it's not always failsafe. A section of plastic bottle, with the top and bottom cut off and inserted into the ground over vulnerable seedlings, can work better (see right).

When you're growing in a container, a copper strip (which is available in plant stores) zaps the molluscs with an electric shock. Get your timing right and an application of a microscopic worm that is a natural enemy to the slug can keep your garden completely clear of the pests. However this biological control won't work against snails.

Birds and mammals

Using a barrier can offer the best method for keeping birds and other animals away from your crop. Keep an eye out for the culprit and then erect a barrier to keep them off your crop. For example, to deter rabbits, you will need a 3-foot (1-m) high barrier of wire fencing, buried an additional 12 inches (30 cm).

Garden diseases
Viruses

Viruses are not common in the garden but can affect certain plants. Tomato mosaic virus and cucumber mosaic virus are probably the most well known. If your plants are afflicted, there is little you can do but the plants should be removed and destroyed as quickly as possible to prevent spreading.

Fungal diseases

There are a wide number of diseases that can affect both fruit and vegetables, but the number of fungicides available to the amateur gardener is becoming fewer and fewer each year.

In reality the best way to avoid diseases building up is by rotation and good hygiene — removing any infected material and washing out pots and the greenhouse each time they're used.

One method that has been shown to help reduce root fungal diseases is by raising the pH. Fungi prefer an acid soil to grow, and as with clubroot, if you add lime to make your soil pH 7 or over, this will limit the effect of fungal diseases on your plants.

MAKING A SLUG AND SNAIL BARRIER

1 Cut the top and bottom off a plastic bottle.

2 Insert into the soil around the young plant to a depth of 2 inches (5 cm) or so.

PART 4: PRESERVING YOUR CROP

Whichever crops you have chosen to cultivate, it is likely that you will have seasonal gluts at various points in the year. Rather than risking the possibility of your lovingly tended crops going to waste simply because you can't eat them fast enough, it is a good idea to preserve them so they can be enjoyed at a later date. This section details popular ways of preserving: how to make jams, jellies, pickles and chutneys, and how to dry and freeze your crops.

Preserving equipment

Equipment used for making preserves containing fruit or vinegar must be made of a nonreactive material, such as stainless steel, plastic, nylon or wood. It is also important to remember to use heatproof utensils for hot preserves.

Pans

A traditional preserving pan, called a maslin, has sloping sides, a lip for pouring and a carrying handle. It is useful, especially when making large quantities of preserves, but it is not essential. The pan you use should have the following characteristics:

• It should be made of a nonreactive material, such as stainless steel, or have a nonstick or enamel lining. Unlined copper or brass pans, or anything made of aluminum, should not be used.

• It should be heavy and have a thick, flat bottom so that heat is conducted evenly and mixtures do not catch and burn.

• If possible, it should have sides that slope outward to provide a large surface area to allow for the rapid evaporation of surplus liquid and steam. If boiling a fairly small quantity of a sauce or syrup, a large, nonstick frying pan or a nonreactive saucepan can be used instead.

• It should have an inner surface free of blemishes, pitting or damage.

• It should have two handles opposite each other to make for easier lifting.

• It should not be more than half full when cooking sweetened mixtures, as they can spit and splutter when boiled.

Scales

Scales are not necessary for making preserves, but they can be very helpful. Try to accurately note the weight of ingredients prior to purchase. To weigh large amounts of ingredients at home, bathroom scales can be used. Put the pan, or another large container, on the scale, re-set to zero and add the ingredients. Alternatively, note the weight of the empty pan, add the ingredients and deduct the pan's weight from the total.

Knives

Using sharp, stainless steel knives of good quality can prevent the discoloration of fruit and vegetables and will ensure quick, easy, neat and safe preparation.

Spice bag

This small bag is usually made of cheesecloth or muslin and has a drawstring top. It can be purchased or improvised at home using a small piece of cheesecloth tied at the top with a long piece of string. The bag is tied to the handle of the pan and is suspended in the preserves to impart flavor. Metal spice balls that clip onto the side of the pan can also be used.

Long-handled wooden spoon

A wooden spoon with a long handle keeps your hands away from very hot liquids, steam and "spitting" mixtures. Wood is essential because metal may react with the acid present and discolor the ingredients.

Slotted spoon

During boiling, jams and jellies frequently produce scum, which must be removed to keep the finished preserves from turning cloudy. A slotted spoon is also useful for scooping out the pits of fruits such as plums and peaches.

Candy thermometer

A candy thermometer clips to the side of the pan and allows the temperature of jams, jellies and marmalades to be easily read, ensuring that the preserves reach the correct setting point. If using a free-standing thermometer, hold it in the center of the preserve mixture for a minute or so before reading it.

Sieves and colanders

These should be made of nylon or plastic.

Bowls

A selection of bowls of various sizes is essential.

Measuring cup

A heatproof measuring cup is necessary for measuring and pouring hot liquids.

Funnel

Two funnels — one a wide-mouthed funnel for filling jars, and another narrow one for filling bottles — are handy and should ideally have a nonstick surface. This facilitates the clean transfer of hot liquids or preserves from one container to another.

Ladle

This is used for transferring preserves from the pan to pour through the funnel.

Jelly bag and stand

A jelly bag, available for purchase at stores that carry a wide variety of home canning supplies, is a bag made of a finely woven material, usually nylon. It is very inexpensive to buy and can be washed and reused. It is chiefly used when making jellies to facilitate the

extraction of juice from the ingredients being used, and is suspended over a bowl to catch the drips of liquid. Some jelly bags are supplied with their own stand, but one can easily be improvised by attaching the bag to a wire coat hanger and hanging from a hook. A homemade jelly bag can be created using two or three layers of cheesecloth or fine cotton. A jelly bag should always be scalded just before it is used.

Pressure cooker

When a recipe calls for precooking the ingredients, a pressure cooker can be used to save time and help retain the color and flavor during the preliminary softening of the fruit, peel or vegetables. Consult the manufacturer's handbook for recipes and timings.

Boiling water canner

Boiling water canners are recommended by the United States Department of Agriculture (USDA) for heat-treating jams, jellies, butters, cheeses, marmalades, chutneys, pickles and some fruits. These canners are made of aluminum or porcelain-covered steel and have removable perforated racks and fitted lids. A canner must be deep enough so that the jars are covered by at least 1 inch (2.5 cm) of briskly bubbling water during processing. If you use an electric stove, the canner must have a flat bottom and should be no more than 4 inches (10 cm) wider than the element on which it will be heated.

Jars and bottles

Wide-mouthed jars with openings of about 3 inches (7.5 cm) are the most useful for pickles because they are easy to fill. For jams, jellies and marmalades, 2½-inch (6-cm) mouthed jars can be used. The best sizes to use for home preserving are 2 cup (450 mL) and 4 cup (950 mL). If they are handled and used carefully, they can be reused several times but you'll need new lids. These jars must be inspected carefully to make sure they are free of cracks, chips or other flaws. If a hot mixture is added to a flawed jar, the jar will immediately shatter. Bacteria can breed in small cracks or chips, which could cause the preserve to spoil.

To sterilize jars and bottles before using them, first wash well in hot, soapy water, then rinse in hot water. Put them, open-side up, in a deep pan, cover with boiling water, and boil rapidly for 10 minutes. Lift them out with tongs and leave to drain upside down on a thick dish towel. Washing in the dishwasher is not recommended. Use warm jars when filling with hot preserves to prevent cracking, but leave them to cool when filling with cold preserves. Always use a container that is appropriate for the amount of preserve so that it is filled to the optimum level (see individual methods).

Covers and lids

Acid-proof screw-top or snap-on lids, or those that have an acid-proof lining (such as plastic) can also be used for the final covering for sweet preserves, while they must be vinegar-proof or have a vinegar-proof lining for chutneys and pickles and other vinegar-containing preserves. If you have only metal lids, cover the top of the jar with plastic wrap before putting on the lid.

For boiling water canning, use two-part lids that are specifically designed for this purpose. The lids have a special seal and cannot be reused; they are held in place by metal screw-bands. The screw-bands and the jars, however, can be recycled. For instructions on how to properly seal the jars, consult the manufacturer's instructions.

The most usual type of self-sealing lid consists of a flat, metal lid with a metal screw-band to hold it in place during processing. The lid has a crimped bottom edge that forms a trough, which is filled with a colored gasket compound. When the jars are processed, the lid gasket softens and flows slightly to cover the jar-sealing surface, yet allows air to escape from the jar. The gasket then forms an airtight seal as the jar cools. Inspect lids carefully before they are used to ensure they are free of defects and that the compound is perfect. Do not keep lids from year to year because the quality of the compound deteriorates with time. These self-sealing lids have a five-year shelf life and it is advisable to buy only the quantity you need each time.

Jams

When making jam, the amount of sugar that is added varies according to the sugar content of the fruit, but it normally accounts for 60 to 65 percent of the weight of the finished jam.

Making jam

1 Put the jars in a low oven to keep warm. Put the sugar into a bowl and place it in the oven as well, and put a saucer in the refrigerator. Make sure the fruit is clean and free of blemishes, and prepare according to type. Put the fruit in the pan with the specified amount of water and heat.

2 Remove the pan from the heat and pour in the warm sugar. Then, heat gently, stirring with a wooden spoon, until the sugar has dissolved. A pat of butter can be added after the sugar to reduce the formation of scum.

3 Increase the heat and boil rapidly, without stirring, until the setting point is reached. This should take between 10 and 15 minutes. The correct temperature should be 220°F (104°C) on the candy thermometer.

4 To test for a set without a thermometer, remove the pan from the heat and try either one of these methods. Drop a little of the jam onto the cold saucer and push it gently with a teaspoon or your fingertip. If the surface wrinkles, the setting point has been reached. Alternatively, lift some of the jam from the pan on a wooden spoon, let it cool slightly, and then allow it to drip back into the pan. If the drops run together along the edge of the spoon and form one unified flake or sheet that breaks off sharply as it falls back into the pan, the jam is ready.

5 Skim any scum from the surface of the jam using a slotted spoon. Leave the jam to stand in the pan for about 10 minutes before filling the jars so the fruit is evenly distributed throughout and does not rise to the top of the jars. Prepare and fill the jars (see page 231), then heat-process in a boiling water canner (see page 231).

JAM-MAKING: WHAT YOU WILL NEED

EQUIPMENT

Sterilized jars (see page 231)
Heatproof bowl
Small plate or saucer
Sharp stainless steel knife (optional)
Cutting board
Large nonreactive pan
Long-handled wooden spoon
Candy thermometer (optional)
Teaspoon
Baking sheet or wooden board
Slotted spoon
Heatproof ladle
Flat, plastic spatula
Clean dishcloth and hot soapy water
Boiling water canner
Labels

INGREDIENTS

Sugar
Slightly underripe, blemish-free fruit, unwashed for
    preference
Lemon juice (optional)
Pat of unsalted butter (optional)

PLUM JAM RECIPE

2½ lb (1.25 kg) plums, halved
1¼ cups (300 mL) water
4½ cups (1 kg) granulated sugar
or preserving sugar
Pat of unsalted butter
Makes about 3½ lb (1.6 kg)

The color of this jam varies depending on the type of plums used. Red-fleshed plums produce a richly red jam, while green-fleshed plums like gages or Italian plums make for a greenish-yellow jam. If the plums are large, cut them into quarters rather than halves.

1 Put the plums in a nonreactive pan and add the water. Bring to a boil, then simmer for about 25 to 30 minutes, stirring occasionally, until the skins are soft and the fruit is really tender. The liquid should be well reduced.
2 Stir in the sugar until dissolved. Add the butter and bring the jam to a boil. Boil rapidly for 10 to 15 minutes, until the setting point is reached (see page 232).
3 Remove the pan from the heat, remove the pits and any scum from the surface with a slotted spoon, and let stand for about 5 minutes. Stir the jam gently.
4 Prepare and fill the jars (see page 231), and heat-process in a boiling water canner (see page 231). Let cool, label and store in a cool, dark, dry place for one month before eating. Keeps for up to two years.

3

5

Jellies

The basic method and principles of making jelly are much the same as for jam, but there are some extra points to watch for, and more time is needed. High-pectin fruits (see below) make the best jellies, although low-pectin fruits can be used if combined with other fruits that have a higher pectin content, or if jam sugar (sugar with pectin) is used.

Making jelly

1 Put the jars in a low oven to keep warm. Put the sugar into a bowl and place in the oven as well, and put the saucer in the refrigerator. Make sure the fruit is clean and that any blemishes have been completely cut out. Prepare the fruit according to type; there is no need to remove the peel, core or seeds. Put the fruit in the pan with the specified amount of water and simmer gently until the fruit is soft, stirring occasionally with a wooden spoon to prevent sticking.

2 Pour boiling water through the jelly bag or cheesecloth to scald it. Tie the bag to a stand and place a large bowl underneath. Pour the contents of the pan into the bag and leave it to drip in a cool place, undisturbed, for 8 to 12 hours until no more liquid comes through.

3 Measure the juice in the bowl and return it to a clean pan. Add 2 cups (450 g) warmed sugar for every 2½ cups (575 mL) juice. Heat gently, stirring with a wooden spoon, until the sugar has dissolved, then raise the heat and boil rapidly until the temperature reaches 220°F (104°C) on a candy thermometer. Alternatively, use the setting point test (see page 232). Avoid stirring unless necessary, as it can cause air bubbles.

4 With the pan off the heat, skim any scum from the surface with a slotted spoon. If the jelly contains particles such as herbs, let it stand for 10 minutes before filling the jars so the particles are evenly distributed throughout the jelly.

5 Prepare and fill the jars (see page 231), then heat-process in a boiling water canner (see page 231).

PECTIN CONTENT OF FRUIT

High: Blackberries (mature but unripe), cooking apples, cranberries, gooseberries, citrus fruit, red currants.
Medium: Eating apples, apricots, blackberries (ripe), loganberries, mulberries, plums, raspberries.
Low: Bananas, blueberries, cherries, figs, grapes, melons, nectarines, peaches, rhubarb, strawberries.

1

2

JELLY-MAKING: WHAT YOU WILL NEED

EQUIPMENT

Sterilized jars (see page 231)
Heatproof bowl
Small plate or saucer
Sharp stainless steel knife (optional)
Cutting board
Large nonreactive pan
Long-handled wooden spoon
Jelly bag or triple thickness of cheesecloth and stand
Large nonreactive bowl
Candy thermometer (optional)
Teaspoon
Slotted spoon
Baking sheet or wooden board
Heatproof ladle
Flat, plastic spatula
Clean dishcloth and hot soapy water
Boiling water canner
Labels

INGREDIENTS

Sugar
Slightly underripe fruit
Water

TARRAGON AND ORANGE JELLY

4 lb (1.8 kg) oranges, halved
   and sliced into semi-circles
1 lb (450 g) lemons, halved
   and sliced into semi-circles
12 cups (2.8 L) water
Granulated sugar or preserving
   sugar (see method)
2 tbsp tarragon leaves
Makes about 5½ lb (2.5 kg)

Golden, fragrant herb jellies like this one are ideal for serving with roast and grilled meats, poultry and game — either spooned on the plate or stirred into the cooking juices to make a light sauce. Herb jellies are also good with pâtés, and this one goes well with fish like salmon and trout. Other herbs, such as thyme or mint, can be used instead of tarragon.

1 Put the oranges and lemons in a nonreactive pan with the water. Bring to a boil, then simmer gently for about 1½ hours, until the fruit is soft.
2 Pour the contents of the pan into a jelly bag suspended over a nonreactive bowl and leave overnight in a cool place to drip.
3 Discard the pulp in the jelly bag. Measure the juice and pour into a clean pan. Add 2¼ cups (450 g) sugar for each 2½ cups (575 mL) juice. Add the tarragon. Heat gently, stirring, until the sugar has dissolved, then boil hard for about 15 minutes until the setting point is reached (see page 232).
4 Remove any scum with a slotted spoon and let the jelly stand for 15 minutes. Stir to distribute the tarragon. Prepare and fill the jars (see page 231), and heat-process in a boiling water canner (see page 231). Leave overnight. Label the cool jars and store in a cool, dark, dry place for up to one year.

Pickles

Pickles are made from fruits and vegetables that have been preserved in vinegar; sometimes the vinegar is spiced or sweetened. Vegetables may be pickled raw or cooked. Most raw vegetables must be brined or salted before being pickled to draw out their moisture, which allows the vinegar to better penetrate the food. When vegetables and fruits are cooked, the cooking boils off excess moisture, and salt is not necessary.

Making pickles

1 Prepare the vegetables or fruits as directed by the recipe. For raw vegetables, there are two options: either layer them, sprinkling salt between each layer, then cover with a plate and leave overnight; or completely cover and soak the vegetables in salted water. Put a weighted plate on the surface to ensure the vegetables are immersed in the brine. Leave overnight.

For cooked fruits and vegetables that are to be pickled, prepare them according to the recipe. Drain very well and leave to dry.

2 Prepare the pickling vinegar according to the recipe. Let the vinegar cool; the spices can be left in or removed, depending on the strength of flavor required. For raw vegetables that were layered with salt, rinse off in cold running water, dry thoroughly with a clean cloth and spread out on another clean, dry cloth and let air-dry completely. For raw vegetables that were soaked in brine, drain the brine, rinse the ingredients under cold running water, and dry thoroughly with a clean cloth to remove the rinsing water.

3 Put the sterilized jars on a baking sheet or wooden board. Pack the vegetables into the sterilized jars to within 1 inch (2.5 cm) of the top. Be sure to pack them firmly so as not to leave too many air pockets, but not too tightly because the vinegar must be able to flow between them.

4 Depending on the type of pickle being made, whether a soft or crunchy result is desired or specified in the recipe, either use the pickling vinegar cold, or bring it to a boil. Pour or ladle into prepared jars (see page 231) to come to within ½ inch (1.5 cm) of the top. Swirl the jars to expel any trapped air bubbles. If the pickles have a tendency to float to the tops of the jars, put a piece of crumpled parchment paper in the top of the jar. Remove it after a couple of weeks. Cover the jars with acid-proof lids (see page 231). Store the pickles in a cool, dark, dry place for about two to three months before eating. The exception is red cabbage, which needs to be eaten within three to four months after it is made, as it softens upon storage.

PICKLE-MAKING: WHAT YOU WILL NEED

EQUIPMENT

Sharp stainless steel knife
Cutting board
Weighted plate (optional)
Nonreactive bowl (optional)
Large, nonreactive pan
Piece of cheesecloth or gauze (optional)
Long piece of string (optional)
Long-handled wooden spoon
Paper towels or dishcloths
Sterilized jars (see page 231)
Baking sheet or wooden board
Heatproof ladle or measuring cup
Nonreactive funnel
Clean dishcloth and hot, soapy water
Clean wide-necked jars, warmed
Parchment paper
Acid-proof lids (see page 231)

INGREDIENTS

Fruit or vegetables
Salt (optional)
Spices
Vinegar
Granulated or brown sugar (optional)

RED CABBAGE WITH ORANGE

1 red cabbage weighing about 2 lb (1 kg), quartered, cored and shredded
1 large onion, peeled and thinly sliced
Kosher salt
3 large oranges, zested and juiced

For the spiced vinegar
1½ cups (350 mL) red wine vinegar
¾ cup (175 mL) raspberry vinegar
1½ tsp whole allspice berries, lightly crushed
1½ tsp black peppercorns
1½ tsp whole cloves
2 bay leaves, torn in half
2-inch (5-cm) long cinnamon stick
1 tbsp brown sugar
½ cup (75 g) raisins
Makes about 2 lb (1 kg)

This preserve is best eaten within three to four months after it is made, as the cabbage softens upon storage. It goes well with bread and cheese, smoked meats and casseroles.

1 Layer the cabbage and onion in a colander, sprinkling salt between each layer. Stand the colander on a plate and leave in a cool place overnight to drain. The next day, rinse the vegetables well, and dry thoroughly with a clean cloth. Spread out on another dry, clean cloth and let air-dry completely.
2 Meanwhile, make the spiced vinegar: put all the ingredients and the orange rind and juice in a nonreactive pan and heat gently, stirring with a wooden spoon, until the sugar has dissolved, then boil for 2 minutes. Remove from the heat and leave to cool.
3 Return the vinegar to a boil, then remove from the heat. Mix the raisins with the cabbage and onion and pack firmly into sterilized jars. Add the vinegar as you go, distributing the raisins and flavorings evenly, and pressing down firmly on the cabbage. Swirl the jars to expel any air bubbles, then seal them and let cool. Label the jars and store in a cool, dark, dry place for at least one month before eating. It will keep for up to one year but is best eaten within three to four months.

Chutneys

Chutneys are mixtures of chopped vegetables and fruit cooked together with vinegar, sugar and spices. The chutney is simmered slowly until the ingredients have softened and nearly all the liquid has evaporated. Test whether the chutney is ready by drawing a spoon across the bottom of a pan; if the channel left by the spoon does not immediately fill with liquid, the chutney is ready. Chutneys vary in their fruitiness, spiciness and sweet-and-sour combination.

Making chutney

1 Prepare the vegetables and fruit; cut into small pieces and put in the pan with the vinegar and spices. If a spice bag is being used, put the spices in a small piece of cheesecloth and tie with string, and then tie the loose end of the string to the handle of the pan to suspend the bag in the contents. Bring to a boil and simmer, uncovered, until the vegetables and fruit are soft but not mushy, anything between 30 minutes and 1½ hours. Stir occasionally to prevent sticking.

2 Over low heat, stir in the sugar until it has dissolved, then return to a boil and cook until the mixture is thick. Stir as necessary to prevent sticking. Lift up the spice bag, press it against the side of the pan to extract the juices, then discard the bag. The chutney is ready when it is thick and no liquid appears in the channel that is left when the spoon is drawn across the bottom of the pan. It will thicken further upon standing.

3 Prepare the jars (see page 231) and fill. Heat-process in a boiling water canner (see page 231).

CHUTNEY-MAKING: WHAT YOU WILL NEED

EQUIPMENT

Sharp stainless steel knife
Cutting board
Small piece of cheesecloth or spice bag (optional)
Long piece of string (optional)
Long-handled wooden spoon
Baking sheet or wooden board
Heatproof ladle or measuring cup
Nonreactive funnel
Clean dishcloth and hot soapy water
Sterilized jars, warmed (see page 231)
Boiling water canner
Labels

INGREDIENTS

Vegetables
Fruit (fresh or dried)
Vinegar
Spices
Sugar

ZUCCHINI CHUTNEY

1½ lb (670 g) zucchini, coarsely chopped or
    thickly sliced
Kosher salt for sprinkling
2 onions, peeled and chopped
3 garlic cloves, peeled and chopped
1 cup (175 g) raisins
½ tbsp black peppercorns, crushed
2 tbsp chopped fresh ginger
1½ tsp celery salt
3¾ cups (900 mL) white wine vinegar
1⅔ cups (300 g) light brown sugar
Makes about 2 lb (1 kg)

For the best flavor, use small
zucchini. Once they grow
large, they become more
watery and therefore
more flavor is lost during
the salting.

1 Layer the zucchini in a
colander, sprinkling the layers
with salt. Place the colander
on a plate and leave overnight
to drain.
2 The next day, rinse the zucchini under cold running
water, drain and pat dry with a clean cloth. Put
the zucchini into a nonreactive pan with the onion,
garlic, raisins, peppercorns, ginger, celery salt and
vinegar. Bring to a boil, and boil gently for about
15 minutes until the onions and zucchini are tender.
3 Stir in the sugar until it has dissolved, then simmer
steadily until the mixture is thick; stir frequently
to prevent sticking. The chutney is ready when
no liquid appears in the channel that is left when a
spoon is drawn across the bottom of the pan. It
will thicken further upon standing.
4 Prepare and fill the jars (see page 231), and
heat-process in a boiling water canner (see page 231).
Let cool, label the jars and store in a cool,
dark, dry place for at least one month before eating.
Keeps for one year.

3

Drying

Traditionally, the drying effect of the sun or wind was used to extend the storage of fruit and vegetables. When home-drying, the choice is limited to specific fruits, vegetables and herbs, as well as some aromatics, such as orange peel.

Oven-drying

1 Select good-quality, firm ingredients that are free of blemishes. Fruit should be just ripe and peeled if necessary with cores or pits removed. Root and tuber vegetables usually dry better than leaves or stalks.

2 Thinly slice and blanch vegetables, except tomatoes, sweet peppers, okra, mushrooms, beets and onions. Remove or trim mushrooms stalks. Halve tomatoes, and halve and pit peaches and plums.

3 Dip foods that discolor, such as apples and pears, in a solution of 6 tablespoons lemon juice to 4⅓ cups (1 L) water.

4 Put a wire rack on a foil-lined baking sheet. Arrange the food on the rack, leaving space between the pieces. Halved fruit should be set cut-side down. Set the oven to its lowest setting (it should not exceed 140°F/60°C); the warming oven of a cast-iron stove is ideal. Put the rack of food in the oven and prop the door slightly open (not applicable for a cast-iron stove).

5 Halfway through drying, turn the food over. If using more than one shelf at a time, swap the trays from one shelf to the other. Leave the food until it is dry and leathery.

6 Leave to cool before packing in layers between sheets of parchment paper in airtight containers. Store in a cool place but not the refrigerator.

Air-drying

1 Prepare the fruit or vegetables, and treat for discoloration, if necessary (see left).

2 Spread on racks on baking sheets. Thread onto lengths of thin sticks, and keep the food slightly separated to allow air to circulate around the pieces. Place across a roasting or baking pan.

3 Leave in a warm, dry place (not a steamy kitchen), for example, in a warm cupboard. The food is ready when it is dried and shriveled.

DRYING: WHAT YOU WILL NEED

EQUIPMENT

Sharp stainless steel knife
Cutting board
Wire rack
Aluminum foil
Parchment paper

INGREDIENTS

Foods to be dried

At home, the choice is limited to specific fruits, vegetables and herbs as well as some aromatics, such as orange peel. Sun and outdoor drying give the best flavor to foods, but most of us do not live in suitable climates with steadily warm, dry temperatures and plenty of ventilation and clean air.

Air-drying herbs

Herbs with firm leaves, such as thyme and rosemary, can be dried more successfully than soft, fleshy herbs like basil.

1 Choose herbs shortly before they come into flower. Pick them in the morning as soon as the dew has lifted but before the sun has become too hot. If drying the herbs in bunches, pick stems as long as possible.

2 To dry in bunches, tie the herbs loosely in small bundles with thick thread and suspend in a warm, dry place out of direct sunlight. They should be ready in three days.

3 Alternatively, spread the herbs on a wire rack covered with cheesecloth (which allows the air to circulate) and leave in a warm place, preferably enclosed, for three to five days.

4 Herbs can also be dried tied in paper bags with small holes cut in the bags, and left in a warm, dry place for three days.

5 Herbs are ready when the stems and leaves are brittle but retain their green color, and crumble easily when rubbed between the fingers. Either keep the stems and leaves intact, or strip the leaves off and store in an airtight container in a cool, dark, dry place.

OVEN-DRYING TIMES

Apple rings	6 to 8 hours
Apricots, halved and stoned	36 to 48 hours
Bananas, peeled and halved lengthways	10 to 16 hours
Berries, left whole	12 to 18 hours
Cherries, stoned	18 to 24 hours
Herbs, tied and bound	12 to 16 hours
Peaches, peeled, halved, stoned and sliced	36 to 48 hours
	12 to 16 hours
Pears, peeled, halved and cored	36 to 48 hours
Pineapple, cored and cut into ¼-inch (5-mm) rings	36 to 48 hours
Plums, halved	18 to 24 hours
Vegetables, cut into ¼-inch (5-mm) slices	2 hours
Vegetables, cut into ¾-inch (1.5-cm) slices	7 to 8 hours

Freezing

Freezing at a temperature below 0°F (-18°C) preserves food by immobilizing the bacteria that can spoil food, and slows down the enzyme activity that can cause quality deterioration. Food should be frozen quickly to prevent the formation of large ice crystals that damage cell walls, so that the thawed food doesn't lose its liquid and "collapse." Conversely, thawing should be done slowly.

1 If freezing more than 2 lb (1 kg) of food, turn the freezer thermostat to "fast-freeze." Choose heavyweight, vapor- and moisture-proof containers and wrappings to protect the food from freezer burn — for example, thick polythene bags, plastic wrap, foil and plastic boxes.

2 Prepare the food as necessary and make sure that it is completely cold.

3 Vegetables should be blanched to preserve their color, flavor, texture and nutritional content, and to destroy the enzymes that would otherwise cause deterioration during frozen storage. Put the prepared vegetables, in batches if necessary so that the pan is not crowded, in a wire basket. Plunge into a large saucepan of boiling water, cover and return quickly to the boil. Boil for the specified time. Remove the basket and immediately plunge it into a large bowl of water with some ice cubes in it. When cold, drain the vegetables very well.

4 Blackberries, black and red currants, blueberries, gooseberries and raspberries can be "open-frozen" by spreading them on trays lined with parchment paper and freezing before packing as normal.

5 Pack the food into suitable containers. If solid food is in a rigid container that it does not fill, fill the gap with crumpled tissue paper. Leave 1-inch (2.5-cm) headspace in rigid containers of liquids to allow for expansion, then fill the space if necessary.

6 Sauces, soups, purées, casseroles, etc. can be poured into polythene bags set in freezer-proof rectangular or square containers, with 1-inch (2.5-cm) headspace to allow for expansion. Freeze until solid, then remove the bag from the container, seal and label.

7 When the food is frozen, return the thermostat to the normal setting.

4

6

8 To freeze herbs, open-freeze the herb sprigs, then pack into freezer-proof polythene bags without crushing the herbs, and tie the bags fairly loosely. Chopped herbs can be frozen individually or combined into blends, such as Provençal — with basil, oregano, thyme, parsley and rosemary — and then either packed into small freezer bags or small containers and put inside a labeled freezer box. Or put the herbs (preferably in useful quantities, such as 2 tablespoonfuls) into ice cube trays, cover with water and freeze. The frozen cubes can be put into freezer bags or boxes. Use frozen herbs straight from the freezer without thawing.

FREEZING: WHAT YOU WILL NEED

EQUIPMENT

Freezer-proof containers
Polythene bags
Plastic wrap
Aluminum foil
Plastic boxes

STORAGE TIMES

VEGETABLES	
Most vegetables	8–12 months
Onions	3–6 months
Herbs	6 months
Not recommended: Lettuce and other salad leaves, spring onions, radishes and corn without husks.	
FRUIT	
Most fruit	8–12 months
Citrus fruit	4–6 months

FREEZER RASPBERRY JAM

1½ lb (700 g) raspberries
4½ cups (1 kg) superfine sugar
½ cup (125 mL) liquid pectin
Makes 7 cups (1.6 kg)

Freezer jams are not boiled, so they have a fresher, more natural taste and a brighter, clearer color than cooked jams. For a change, instead of using ordinary superfine sugar, try using vanilla sugar, which can be bought or homemade. Simply insert a vanilla bean in a jar of sugar and leave for two weeks before using; the vanilla bean can be left in the jar, or used in another recipe.

1 Place the raspberries in a bowl and gently stir in the sugar using a fork, lightly mashing the berries. Leave for 20 minutes, stirring occasionally.
2 Pour in the liquid pectin and stir continuously for three minutes.
3 Ladle the jam into clean, freezer-proof containers, filling them to ½ inch (1 cm) from the top. Seal, label and let cool for about 5 hours.
4 Put the containers in the refrigerator and leave for 24 to 48 hours until the jam gels.
5 Put the containers in the freezer and store for up to six months.
6 To serve, leave at room temperature for about one hour, depending on the size of the container.

Sowing summary

A quick-reference guide to vegetable sowing information to help you plan your food garden calendar.

VEGETABLE	DEPTH OF SOWING	DISTANCE APART	DISTANCE BETWEEN ROWS	SOWING SEASON	CROPPING SEASON
Asparagus crowns	4 inches (10 cm)	17¾ inches (45 cm)	36 inches (90 cm)	Mid-spring	Mid-spring–Late spring
Arugula	½ inch (1 cm)	½ inch (1 cm)	8–12 inches (20–30 cm)	Mid-spring–Early fall	Late spring–Mid-fall
Beet	⅝ inch (1.5 cm)	1 inch (2.5 cm)	8–12 inches (20–30 cm)	Mid-spring–Early summer	Early summer–Mid-fall
Bok choi	½ inch (1 cm)	8 inches (20 cm)	12 inches (30 cm)	Mid-spring–Late summer	Late summer–Early winter
Broccoli	½ inch (1 cm)	16–24 inches (40–60 cm)	16–24 inches (40–60 cm)	Early spring–Late spring	Midsummer–Mid-spring
Brussels sprouts	½ inch (1 cm)	3 feet (90 cm)	32–36 inches (80–90 cm)	Late spring	Mid-fall–Late-winter
Bush beans	¾ inch (2 cm)	2 inches (5 cm)	12 inches (30 cm)	Mid spring–Midsummer	Early summer–Mid-fall
Cabbage	½ inch (1 cm)	6–20 inches (15–50 cm)	32–36 inches (80–90 cm)	Early spring	All year round
Carrot	½ inch (1 cm)	1 inch (2.5 cm)	20 inches (50 cm)	Early spring–Early summer	Late spring–Late fall
Cauliflower	½ inch (1 cm)	16 inches (40 cm)	34 inches (85 cm)	Spring	All year round
Celeriac	Surface	12 inches (30 cm)	12 inches (30 cm)	Early spring	Early fall–Late winter
Celery	Surface	8 inches (20 cm)	28 inches (70 cm)	Spring	Early summer–Late fall
Chicory and Endive	½ inch (1 cm)	12 inches (30 cm)	8–16 inches (20–40 cm)	Mid-spring–Early summer	Midsummer–Early winter
Chili	½ inch (1 cm)	12 inches (30 cm)	12 inches (30 cm)	Early spring	Midsummer–Mid-fall
Chinese cabbage	½ inch (1 cm)	12 inches (30 cm)	12 inches (30 cm)	Early summer–Midsummer	Late summer–Early winter
Corn	1 inch (2.5 cm)	blocks of 3 x 3 or 5 x 5	14 inches (35 cm)	Mid-spring	Late summer–Early fall
Cucumber	1 inch (2.5 cm)	6 inches (15 cm)	4–6 inches (10–12 cm)	Late spring	Midsummer–Mid-fall
Edible flowers	Check specific instructions on your seed packet				All year round
Eggplant	¼ inch (0.5 cm)	18 inches (46 cm)	20–30 inches (50–75 cm)	Early spring–Mid-spring	Late summer–Mid-fall
Fava beans	2 inches (5 cm)	8 inches (20 cm)	8–12 inches (20–30 cm)	Late fall or Mid-spring	Early summer–Late summer
Florence fennel	½ inch (1 cm)	12 inches (30 cm)	12 inches (30 cm)	Mid-spring–Late spring	Late spring–Early fall
Garlic	1¼ inches (3 cm)	3 inches (7.5 cm)	16 inches (40 cm)	Fall or Early winter	Late spring–Early fall
Globe artichoke and Cardoon	½ inch (1 cm)	30 inches (75 cm)	30 inches (75 cm)	Late winter	Late spring–Early summer
Jerusalem artichoke tubers	4–6 inches (10–15 cm)	12 inches (30 cm)	12 inches (30 cm)	Late winter–Mid-spring	Late fall–Winter
Kale	½ inch (1 cm)	17¾ inches (45 cm)	17¾ inches (45 cm)	Mid-spring	Early fall–Late winter
Kohlrabi	½ inch (1 cm)	4 inches (10 cm)	16 inches (40 cm)	Spring–Early summer	Late spring–Early winter

VEGETABLE	DEPTH OF SOWING	DISTANCE APART	DISTANCE BETWEEN ROWS	SOWING SEASON	CROPPING SEASON
Leek	¼ inch (0.5 cm)	6 inches (15 cm)	24 inches (60 cm)	Spring	Late summer–Early spring
Lettuce	¼ inch (0.5 cm)	⅝ inch (1.5 cm)	12 inches (30 cm)	Early spring–Fall	Early summer–Late fall
Marrow	½ inch (1 cm)	20 inches (50 cm)	3 ft. 2 inches (1 m)	Late spring	Midsummer–Mid-fall
Microgreens	¼ inch (0.5 cm)	¹⁄₁₆ inch (2 mm)	N/A	All year round	All year round
Mizuna	½ inch (1 cm)	1 inch (2.5 cm)	16 inches (40 cm)	Early spring–Early fall	Midsummer–Mid-winter
New Zealand spinach and Swiss chard	⅝ inch (1.5 cm)	12–20 inches (30–50 cm)	12–20 inches (30–50 cm)	Mid-spring	Early spring–Late fall
Onion	½ inch (1 cm)	4 inches (10 cm)	8 inches (20 cm)	Spring and Fall	Early summer–Early fall
Parsnip	½ inch (1 cm)	6 inches (15 cm)	8–12 inches (20–30 cm)	Early spring	Early fall–Late winter
Peas	1 inch (2.5 cm)	2–4 inches (5–10 cm)	3–6 inches (7.5–15 cm)	Early spring–Midsummer	Late spring–Mid-fall
Pole beans	2 inches (5 cm)	16 inches (40 cm)	20 inches (50 cm)	Mid-spring	Early summer–Mid-fall
Potato (earlies)	4 inches (10 cm)	16 inches (40 cm)	20 inches (50 cm)	Early spring–Mid-spring	Early summer–Late summer
Potato (second earlies)	4 inches (10 cm)	16 inches (40 cm)	60 inches (24 cm)	Early spring–Mid-spring	Midsummer–Early fall
Potato (maincrop)	4 inches (10 cm)	16 inches (40 cm)	30 inches (75 cm)	Early spring–Mid-spring	Late summer–Late fall
Radish	½ inch (1 cm)	1 inch (2.5 cm)	6 inches (15 cm)	Early spring onward	Late spring–Late fall
Rutabaga	½ inch (1 cm)	12 inches (30 cm)	26 inches (65 cm)	Mid-spring–Late spring	Mid-fall–Early winter
Shallot	½ inch (1 cm)	6 inches (15 cm)	12 inches (30 cm)	Early spring	Late summer–Mid-fall
Snow peas and Snap peas	2 inches (5 cm)	4 inches (10 cm)	3–6 inches (7.5–15 cm)	Early spring–Midsummer	Late spring–Mid-fall
Spinach	½ inch (1 cm)	8 inches (20 cm)	12 inches (30 cm)	Early spring	Early summer–Mid-fall
Spring onion	½ inch (1 cm)	¾–2 inches (2–5 cm)	12 inches (30 cm)	Early spring–Midsummer	Late spring–Late fall
Sprouting seeds	N/A	N/A	N/A	All year round	All year round
Squash and Pumpkin	1 inch (2.5 cm)	6 inches (15 cm)	40 inches (1 m)	Spring	Midsummer–Mid-fall
Sweet pepper	½ inch (1 cm)	12 inches (30 cm)	12 inches (30 cm)	Early spring	Midsummer–Mid-fall
Sweet potato	Grow as plants	17¾ inches (45 cm)	17¾ inches (45 cm)	N/A	Mid-fall–Late fall
Tomato	¼ inch (0.5 cm)	17¾–23 inches (45–60 cm)	40 inches (1 m)	Late spring	Midsummer–Mid-fall
Turnip	¾ inch (2 cm)	8 inches (20 cm)	6 inches (15 cm)	Early spring onward	Early summer–Mid-fall
Zucchini	½ inch (1 cm)	20 inches (50 cm)	40 inches (1 m)	Late spring	Early summer–Mid-fall

Crop selection summary

A quick-reference guide to the characteristics of each crop to help you decide what to grow.

VEGETABLE	VALUE FOR MONEY	MAINTENANCE	FREEZE/ STORE
Arugula	●●●●●	●●●●	●●
Asparagus	●●●●●	●●●●	●●
Beet	●●●●●	●●●●	●●●
Bok choi	●●●●	●●	●●
Broccoli	●●●●	●●●	●●
Brussels sprouts	●●●●	●●●	●●
Bush beans	●●●●●	●●●●	●●●●
Cabbage	●●●●	●●●	●●●
Cardoon	●●●	●●●●	●●
Carrot	●●●●●	●●●●	●●●●●
Cauliflower	●●●	●●●	●●
Celeriac	●●●●	●●●	●●●
Celery	●●●	●●●	●●
Chicory	●●●●●	●●●	●●
Chili	●●●●	●●	●●●●
Chinese cabbage	●●●●	●●	●●
Corn	●●●●	●●●●	●●
Cucumber	●●●●●	●●●	●●
Eggplant	●●●●	●●	●●
Endive	●●●●●	●●●	●●
Fava beans	●●●●●	●●●●	●●●●
Florence fennel	●●●	●●●	●●
Garlic	●●●●●	●●●●	●●●●●
Globe artichoke	●●●	●●●●	●●
Jerusalem artichoke	●●●●●	●●●●	●●●●
Kale	●●●●●	●●●●	●●
Kohlrabi	●●●●	●●●	●●●

VEGETABLE	VALUE FOR MONEY	MAINTENANCE	FREEZE/ STORE
Leek	●●●●●	●●●●	●●●
Lettuce	●●●●●	●●●●	●●
Marrow	●●●●●	●●●●	●●●
Microgreens	●●●	●●	●●
Mizuna	●●●●●	●●●●	●●
New Zealand spinach	●●●●●	●●●●	●●
Onion	●●●●●	●●●●	●●●●●
Parsnip	●●●●●	●●●●	●●●●●
Peas	●●●●●	●●●●	●●●●
Pole beans	●●●●●	●●●●	●●●●
Potato	●●●●●	●●●●	●●●●●
Pumpkin	●●●●●	●●●●	●●●●
Radish	●●●●●	●●●●	●●
Rutabaga	●●●●	●●●	●●●
Shallot	●●●●●	●●●●	●●●●●
Snap peas	●●●●	●●●	●●●●
Snow peas	●●●●	●●●	●●●●
Spinach	●●●●●	●●●●	●●
Spring onion	●●●●●	●●●●	●●
Sprouting seeds	●●●●	●●	●●
Squash	●●●●●	●●●●	●●●●
Sweet pepper	●●●	●●	●●
Sweet potato	●●●	●●●	●●
Swiss chard	●●●●●	●●●●	●●
Tomato	●●●●●	●●	●●●
Turnip	●●●●●	●●●	●●●
Zucchini	●●●●●	●●●●	●●

HERB	VALUE FOR MONEY	MAINTENANCE	FREEZE/ STORE
Basil	✿✿✿✿✿	✿✿	✿✿✿
Bay	✿✿✿✿✿	✿✿✿✿✿	✿✿✿
Chervil	✿✿✿✿	✿✿✿✿	✿✿✿
Chives	✿✿✿✿✿	✿✿✿✿	✿✿✿
Cilantro	✿✿✿✿✿	✿✿✿	✿✿✿
Dill	✿✿✿✿	✿✿✿	✿✿✿
Fennel	✿✿✿✿	✿✿✿	✿✿✿
Lovage	✿✿✿✿	✿✿✿✿	✿✿✿
Mint	✿✿✿✿✿	✿✿✿✿	✿✿✿
Oregano	✿✿✿✿✿	✿✿✿✿	✿✿✿
Parsley	✿✿✿✿✿	✿✿✿✿	✿✿✿
Rosemary	✿✿✿✿✿	✿✿✿✿✿	✿✿✿
Sage	✿✿✿✿✿	✿✿✿✿	✿✿✿
Tarragon	✿✿✿✿✿	✿✿✿✿	✿✿✿
Thyme	✿✿✿✿✿	✿✿✿✿	✿✿✿

FRUIT AND NUTS	VALUE FOR MONEY	MAINTENANCE	FREEZE/ STORE
Almond	✿✿✿✿	✿✿✿	✿✿✿✿
Apple	✿✿✿✿✿	✿✿✿	✿✿✿✿✿
Apricot	✿✿✿	✿✿✿	✿✿
Black currant	✿✿✿✿	✿✿✿✿	✿✿✿
Blackberry and hybrid berries	✿✿✿	✿✿✿	✿✿✿
Blueberry	✿✿✿	✿✿✿✿	✿✿✿
Cape gooseberry	✿✿✿	✿✿✿	✿✿
Citrus	✿✿✿	✿✿	✿✿✿
Cranberry	✿✿✿✿	✿✿	✿✿✿
Damson	✿✿✿✿✿	✿✿✿	✿✿✿
Fig	✿✿✿✿	✿✿✿✿	✿✿✿
Filbert	✿✿✿	✿✿✿✿	✿✿✿
Gage	✿✿✿✿✿	✿✿✿	✿✿✿
Gooseberry	✿✿✿✿	✿✿✿	✿✿✿
Grapes	✿✿✿✿	✿✿✿	✿✿✿
Hazelnut	✿✿✿	✿✿✿✿	✿✿✿
Kiwi	✿✿✿	✿✿✿	✿✿
Melon	✿✿✿✿	✿✿✿✿	✿✿
Nectarine	✿✿✿	✿✿✿	✿✿
Passion fruit	✿✿✿	✿✿✿	✿✿
Peach	✿✿✿	✿✿✿	✿✿
Pear	✿✿✿✿✿	✿✿✿	✿✿✿✿
Plum	✿✿✿✿✿	✿✿✿	✿✿✿
Raspberry	✿✿✿✿✿	✿✿✿✿	✿✿✿
Red currant	✿✿✿✿	✿✿✿✿	✿✿✿
Rhubarb	✿✿✿✿✿	✿✿✿✿	✿✿
Strawberry	✿✿✿✿✿	✿✿✿✿	✿✿✿
Sweet cherry	✿✿✿✿✿	✿✿✿	✿✿✿
Tart cherry	✿✿✿✿✿	✿✿✿	✿✿✿
Walnut	✿✿✿✿	✿✿✿✿	✿✿✿
White currant	✿✿✿✿	✿✿✿✿	✿✿✿

Hardiness zones

Remember that hardiness is not just a question of minimum temperatures. A plant's ability to survive certain temperatures is affected by many factors, such as the amount of shelter given and its position in your garden.

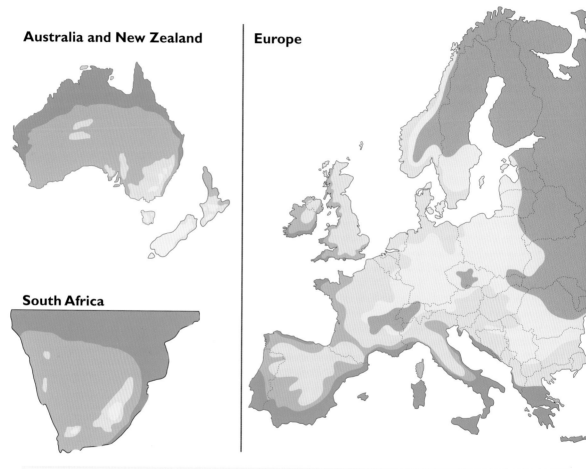

Australia and New Zealand

Europe

South Africa

KEY
Average annual minimum temperature

Zone 1	Below -50°F (-45°C)		**Zone 6**	-10 to 0°F (-23 to -18°C)
Zone 2	-50 to -40°F (-45 to -40°C)		**Zone 7**	0 to 10°F (-18 to -12°C)
Zone 3	-40 to -30°F (-40 to -34°C)		**Zone 8**	10 to 20°F (-12 to -7°C)
Zone 4	-30 to -20°F (-34 to -29°C)		**Zone 9**	20 to 30°F (-7 to -1°C)
Zone 5	-20 to -10°F (-29 to -23°C)		**Zone 10**	30 to 40°F (-1 to 5°C)

United States of America

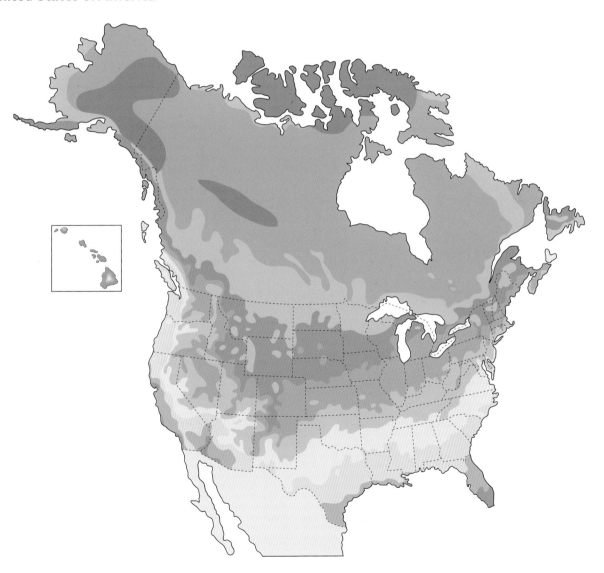

Index

Acknowledgments

Quarto would like to thank the following photographers and agencies for supplying images for inclusion in this book:

Jenny & Colin Guest
p.32b–33b, 34, 36, 37, 38bl/br, 39t/bl, 40, 40b, 42b, 43b, 44b, 46b, 47bl, 48t, 49b, 54, 56br, 58, 59cr, 62cr, 64b–65b, 65t, 70, 71b, 72b, 73, 74b–75b, 78b, 79b, 82t, 84b, 87, 88b, 90bl, 100, 101br, 104bc, 105br, 106b–107b, 120b, 122b, 123b, 124bl/bc, 127b, 132b, 133b, 134b, 135t, 161t, 168b, 169b, 183, 214, 215, 227

Mark Winwood
p.31, 35, 45t, 47br, 48b, 52, 53b, 60b, 63bl, 66, 69, 77, 82b, 83, 86, 88t, 89br, 93br, 96bc/br, 97t, 98, 104, 108b, 110b, 112, 113b, 119b, 124br, 135b, 140, 146b, 152bl, 154b, 155, 158t/bl, 171b, 177b, 178b, 179b, 185, 199t, 204

John Grain
p.2, 3c/b, 11, 80b, 154t, 162b, 163bl

Jenny Steel www.wildlife-gardening.co.uk
p.216

Key Sexton http://blog.gardening-tools-direct.co.uk
p.226

Photolibrary
p.12–13, 16, 17, 19t, 50b, 61, 81, 92, 94br, 95b, 111t, 128, 129tl/tr, 129bl, 130, 131bl, 150, 162, 163br, 165, 198b, 213, 223t/bl/br

Getty Images
p.33tl/tr, 43t, 103b, 106t

Quintet Publishing
Images: p.230tl/br, 231tl, 232, 233, 234, 235, 236, 237, 238, 239, 240, 241, 242, 243
Text: p.230–243

All other images are the copyright of Quarto Publishing plc. While every effort has been made to credit contributors, Quarto would like to apologize should there have been any omissions or errors — and would be pleased to make the appropriate correction for future editions of the book.